RODDENBERRY PRESENTS

WORTH

WORTH

Written by Aubrey Sitterson
Art by Chris Moreno
Cover by Chris Moreno

Colors by Cirque Studios
Letters by Troy Peteri
Edited by Paul Morrissey
Executive Editors Trevor Roth & Eugene "Rod" Roddenberry
Created by Trevor Roth

Published by **Arcana**

Sean Patrick O'Reilly, *CEO and Founder*
Erik Hendrix, *VP of Publishing*
Michelle Meyers, *VP of Sales*
Dan Forcey, *VP of Film & TV*
Amanda Hendrix, *Senior Editor*
Emma Waddell, *Marketing*
Mia Divac, *Story Editor*
www.arcana.com

Roddenberry Entertainment

Tory Ireland Mell, *Producer*
Brent Beaudette, *Product Manager*
Ryan Harvie, *Executive Assistant*
H. Jay Roth, *Creative Consultant*

www.WheresYourWorth.com
www.roddenberry.com

RODDENBERRY
ENTERTAINMENT

ARCANA

CHAPTER 1

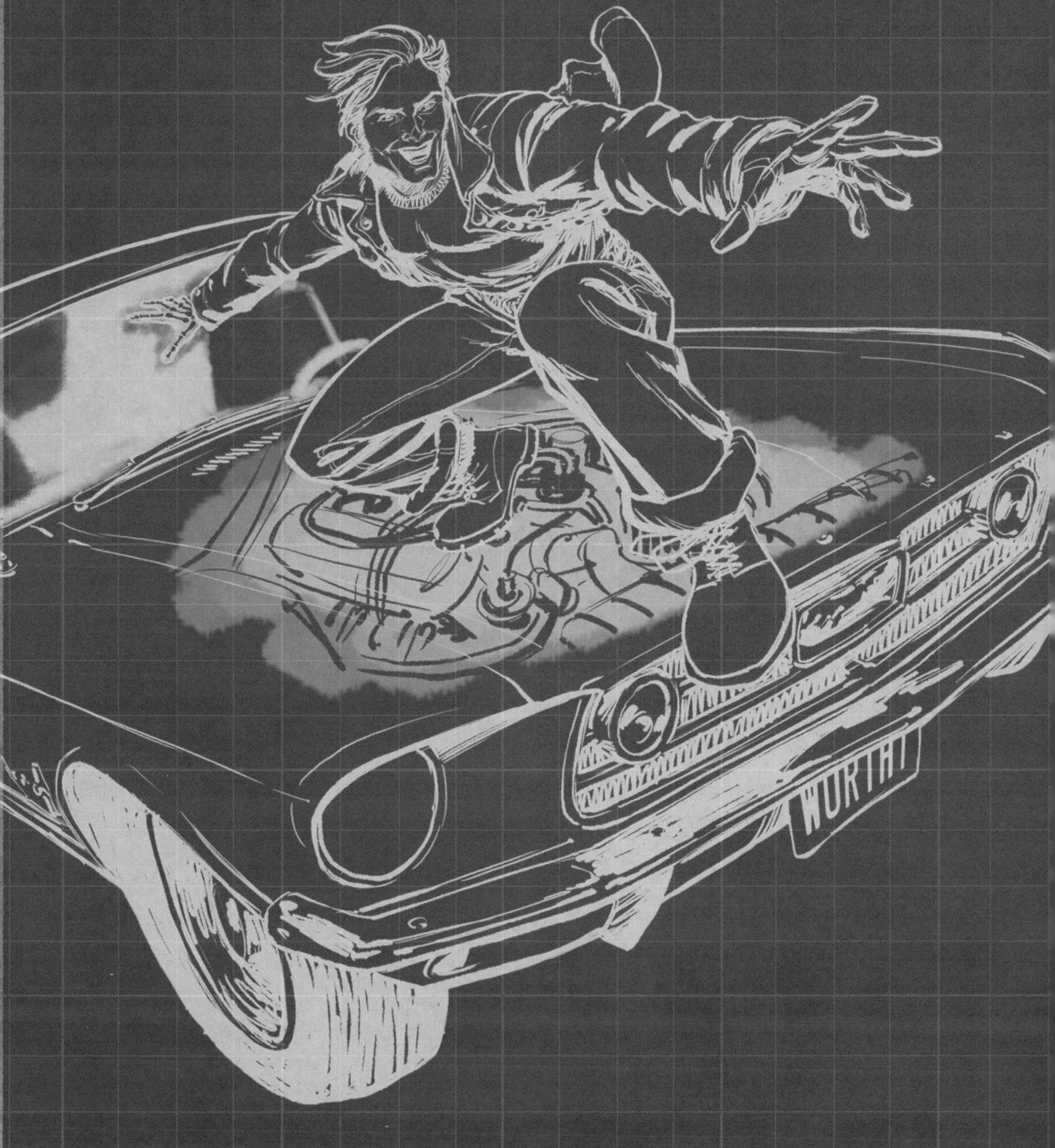
WORTHY

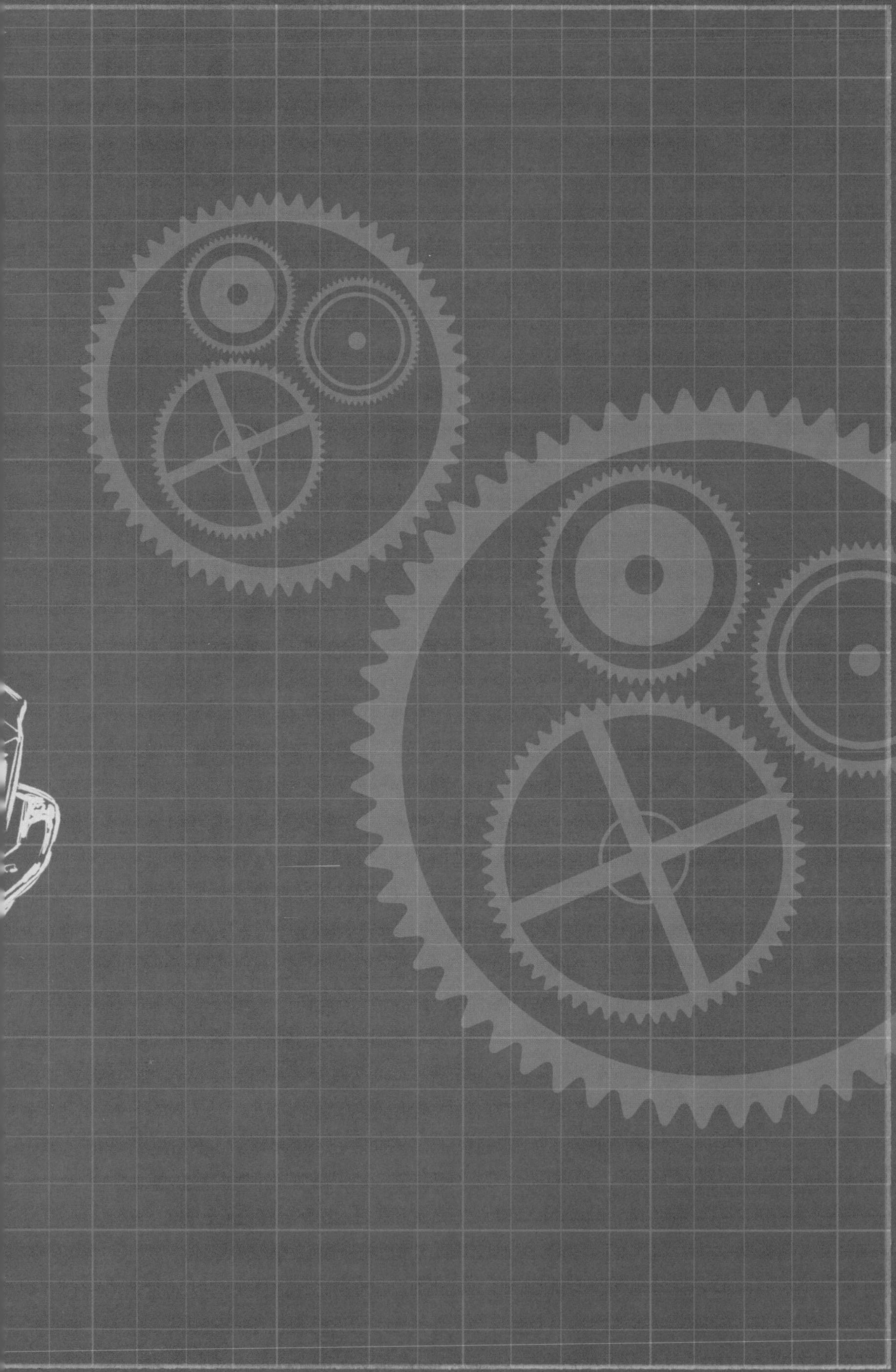

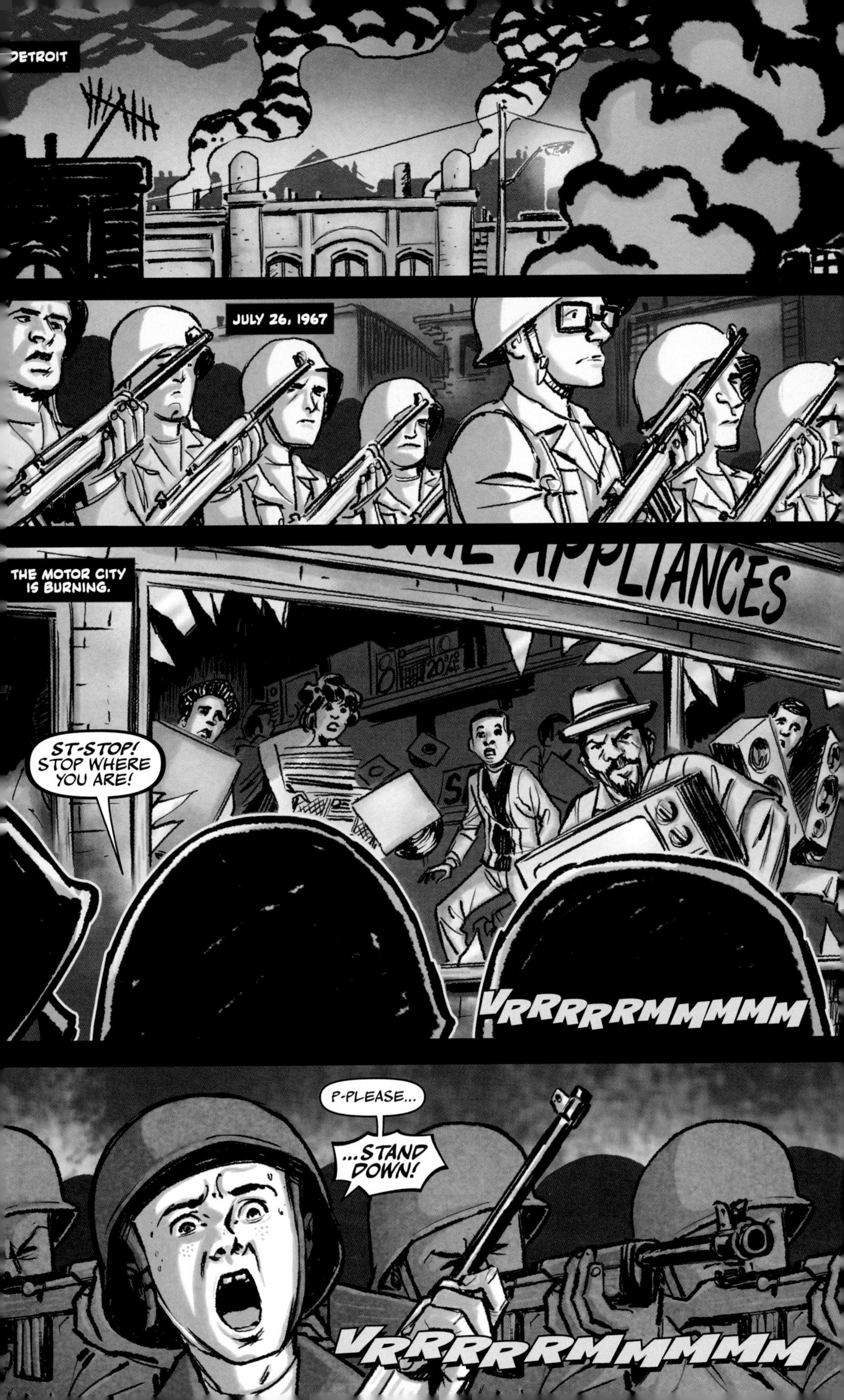
DETROIT
JULY 26, 1967
THE MOTOR CITY IS BURNING.
APPLIANCES
ST-STOP! STOP WHERE YOU ARE!
VRRRRRMMMMM
P-PLEASE...
...STAND DOWN!
VRRRRRMMMMM

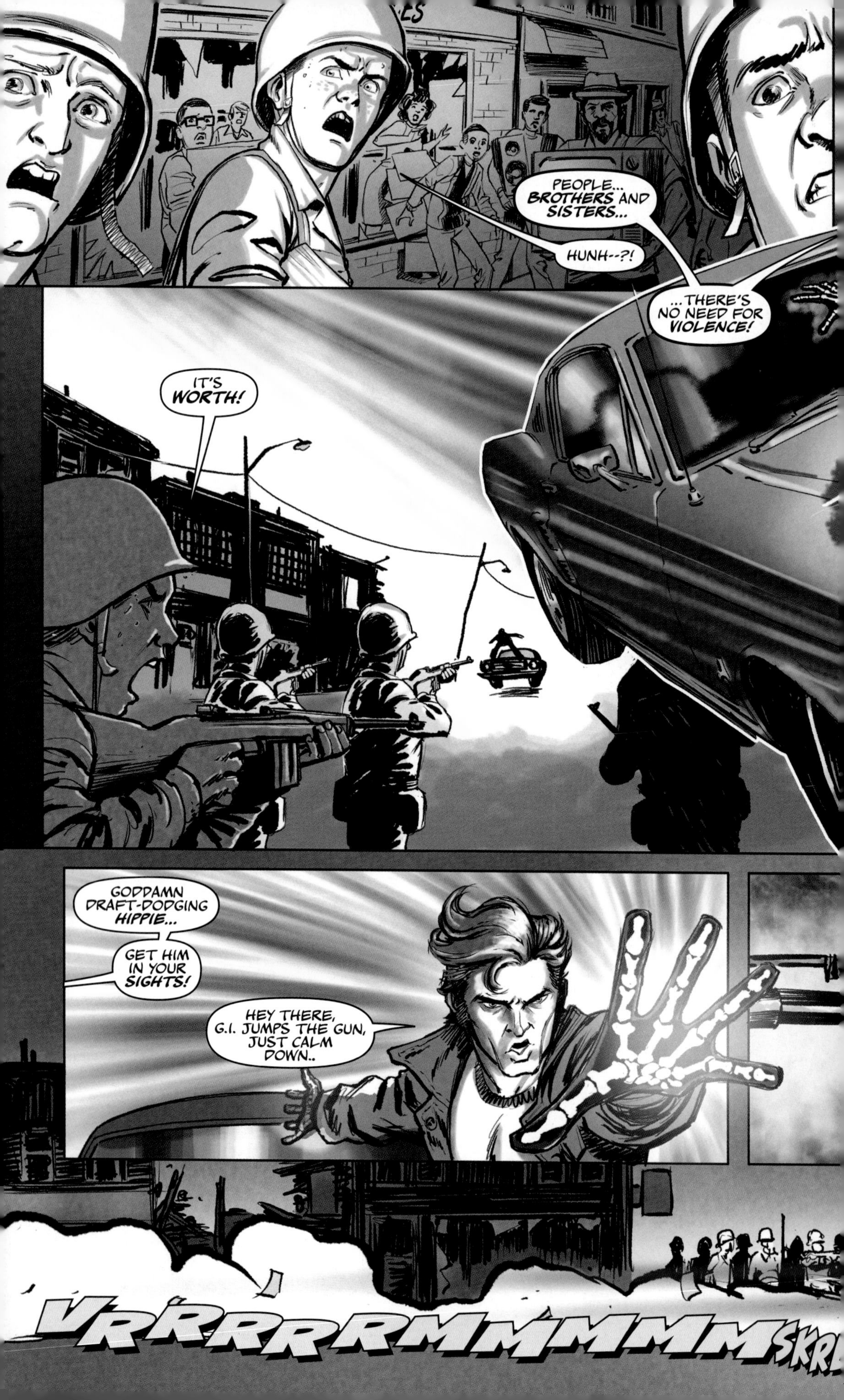
PEOPLE... BROTHERS AND SISTERS...
HUNH--?!
...THERE'S NO NEED FOR VIOLENCE!
IT'S WORTH!
GODDAMN DRAFT-DODGING HIPPIE...
GET HIM IN YOUR SIGHTS!
HEY THERE, G.I. JUMPS THE GUN, JUST CALM DOWN..
VRRRRRMMMMMMSKR

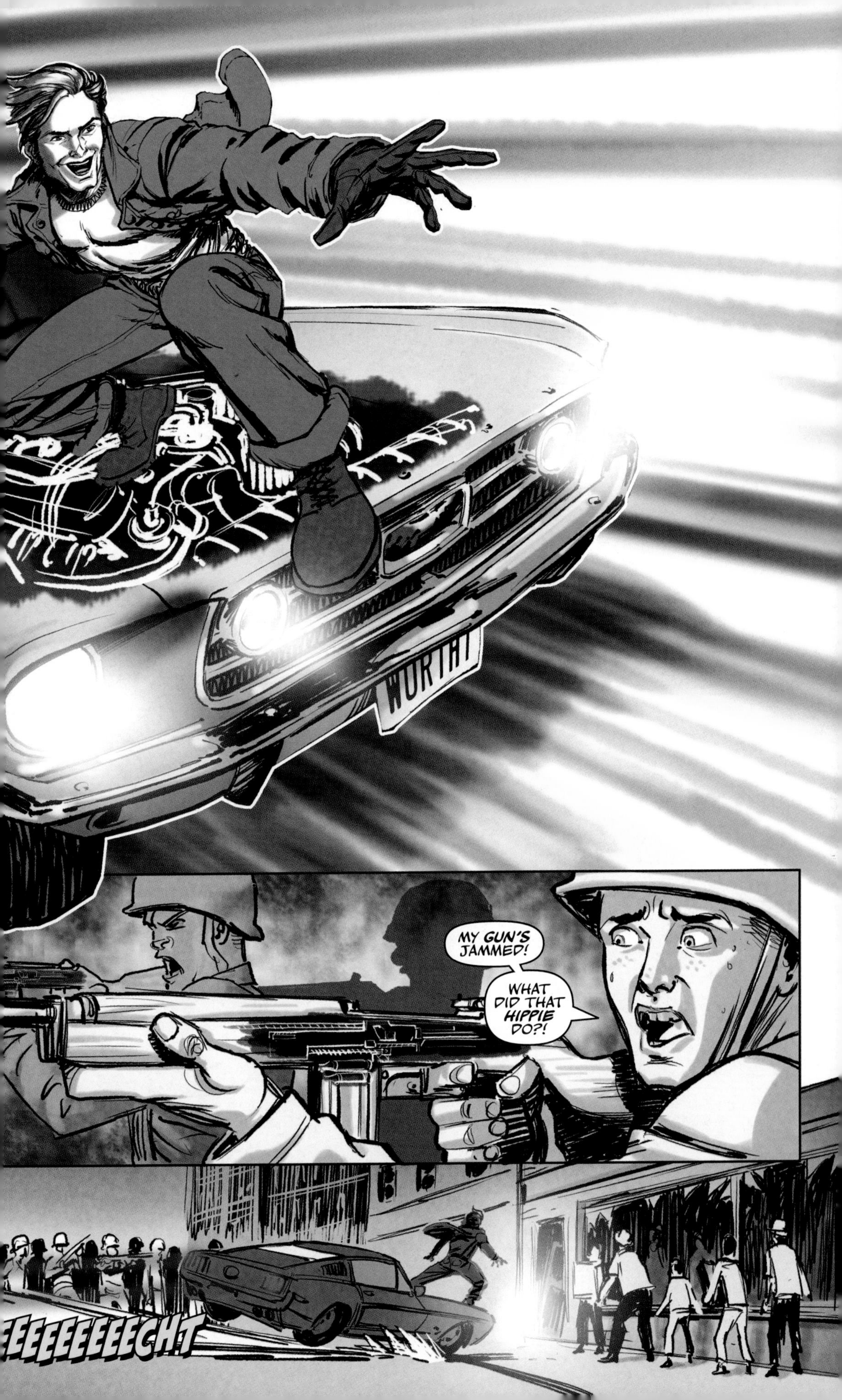
WORTHY
MY GUN'S JAMMED!
WHAT DID THAT HIPPIE DO?!
EEEEEEEEECHT

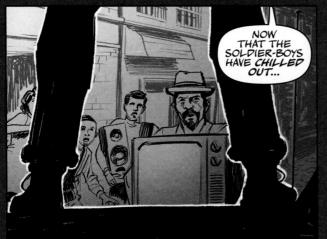

NOW THAT THE SOLDIER-BOYS HAVE *CHILLED OUT*...

...I'D LIKE TO THANK YOU FINE, UPSTANDING CITIZENS FOR HELPING SAVE ALL THAT MERCHANDISE.

YOU CAN JUST SET IT DOWN ON THE *SIDEWALK* THERE.

"I DIDN'T SLEEP FOR DAYS.

"BETWEEN THE LOOTERS, THE SNIPERS, THE NATIONAL GUARD, THE ARMY, THE STATE POLICE AND THE LOCAL COPS...

"...THE *ENTIRE* CITY WAS UNDER SIEGE.

"THERE WERE TOO MANY FIRES TO *PUT OUT*.

"TOO MANY LIVES TO PROTECT."

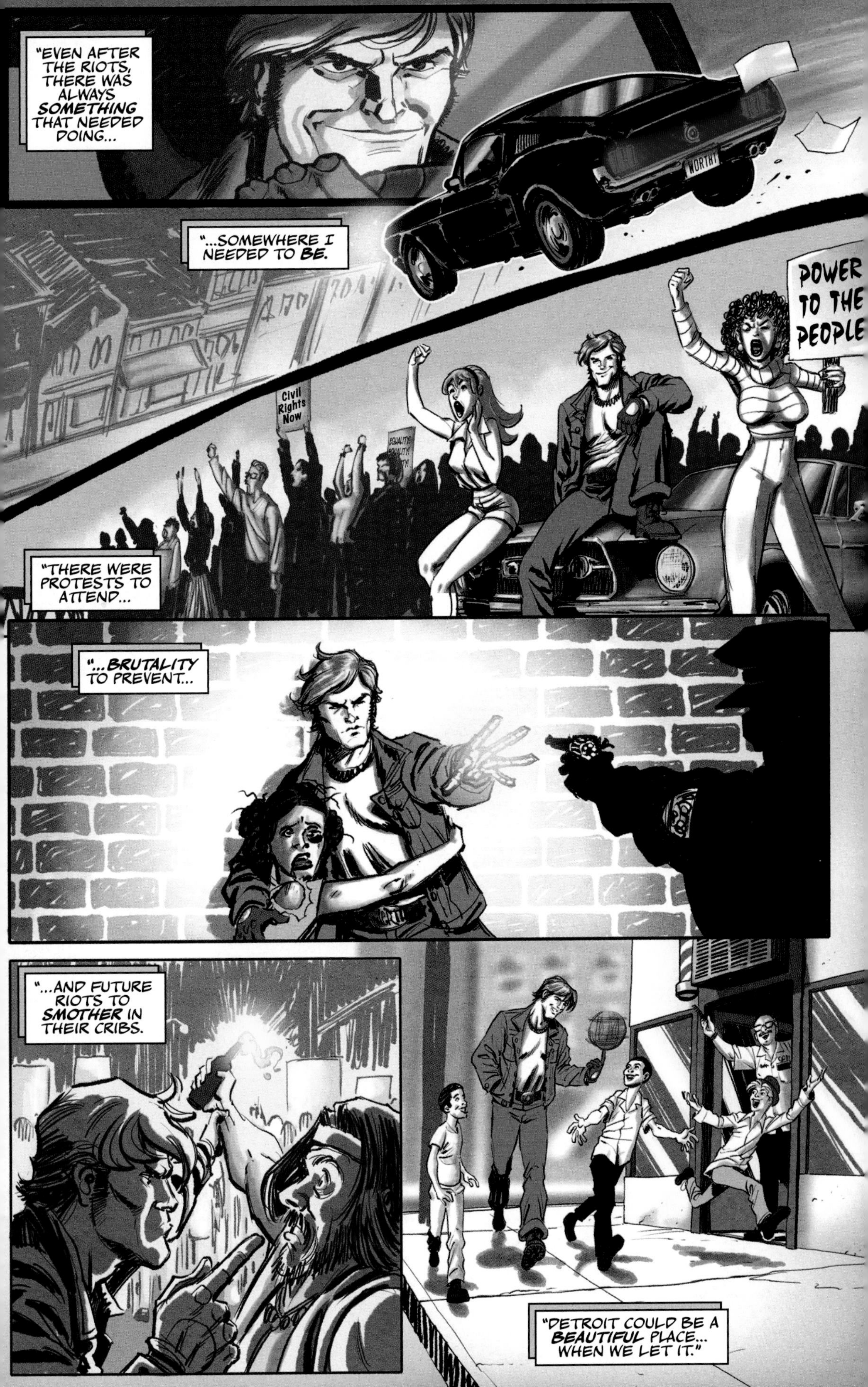
"EVEN AFTER THE RIOTS, THERE WAS ALWAYS *SOMETHING* THAT NEEDED DOING...
WORTHY
"...SOMEWHERE I NEEDED TO *BE*.
Civil Rights Now
POWER TO THE PEOPLE
"THERE WERE PROTESTS TO ATTEND...
"...*BRUTALITY* TO PREVENT...
"...AND FUTURE RIOTS TO *SMOTHER* IN THEIR CRIBS.
"DETROIT COULD BE A *BEAUTIFUL* PLACE... WHEN WE LET IT."

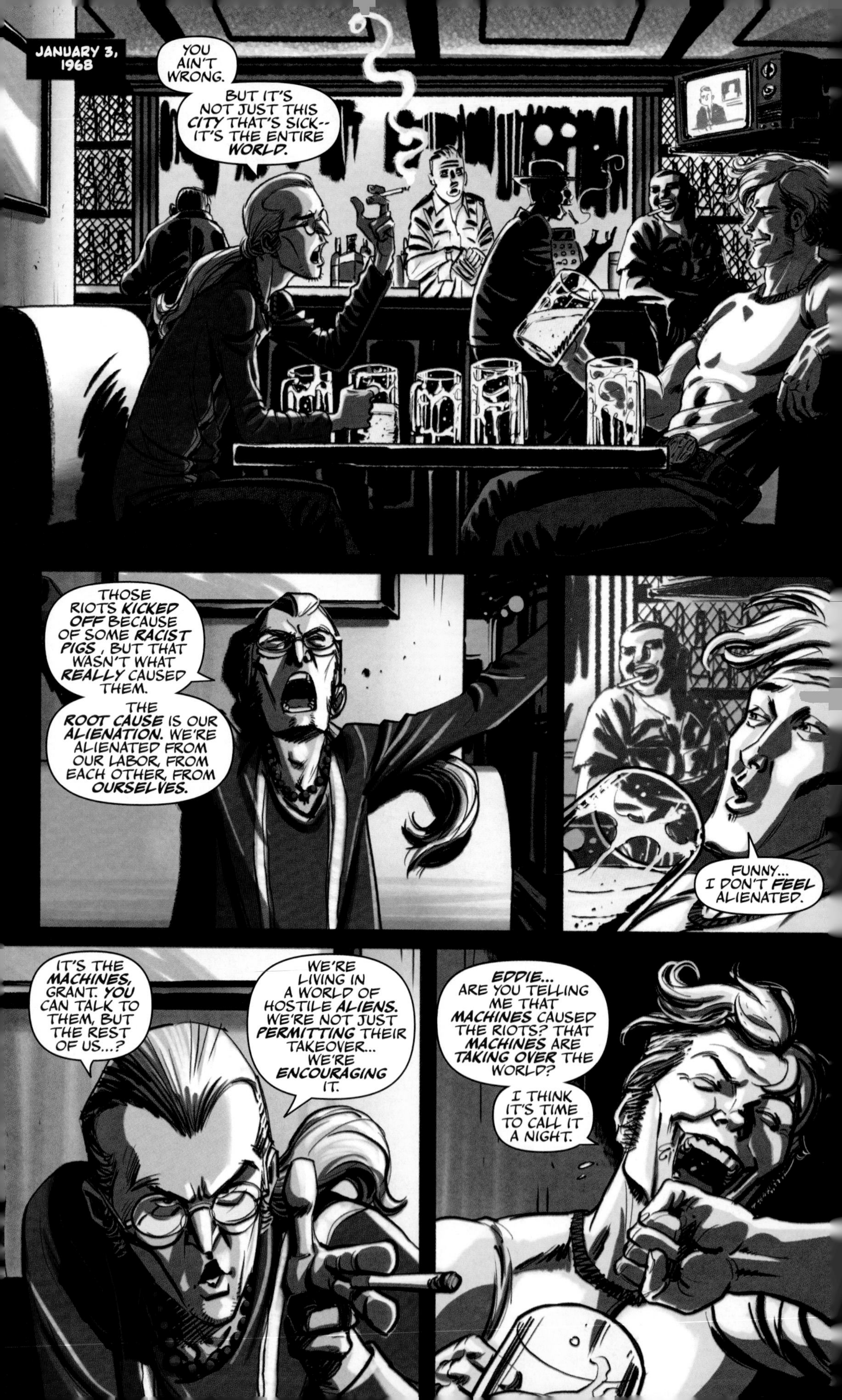
JANUARY 3, 1968
YOU AIN'T WRONG.
BUT IT'S NOT JUST THIS CITY THAT'S SICK-- IT'S THE ENTIRE WORLD.
THOSE RIOTS KICKED OFF BECAUSE OF SOME RACIST PIGS, BUT THAT WASN'T WHAT REALLY CAUSED THEM.
THE ROOT CAUSE IS OUR ALIENATION. WE'RE ALIENATED FROM OUR LABOR, FROM EACH OTHER, FROM OURSELVES.
FUNNY... I DON'T FEEL ALIENATED.
IT'S THE MACHINES, GRANT. YOU CAN TALK TO THEM, BUT THE REST OF US...?
WE'RE LIVING IN A WORLD OF HOSTILE ALIENS. WE'RE NOT JUST PERMITTING THEIR TAKEOVER... WE'RE ENCOURAGING IT.
EDDIE... ARE YOU TELLING ME THAT MACHINES CAUSED THE RIOTS? THAT MACHINES ARE TAKING OVER THE WORLD?
I THINK IT'S TIME TO CALL IT A NIGHT.

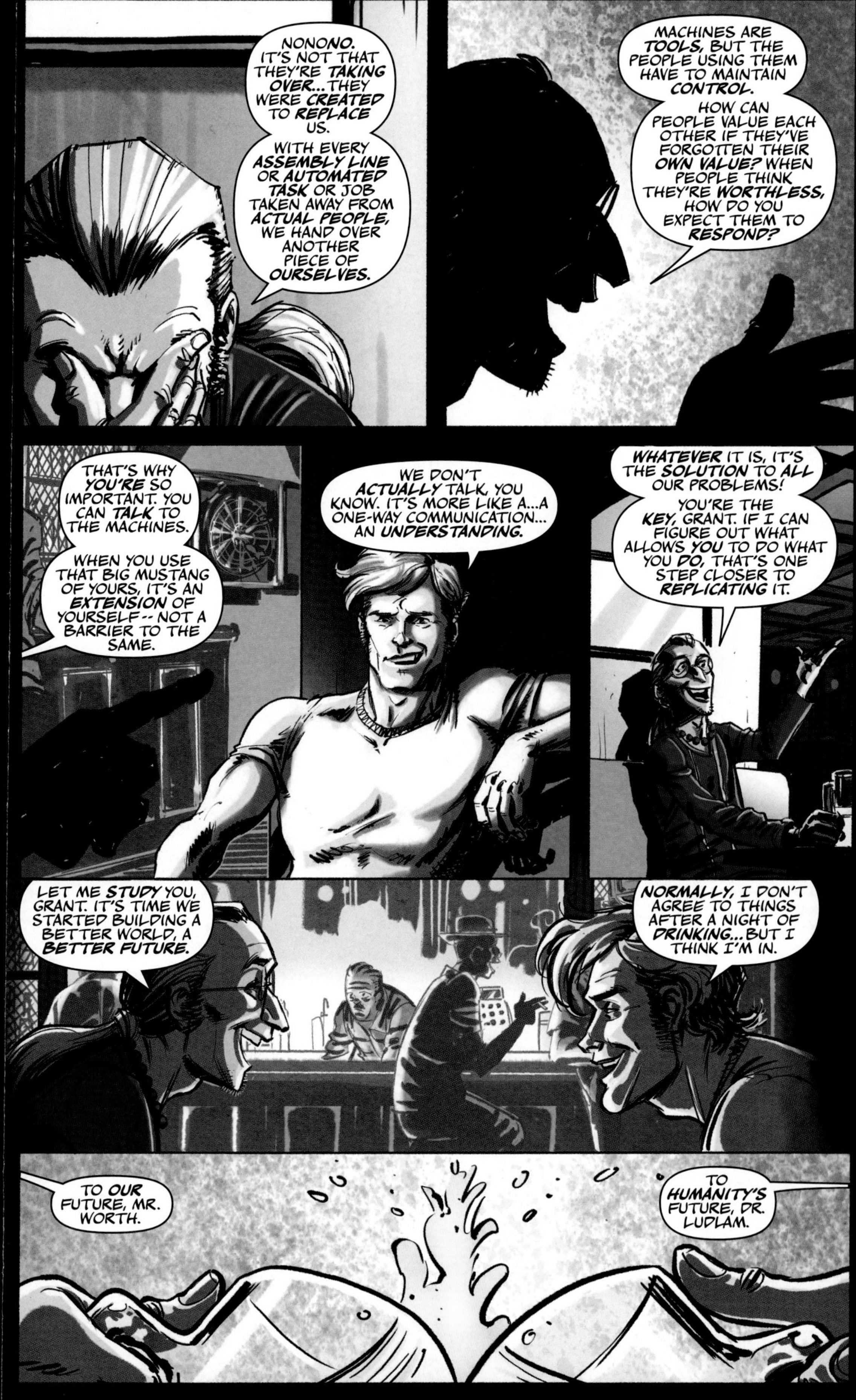
NONONO. IT'S NOT THAT THEY'RE TAKING OVER... THEY WERE CREATED TO REPLACE US.
WITH EVERY ASSEMBLY LINE OR AUTOMATED TASK OR JOB TAKEN AWAY FROM ACTUAL PEOPLE, WE HAND OVER ANOTHER PIECE OF OURSELVES.
MACHINES ARE TOOLS, BUT THE PEOPLE USING THEM HAVE TO MAINTAIN CONTROL.
HOW CAN PEOPLE VALUE EACH OTHER IF THEY'VE FORGOTTEN THEIR OWN VALUE? WHEN PEOPLE THINK THEY'RE WORTHLESS, HOW DO YOU EXPECT THEM TO RESPOND?
THAT'S WHY YOU'RE SO IMPORTANT. YOU CAN TALK TO THE MACHINES.
WHEN YOU USE THAT BIG MUSTANG OF YOURS, IT'S AN EXTENSION OF YOURSELF-- NOT A BARRIER TO THE SAME.
WE DON'T ACTUALLY TALK, YOU KNOW. IT'S MORE LIKE A...A ONE-WAY COMMUNICATION... AN UNDERSTANDING.
WHATEVER IT IS, IT'S THE SOLUTION TO ALL OUR PROBLEMS!
YOU'RE THE KEY, GRANT. IF I CAN FIGURE OUT WHAT ALLOWS YOU TO DO WHAT YOU DO, THAT'S ONE STEP CLOSER TO REPLICATING IT.
LET ME STUDY YOU, GRANT. IT'S TIME WE STARTED BUILDING A BETTER WORLD, A BETTER FUTURE.
NORMALLY, I DON'T AGREE TO THINGS AFTER A NIGHT OF DRINKING... BUT I THINK I'M IN.
TO OUR FUTURE, MR. WORTH.
TO HUMANITY'S FUTURE, DR. LUDLAM.

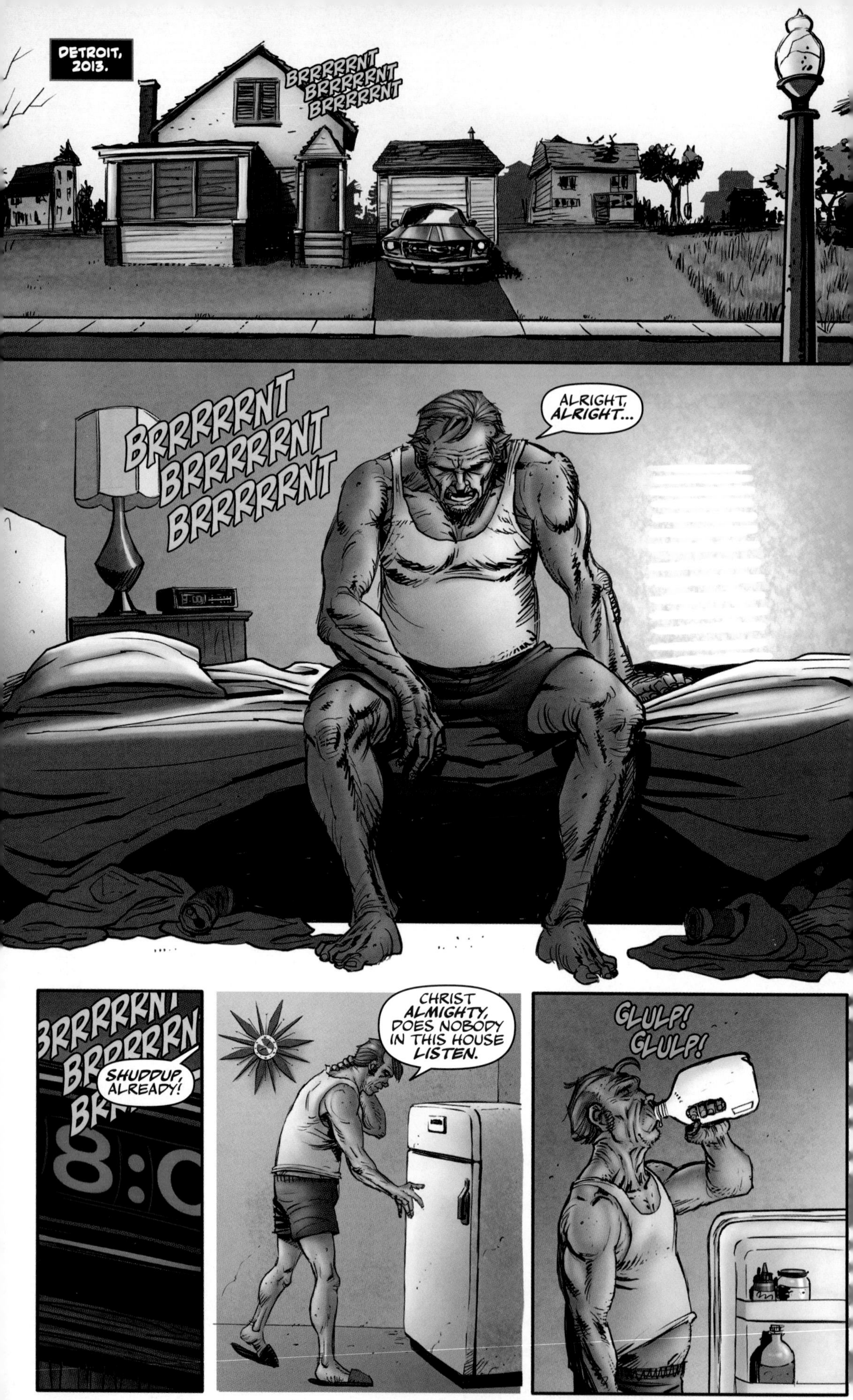
DETROIT, 2013.
BRRRRRNT BRRRRRNT BRRRRRNT
ALRIGHT, ALRIGHT...
BRRRRRNT BRRRRRNT BRRRRRNT
SHUDDUP, ALREADY!
CHRIST ALMIGHTY, DOES NOBODY IN THIS HOUSE LISTEN.
GLULP! GLULP!

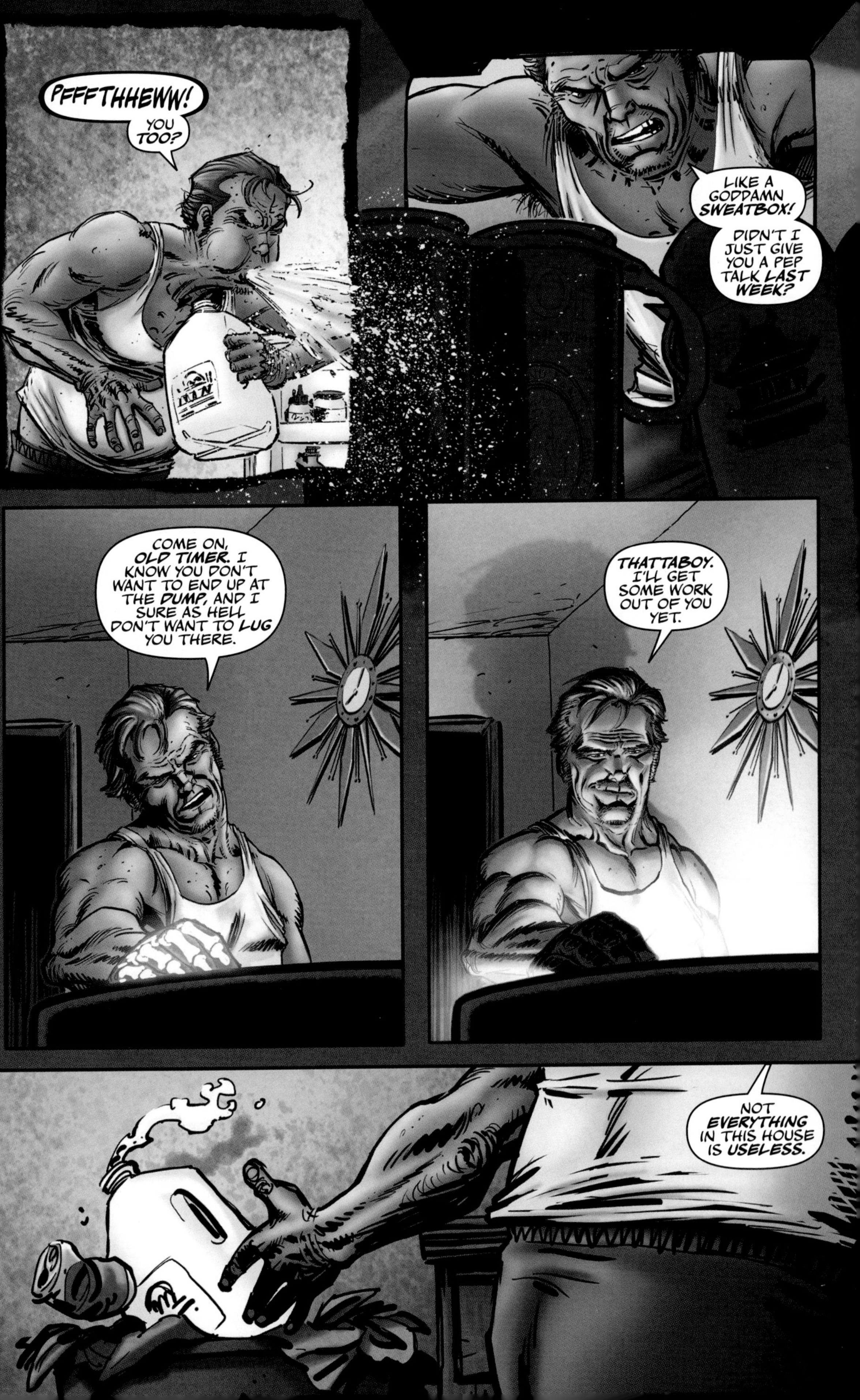
PFFFTHHEWW!
YOU TOO?
LIKE A GODDAMN SWEATBOX!
DIDN'T I JUST GIVE YOU A PEP TALK LAST WEEK?
COME ON, OLD TIMER. I KNOW YOU DON'T WANT TO END UP AT THE DUMP, AND I SURE AS HELL DON'T WANT TO LUG YOU THERE.
THATTABOY. I'LL GET SOME WORK OUT OF YOU YET.
NOT EVERYTHING IN THIS HOUSE IS USELESS.

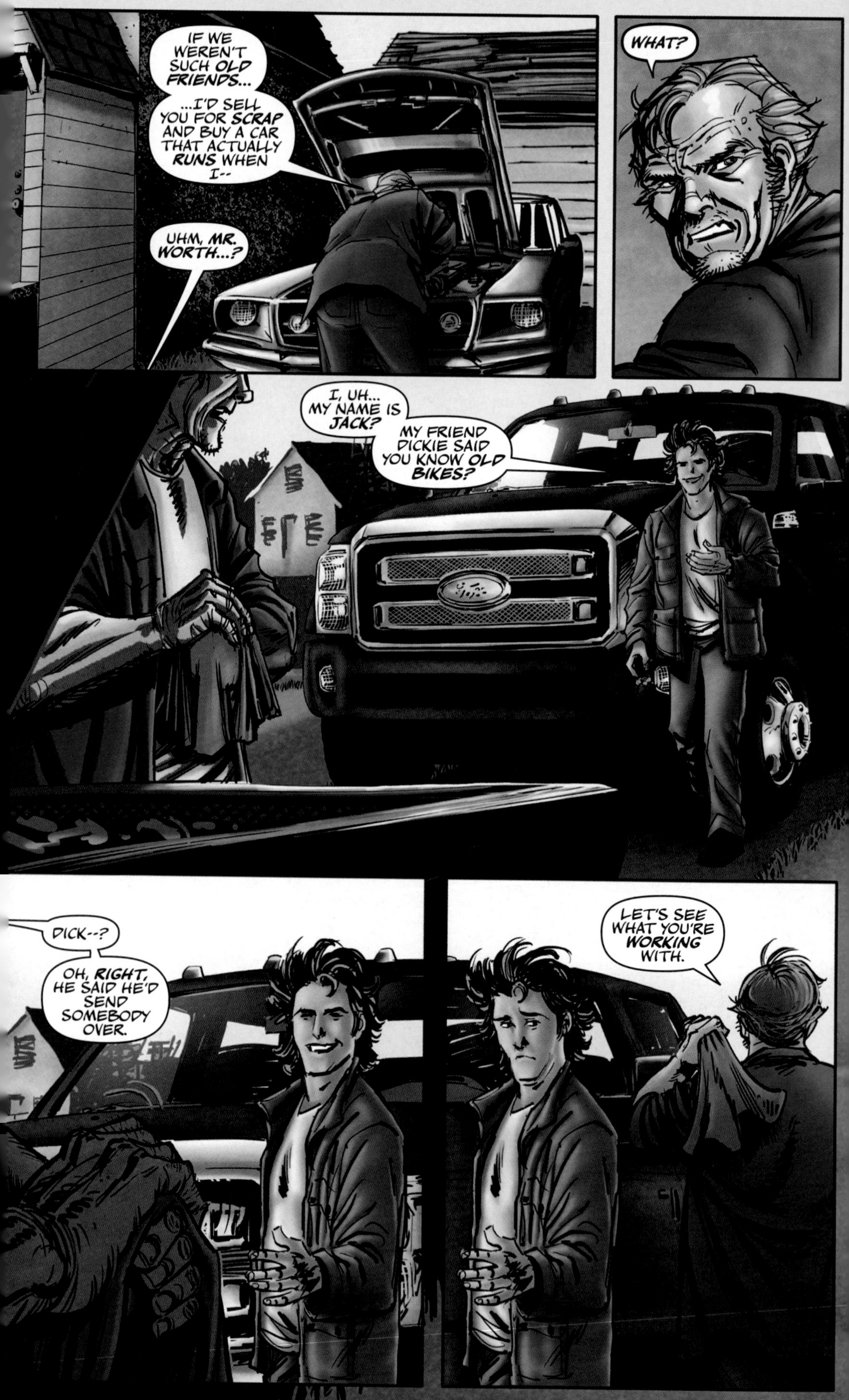
IF WE WEREN'T SUCH OLD FRIENDS...
...I'D SELL YOU FOR SCRAP AND BUY A CAR THAT ACTUALLY RUNS WHEN I--
UHM, MR. WORTH...?
WHAT?
I, UH... MY NAME IS JACK?
MY FRIEND DICKIE SAID YOU KNOW OLD BIKES?
DICK--?
OH, RIGHT, HE SAID HE'D SEND SOMEBODY OVER.
LET'S SEE WHAT YOU'RE WORKING WITH.

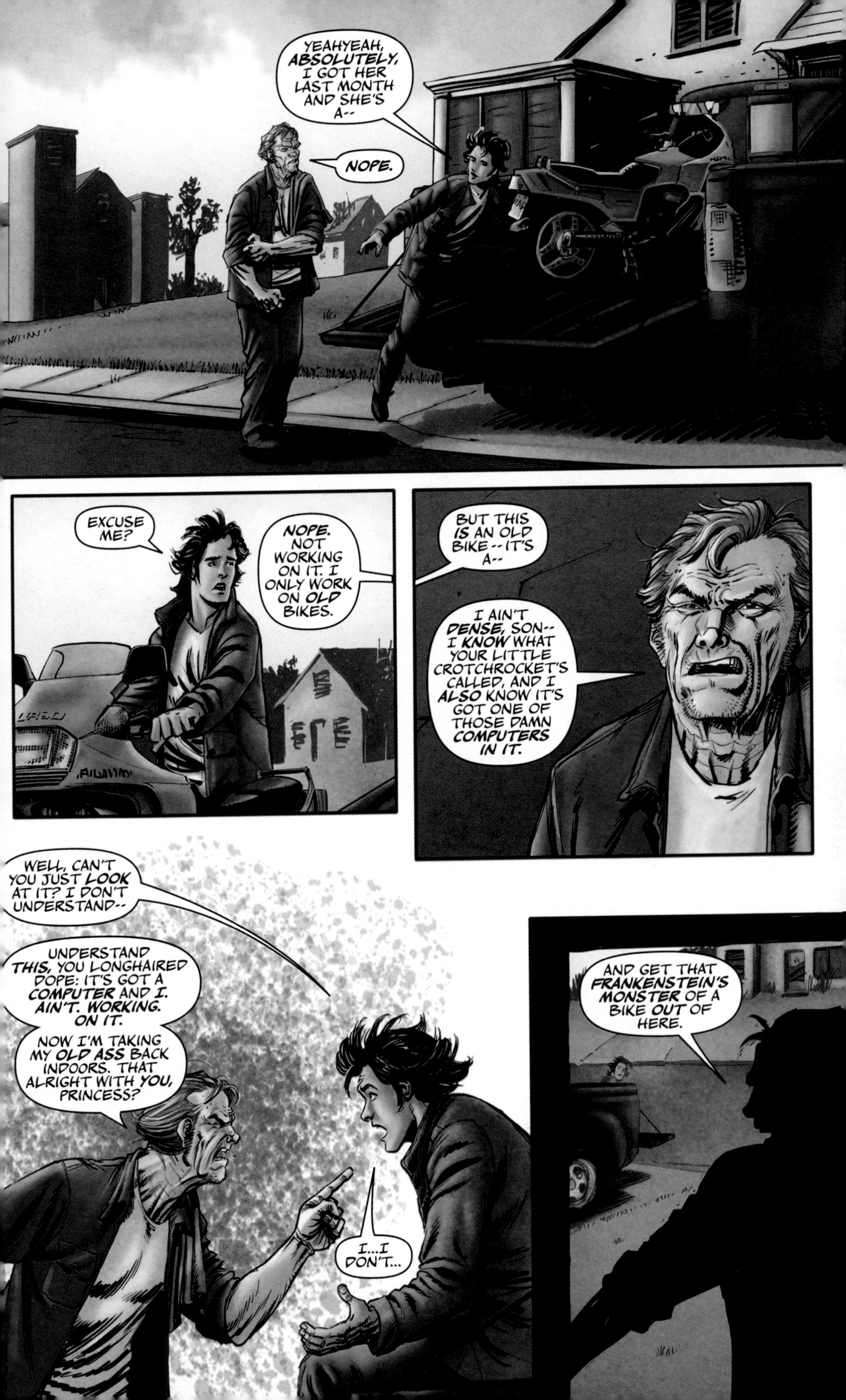
YEAHYEAH, ABSOLUTELY, I GOT HER LAST MONTH AND SHE'S A--
NOPE.
EXCUSE ME?
NOPE. NOT WORKING ON IT. I ONLY WORK ON OLD BIKES.
BUT THIS IS AN OLD BIKE -- IT'S A--
I AIN'T DENSE, SON-- I KNOW WHAT YOUR LITTLE CROTCHROCKET'S CALLED, AND I ALSO KNOW IT'S GOT ONE OF THOSE DAMN COMPUTERS IN IT.
WELL, CAN'T YOU JUST LOOK AT IT? I DON'T UNDERSTAND--
UNDERSTAND THIS, YOU LONGHAIRED DOPE: IT'S GOT A COMPUTER AND I. AIN'T. WORKING. ON IT.
NOW I'M TAKING MY OLD ASS BACK INDOORS. THAT ALRIGHT WITH YOU, PRINCESS?
I...I DON'T...
AND GET THAT FRANKENSTEIN'S MONSTER OF A BIKE OUT OF HERE.

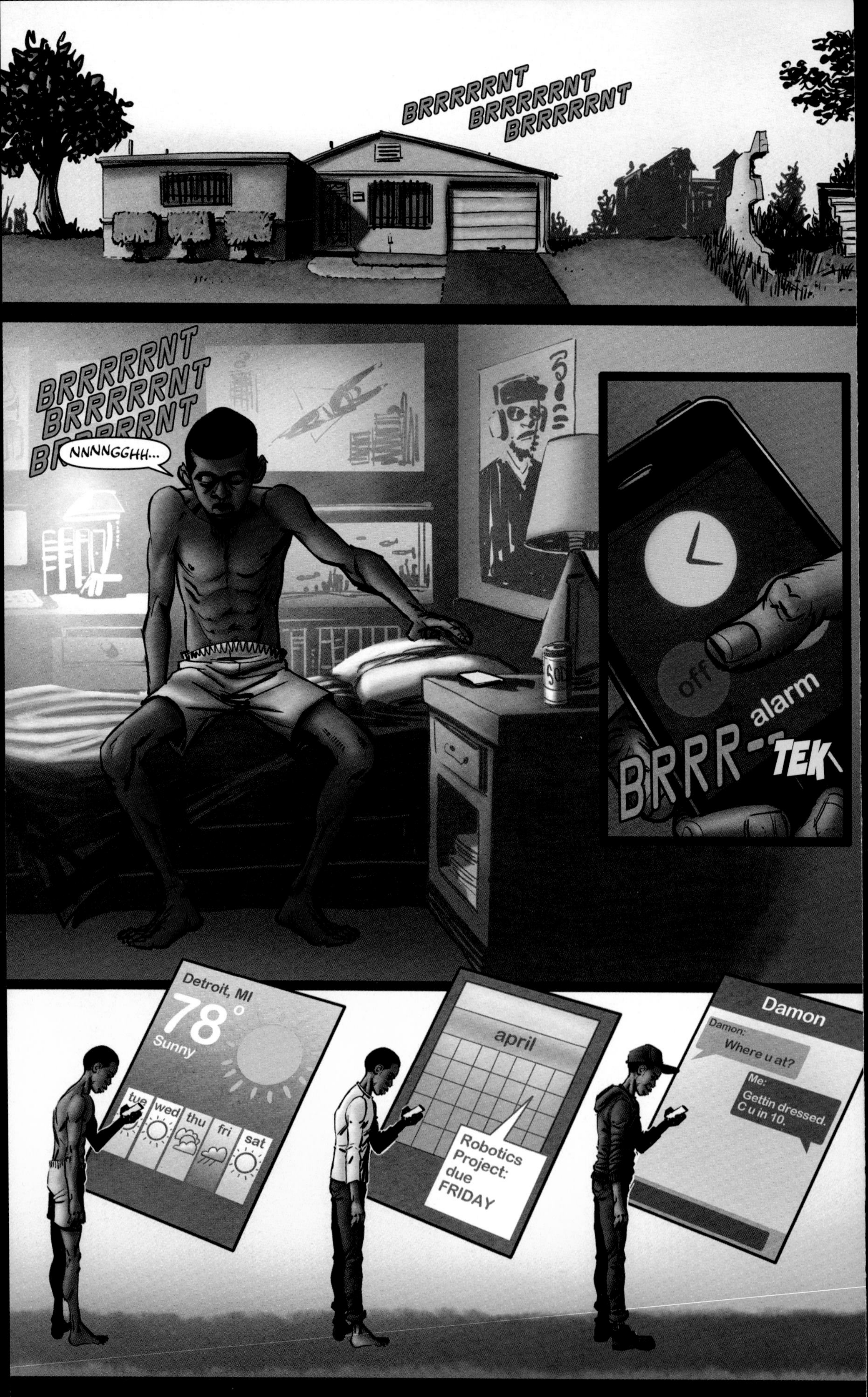
BRRRRRNT BRRRRRNT BRRRRRNT
BRRRRRNT BRRRRRNT BRRRRRNT
NNNNGGHH...
off
alarm
BRRR-
TEK
Detroit, MI
78°
Sunny
tue
wed
thu
fri
sat
april
Robotics Project: due FRIDAY
Damon
Damon:
Where u at?
Me:
Gettin dressed. C u in 10.

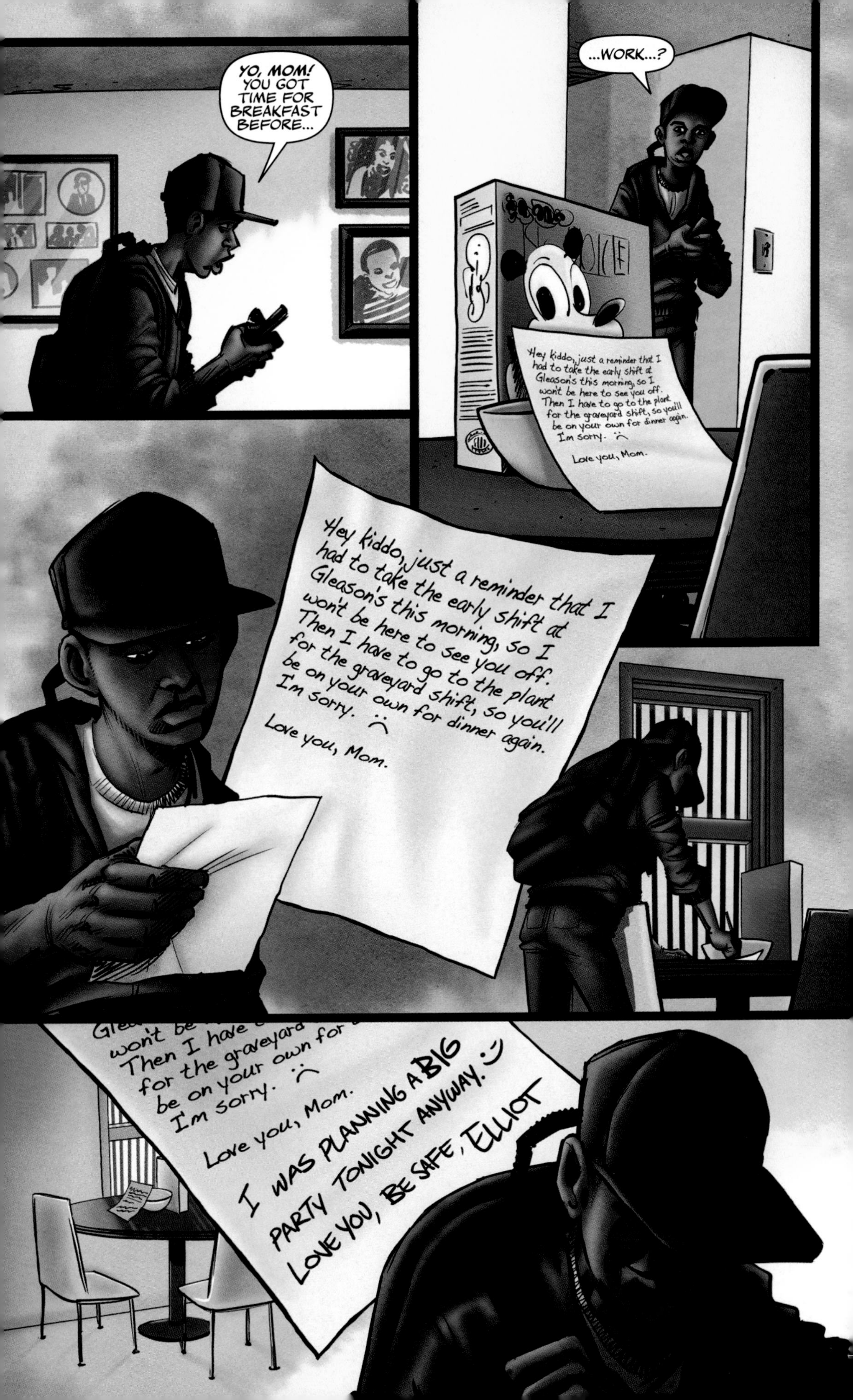
YO, MOM! YOU GOT TIME FOR BREAKFAST BEFORE...
...WORK...?
Hey kiddo, just a reminder that I had to take the early shift at Gleason's this morning, so I won't be here to see you off. Then I have to go to the plant for the graveyard shift, so you'll be on your own for dinner again. I'm sorry. :(
Love you, Mom.
Hey kiddo, just a reminder that I had to take the early shift at Gleason's this morning, so I won't be here to see you off. Then I have to go to the plant for the graveyard shift, so you'll be on your own for dinner again. I'm sorry. :(
Love you, Mom.
I WAS PLANNING A BIG PARTY TONIGHT ANYWAY. :)
LOVE YOU, BE SAFE, ELLIOT

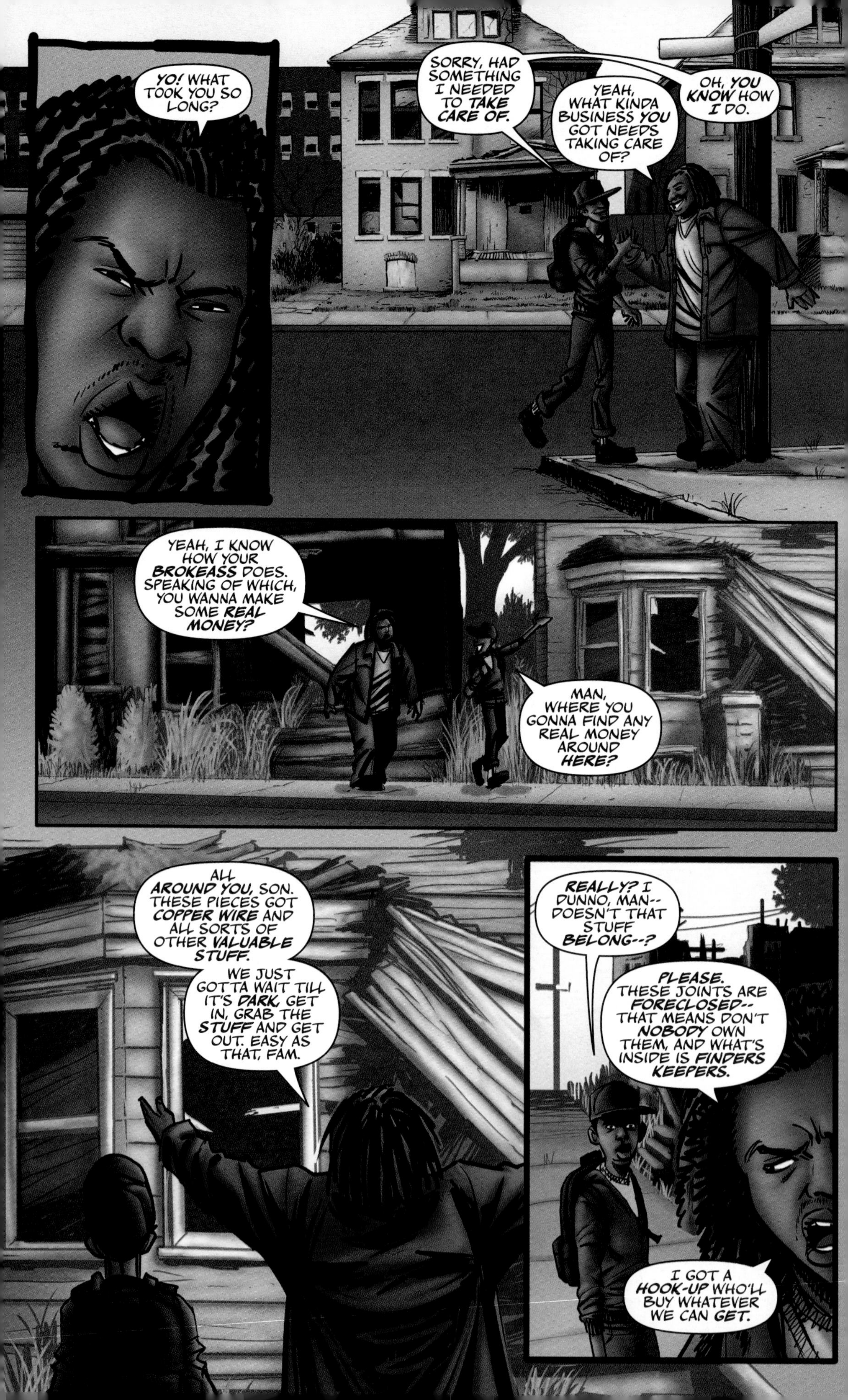

YO! WHAT TOOK YOU SO LONG?
SORRY, HAD SOMETHING I NEEDED TO TAKE CARE OF.
YEAH, WHAT KINDA BUSINESS YOU GOT NEEDS TAKING CARE OF?
OH, YOU KNOW HOW I DO.
YEAH, I KNOW HOW YOUR BROKEASS DOES. SPEAKING OF WHICH, YOU WANNA MAKE SOME REAL MONEY?
MAN, WHERE YOU GONNA FIND ANY REAL MONEY AROUND HERE?
ALL AROUND YOU, SON. THESE PIECES GOT COPPER WIRE AND ALL SORTS OF OTHER VALUABLE STUFF.
WE JUST GOTTA WAIT TILL IT'S DARK, GET IN, GRAB THE STUFF AND GET OUT. EASY AS THAT, FAM.
REALLY? I DUNNO, MAN-- DOESN'T THAT STUFF BELONG--?
PLEASE. THESE JOINTS ARE FORECLOSED-- THAT MEANS DON'T NOBODY OWN THEM, AND WHAT'S INSIDE IS FINDERS KEEPERS.
I GOT A HOOK-UP WHO'LL BUY WHATEVER WE CAN GET.

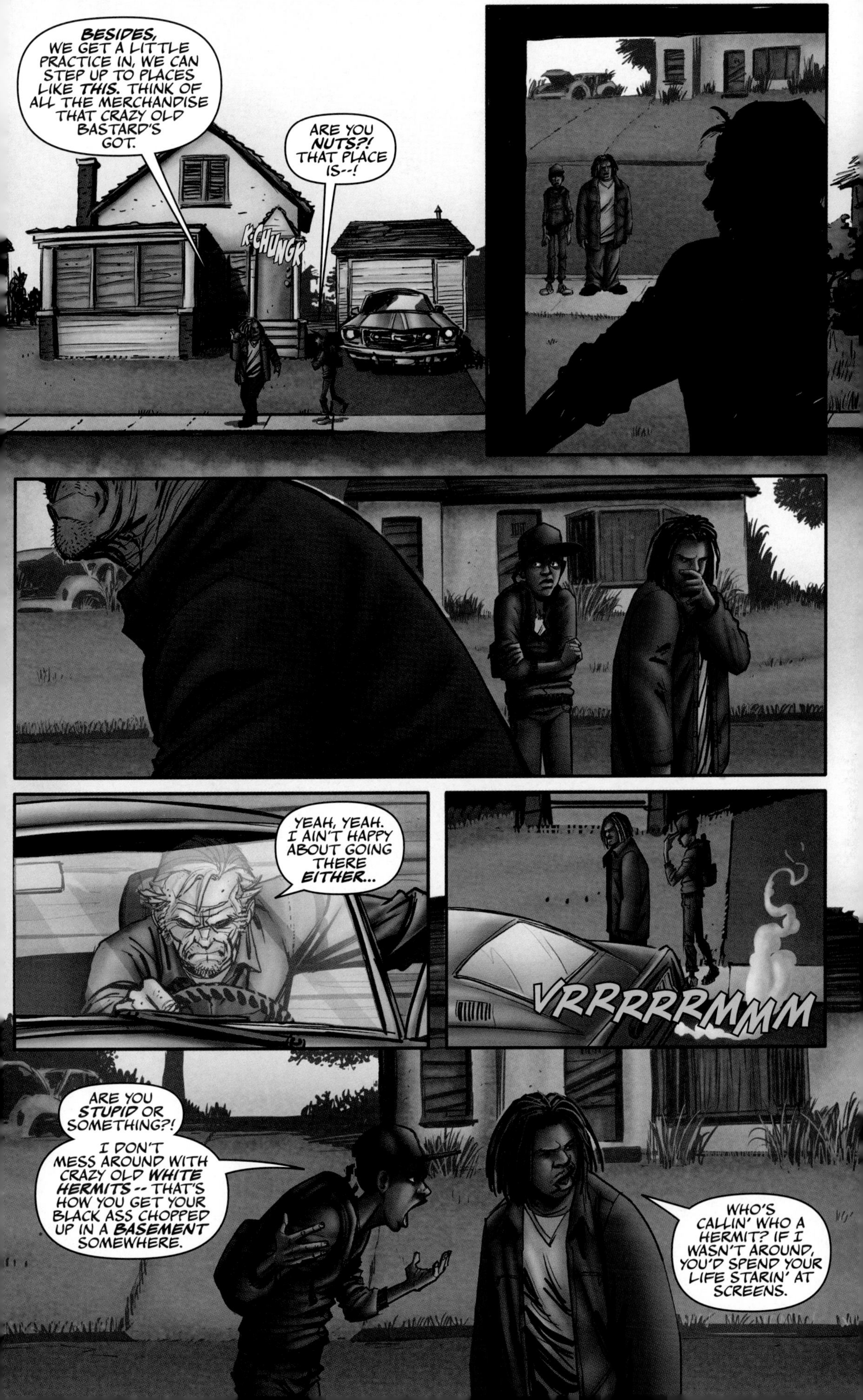
BESIDES, WE GET A LITTLE PRACTICE IN, WE CAN STEP UP TO PLACES LIKE THIS. THINK OF ALL THE MERCHANDISE THAT CRAZY OLD BASTARD'S GOT.
K-CHUNGK
ARE YOU NUTS?! THAT PLACE IS--!
YEAH, YEAH. I AIN'T HAPPY ABOUT GOING THERE EITHER...
VRRRRRMMM
ARE YOU STUPID OR SOMETHING?!
I DON'T MESS AROUND WITH CRAZY OLD WHITE HERMITS -- THAT'S HOW YOU GET YOUR BLACK ASS CHOPPED UP IN A BASEMENT SOMEWHERE.
WHO'S CALLIN' WHO A HERMIT? IF I WASN'T AROUND, YOU'D SPEND YOUR LIFE STARIN' AT SCREENS.

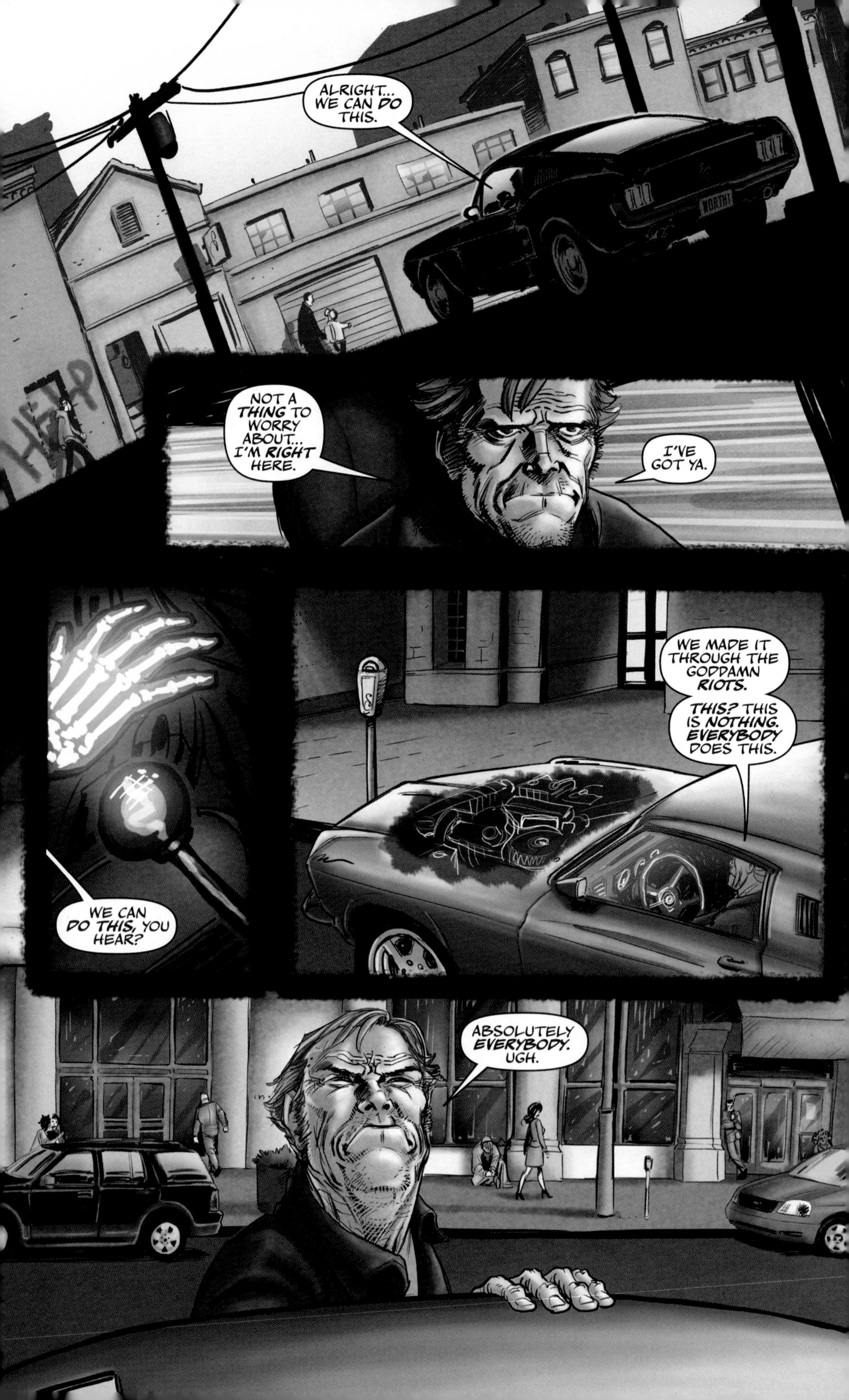
ALRIGHT... WE CAN DO THIS.
NOT A THING TO WORRY ABOUT... I'M RIGHT HERE.
I'VE GOT YA.
WE CAN DO THIS, YOU HEAR?
WE MADE IT THROUGH THE GODDAMN RIOTS.
THIS? THIS IS NOTHING. EVERYBODY DOES THIS.
ABSOLUTELY EVERYBODY. UGH.

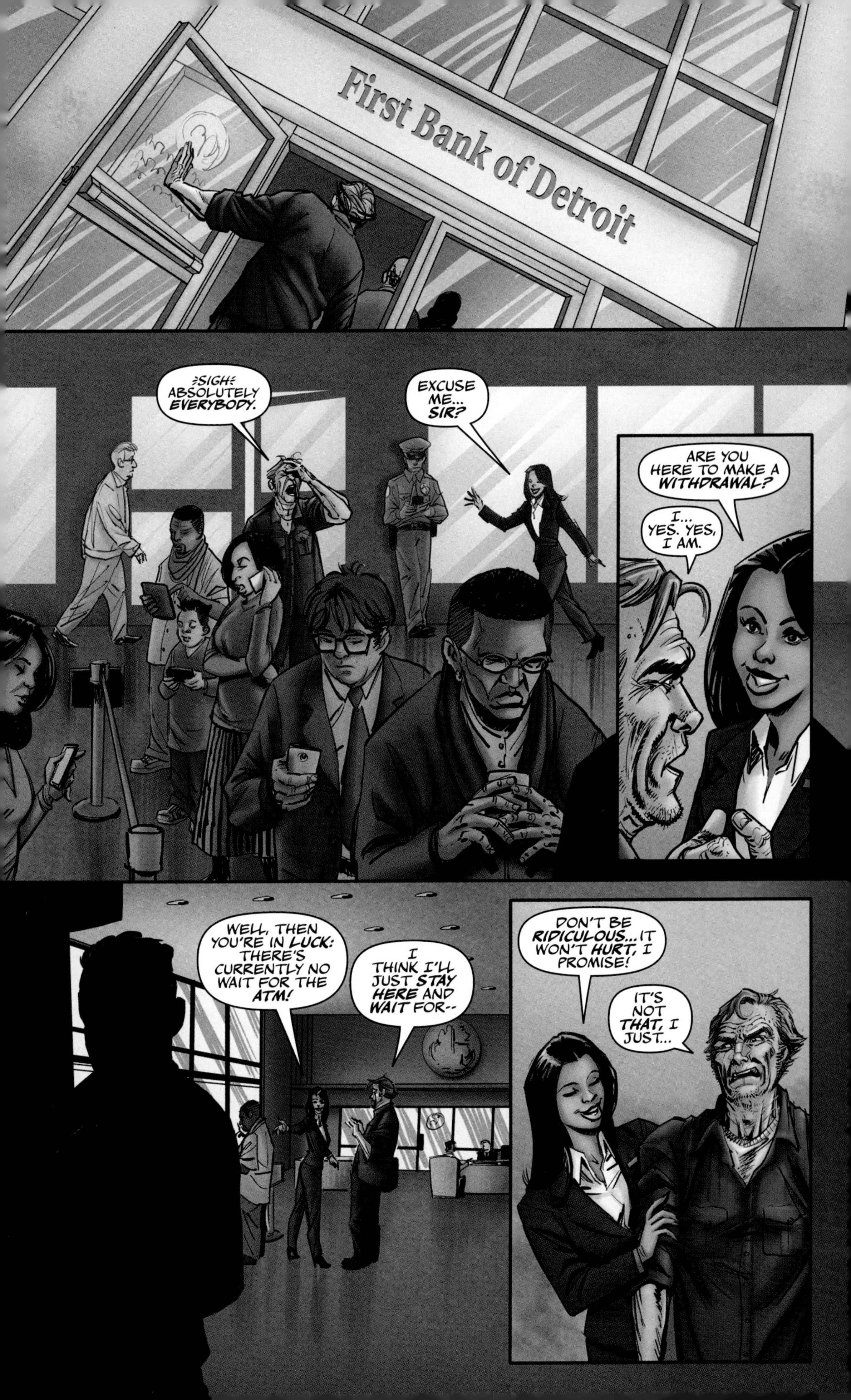
First Bank of Detroit
SIGH ABSOLUTELY EVERYBODY.
EXCUSE ME... SIR?
ARE YOU HERE TO MAKE A WITHDRAWAL?
I... YES. YES, I AM.
WELL, THEN YOU'RE IN LUCK: THERE'S CURRENTLY NO WAIT FOR THE ATM!
I THINK I'LL JUST STAY HERE AND WAIT FOR--
DON'T BE RIDICULOUS... IT WON'T HURT, I PROMISE!
IT'S NOT THAT, I JUST...

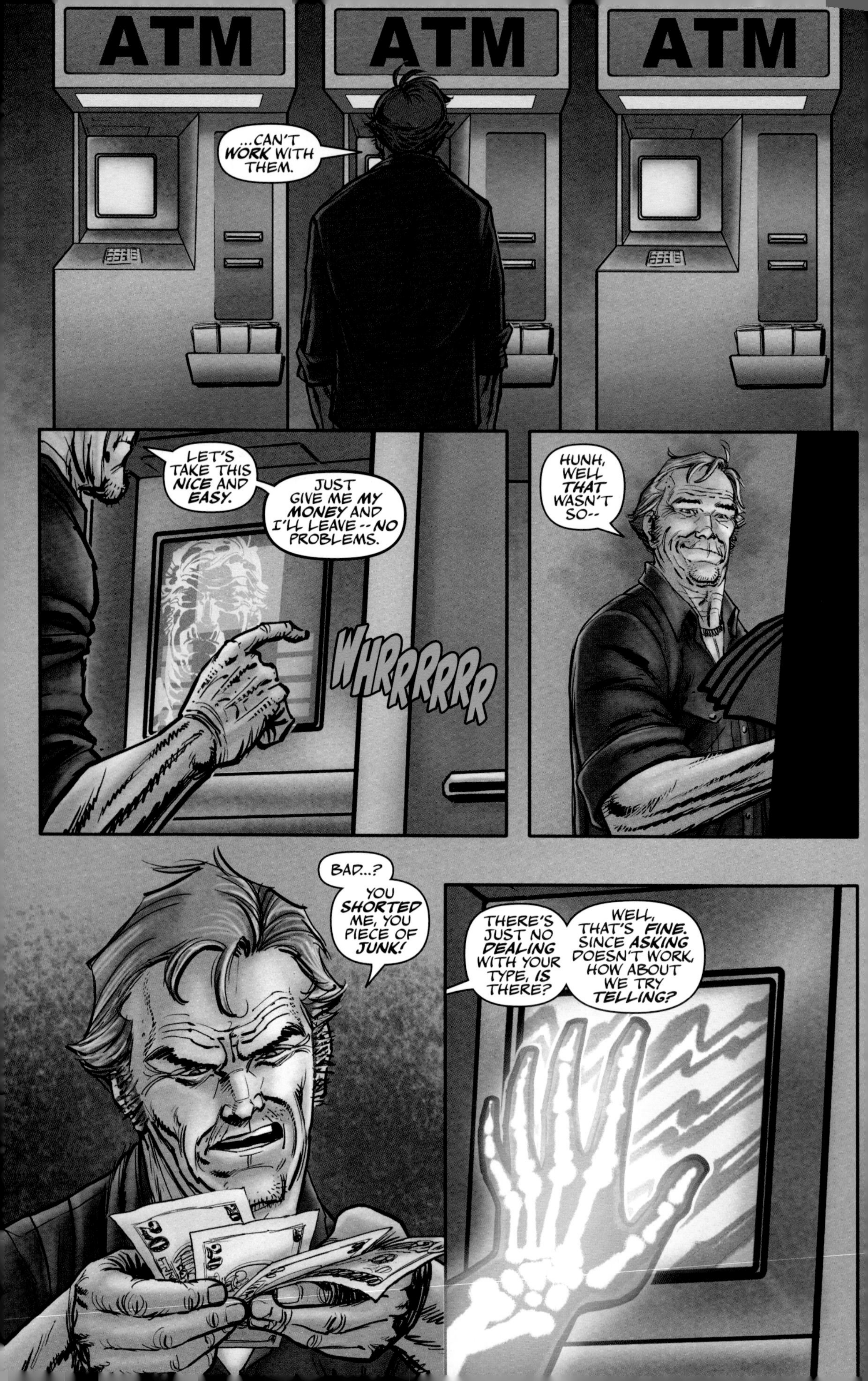
ATM
ATM
ATM
...CAN'T WORK WITH THEM.
LET'S TAKE THIS NICE AND EASY.
JUST GIVE ME MY MONEY AND I'LL LEAVE -- NO PROBLEMS.
WHRRRRRR
HUNH, WELL THAT WASN'T SO--
BAD...?
YOU SHORTED ME, YOU PIECE OF JUNK!
THERE'S JUST NO DEALING WITH YOUR TYPE, IS THERE?
WELL, THAT'S FINE. SINCE ASKING DOESN'T WORK, HOW ABOUT WE TRY TELLING?

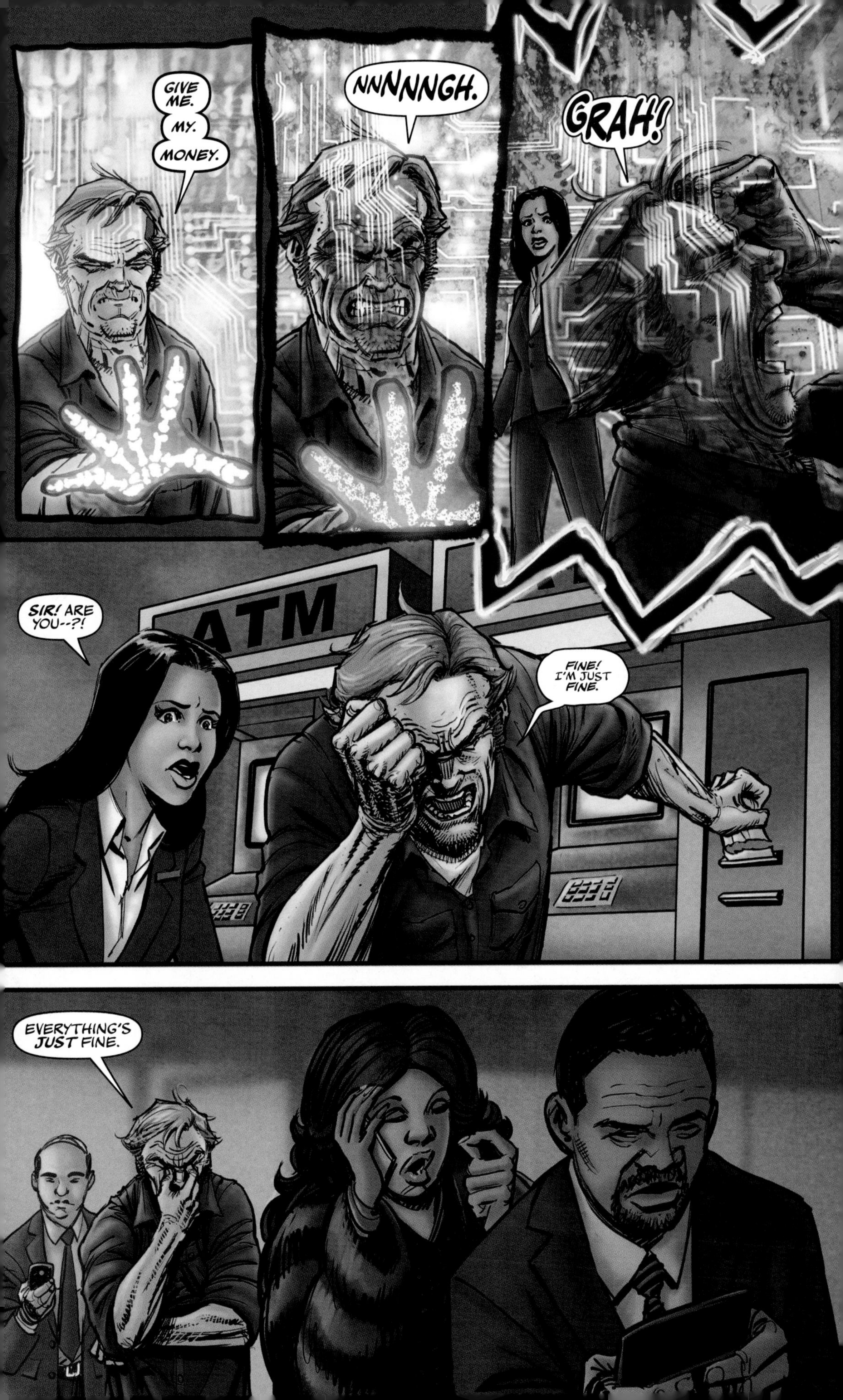
GIVE ME.
MY.
MONEY.
NNNNNGH.
GRAH!
SIR! ARE YOU--?!
FINE! I'M JUST FINE.
EVERYTHING'S JUST FINE.

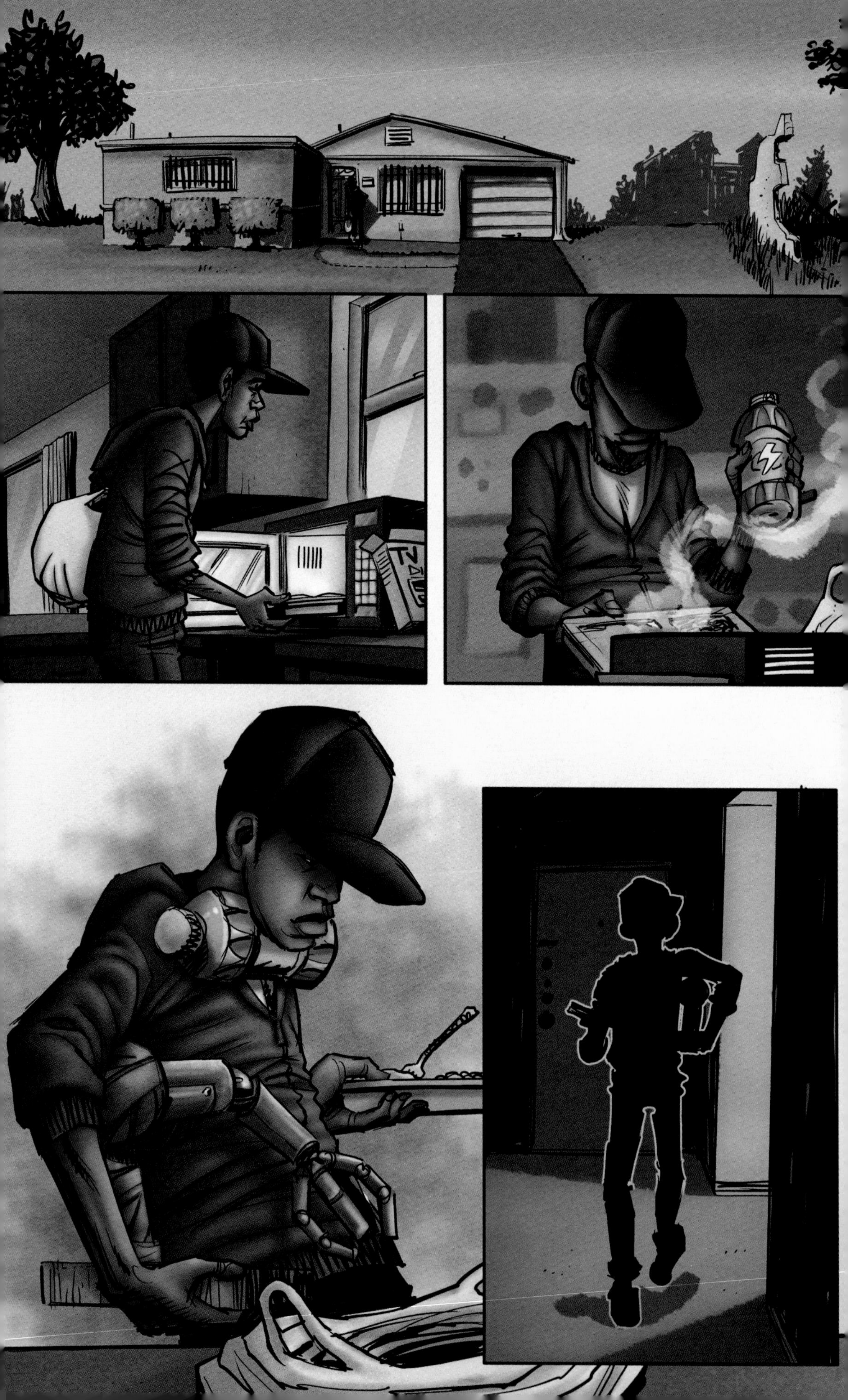

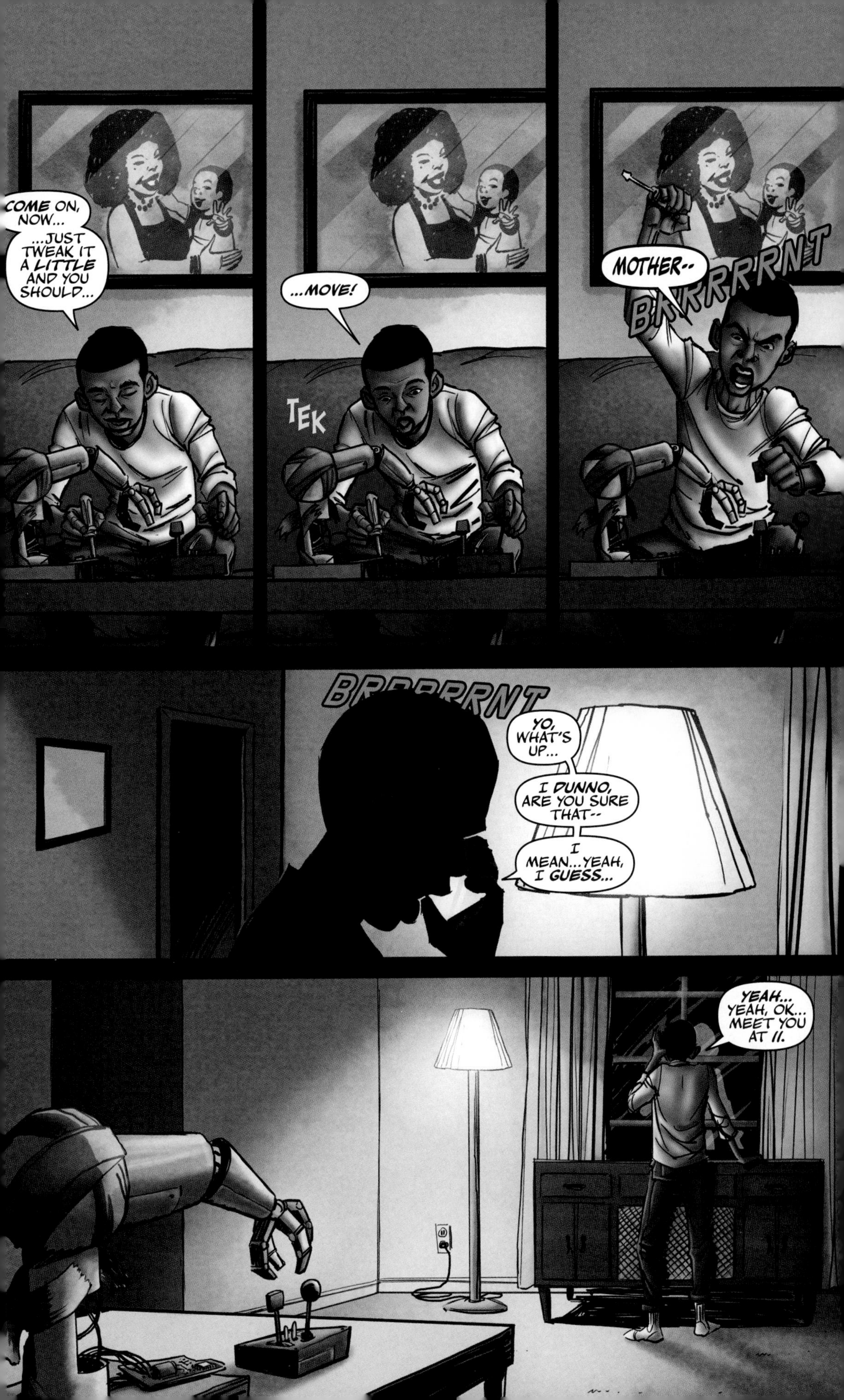
COME ON, NOW...
...JUST TWEAK IT A LITTLE AND YOU SHOULD...
TEK
...MOVE!
MOTHER--
BRRRRRNT
BRRRRRNT
YO, WHAT'S UP...
I DUNNO, ARE YOU SURE THAT--
I MEAN...YEAH, I GUESS...
YEAH... YEAH, OK... MEET YOU AT 11.

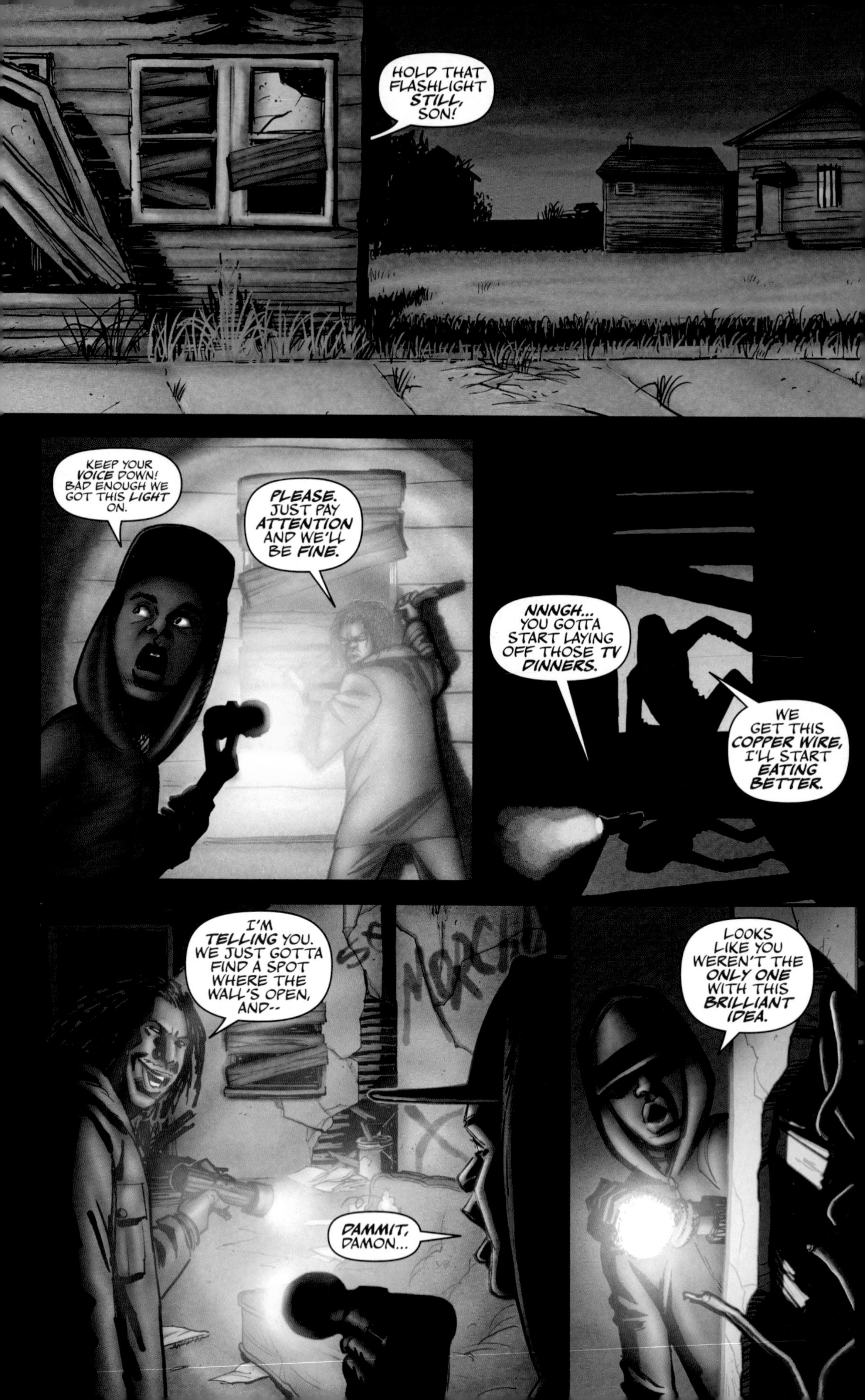
HOLD THAT FLASHLIGHT STILL, SON!
KEEP YOUR VOICE DOWN! BAD ENOUGH WE GOT THIS LIGHT ON.
PLEASE. JUST PAY ATTENTION AND WE'LL BE FINE.
NNNGH... YOU GOTTA START LAYING OFF THOSE TV DINNERS.
WE GET THIS COPPER WIRE, I'LL START EATING BETTER.
I'M TELLING YOU. WE JUST GOTTA FIND A SPOT WHERE THE WALL'S OPEN, AND--
DAMMIT, DAMON...
LOOKS LIKE YOU WEREN'T THE ONLY ONE WITH THIS BRILLIANT IDEA.

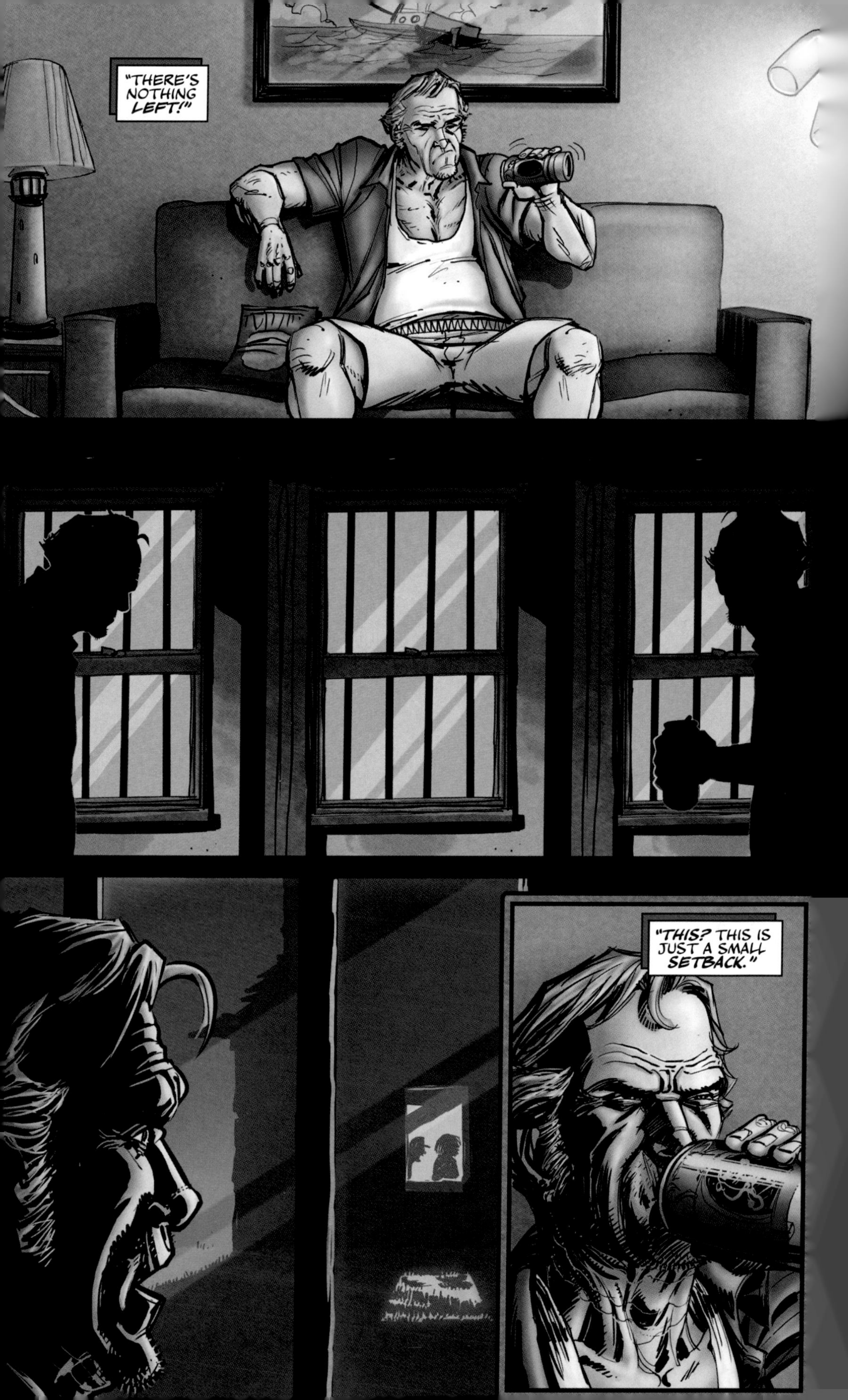
"THERE'S NOTHING LEFT!"
"THIS? THIS IS JUST A SMALL SETBACK."

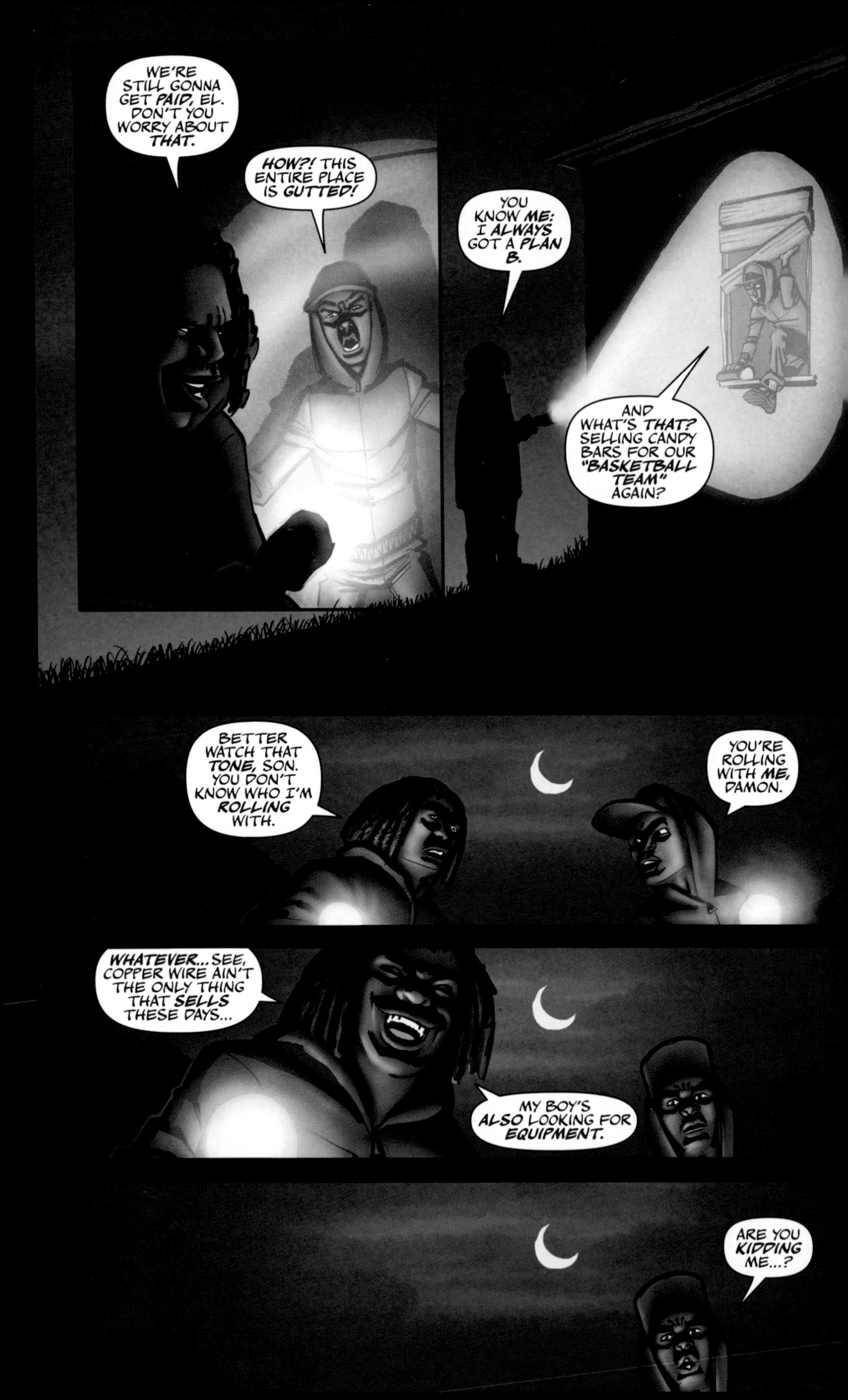
WE'RE STILL GONNA GET PAID, EL. DON'T YOU WORRY ABOUT THAT.
HOW?! THIS ENTIRE PLACE IS GUTTED!
YOU KNOW ME: I ALWAYS GOT A PLAN B.
AND WHAT'S THAT? SELLING CANDY BARS FOR OUR "BASKETBALL TEAM" AGAIN?
BETTER WATCH THAT TONE, SON. YOU DON'T KNOW WHO I'M ROLLING WITH.
YOU'RE ROLLING WITH ME, DAMON.
WHATEVER... SEE, COPPER WIRE AIN'T THE ONLY THING THAT SELLS THESE DAYS...
MY BOY'S ALSO LOOKING FOR EQUIPMENT.
ARE YOU KIDDING ME...?

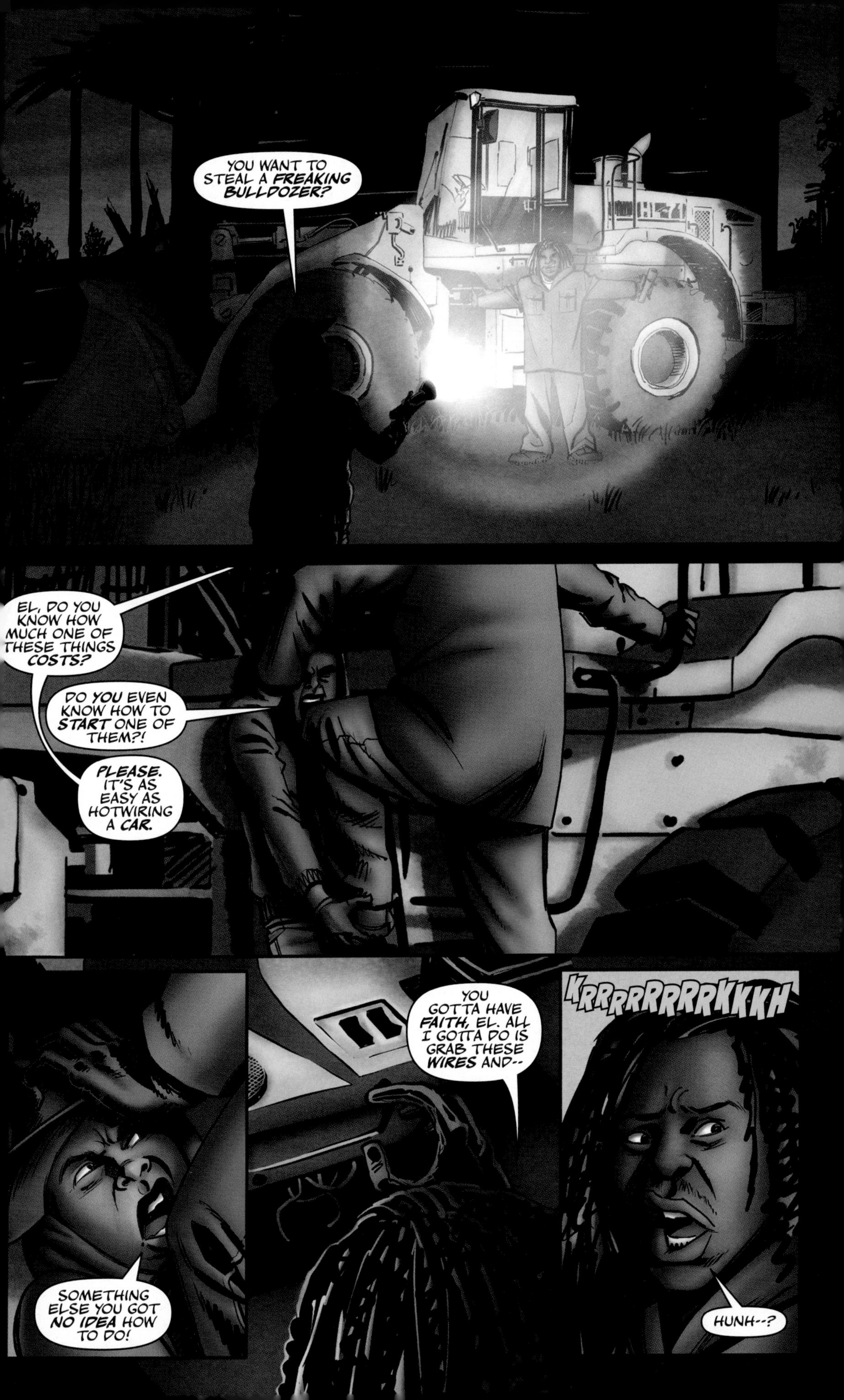
YOU WANT TO STEAL A FREAKING BULLDOZER?
EL, DO YOU KNOW HOW MUCH ONE OF THESE THINGS COSTS?
DO YOU EVEN KNOW HOW TO START ONE OF THEM?!
PLEASE. IT'S AS EASY AS HOTWIRING A CAR.
SOMETHING ELSE YOU GOT NO IDEA HOW TO DO!
YOU GOTTA HAVE FAITH, EL. ALL I GOTTA DO IS GRAB THESE WIRES AND--
KRRRRRRRRKKKH
HUNH--?

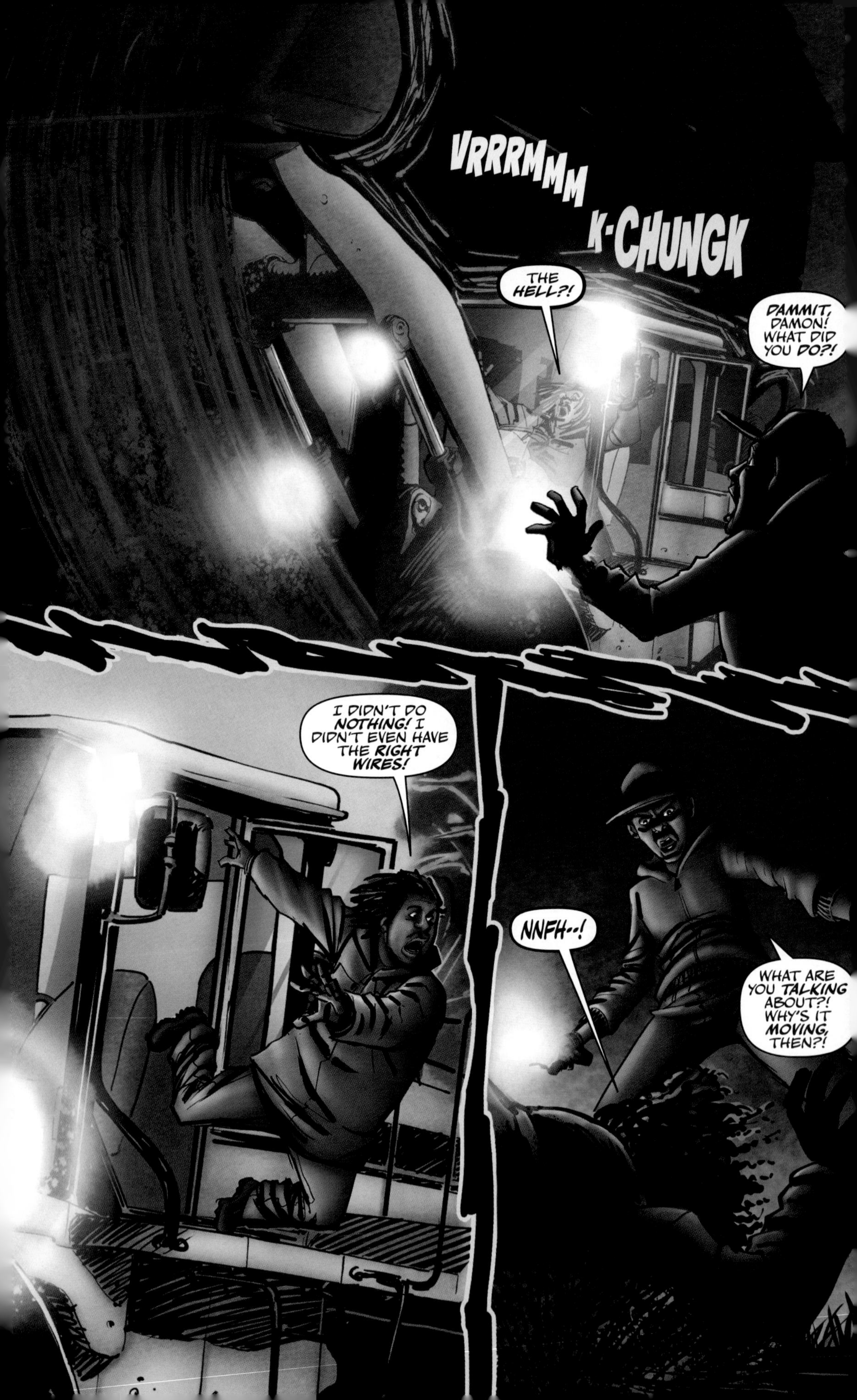
VRRRMMM
K-CHUNGK
THE HELL?!
DAMMIT, DAMON! WHAT DID YOU DO?!
I DIDN'T DO NOTHING! I DIDN'T EVEN HAVE THE RIGHT WIRES!
NNFH--!
WHAT ARE YOU TALKING ABOUT?! WHY'S IT MOVING, THEN?!

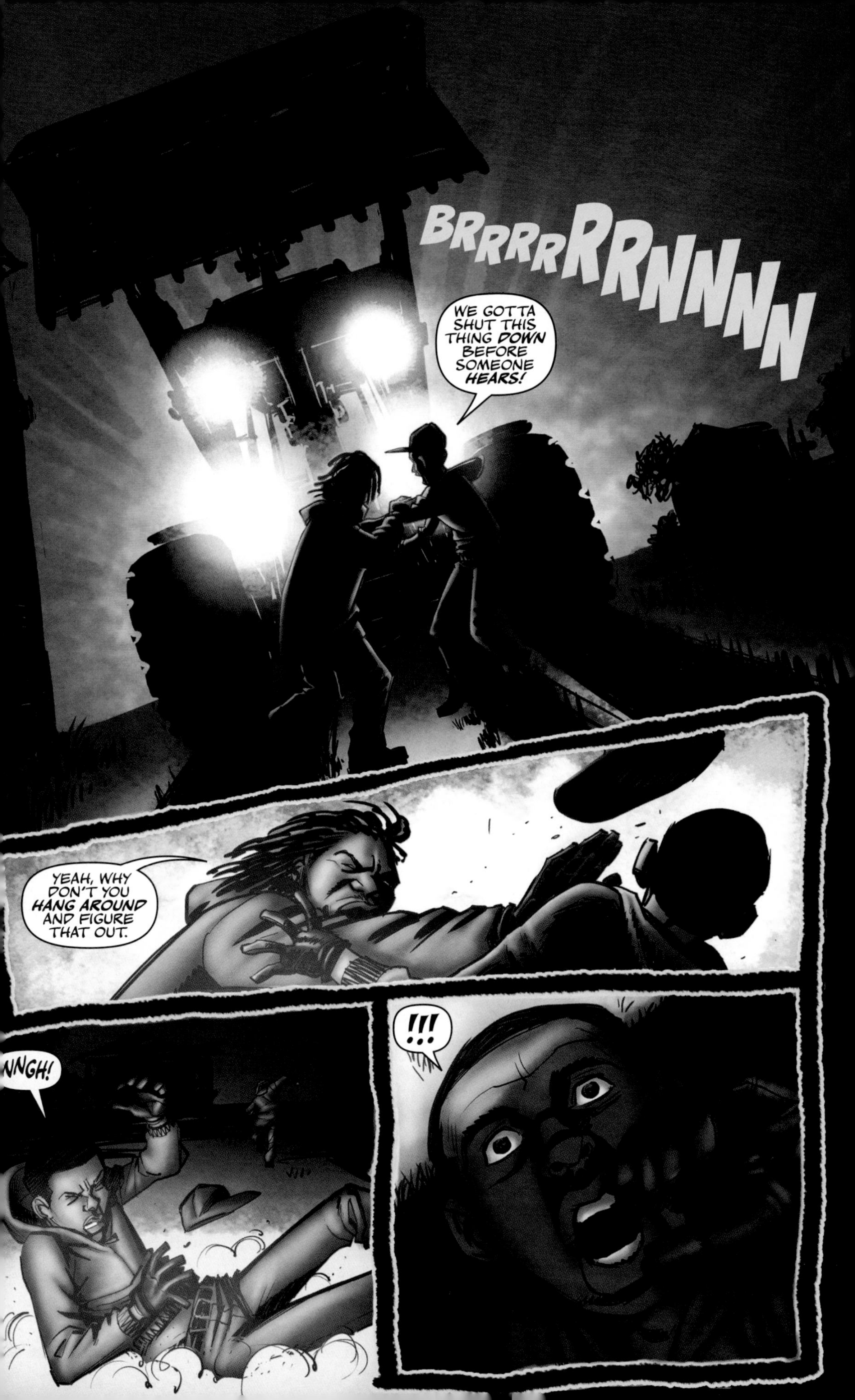
BRRRRRRNNNNN
WE GOTTA SHUT THIS THING DOWN BEFORE SOMEONE HEARS!
YEAH, WHY DON'T YOU HANG AROUND AND FIGURE THAT OUT.
NNGH!
!!!

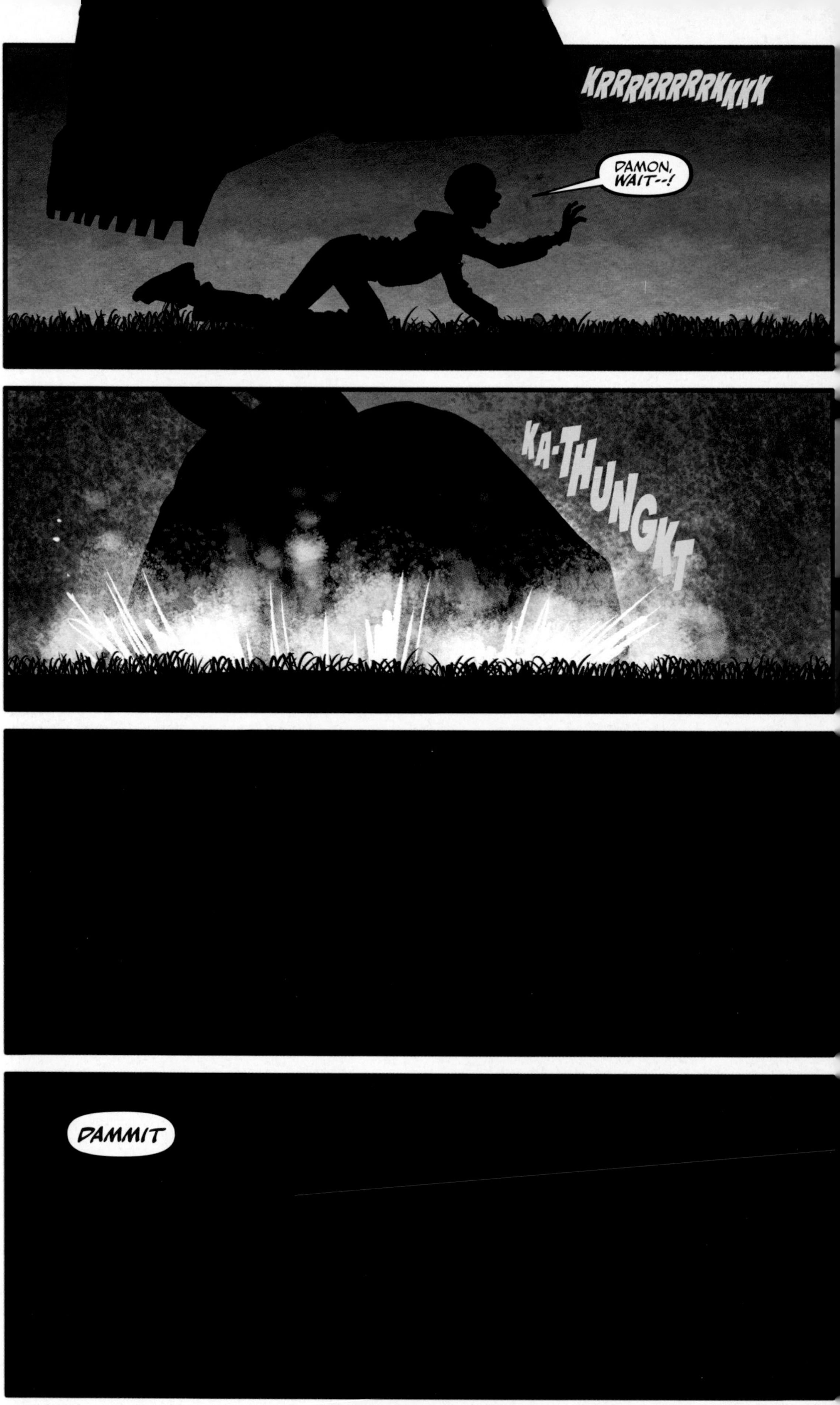
KRRRRRRRRKKKK
DAMON, WAIT--!
KA-THUNGKT
DAMMIT

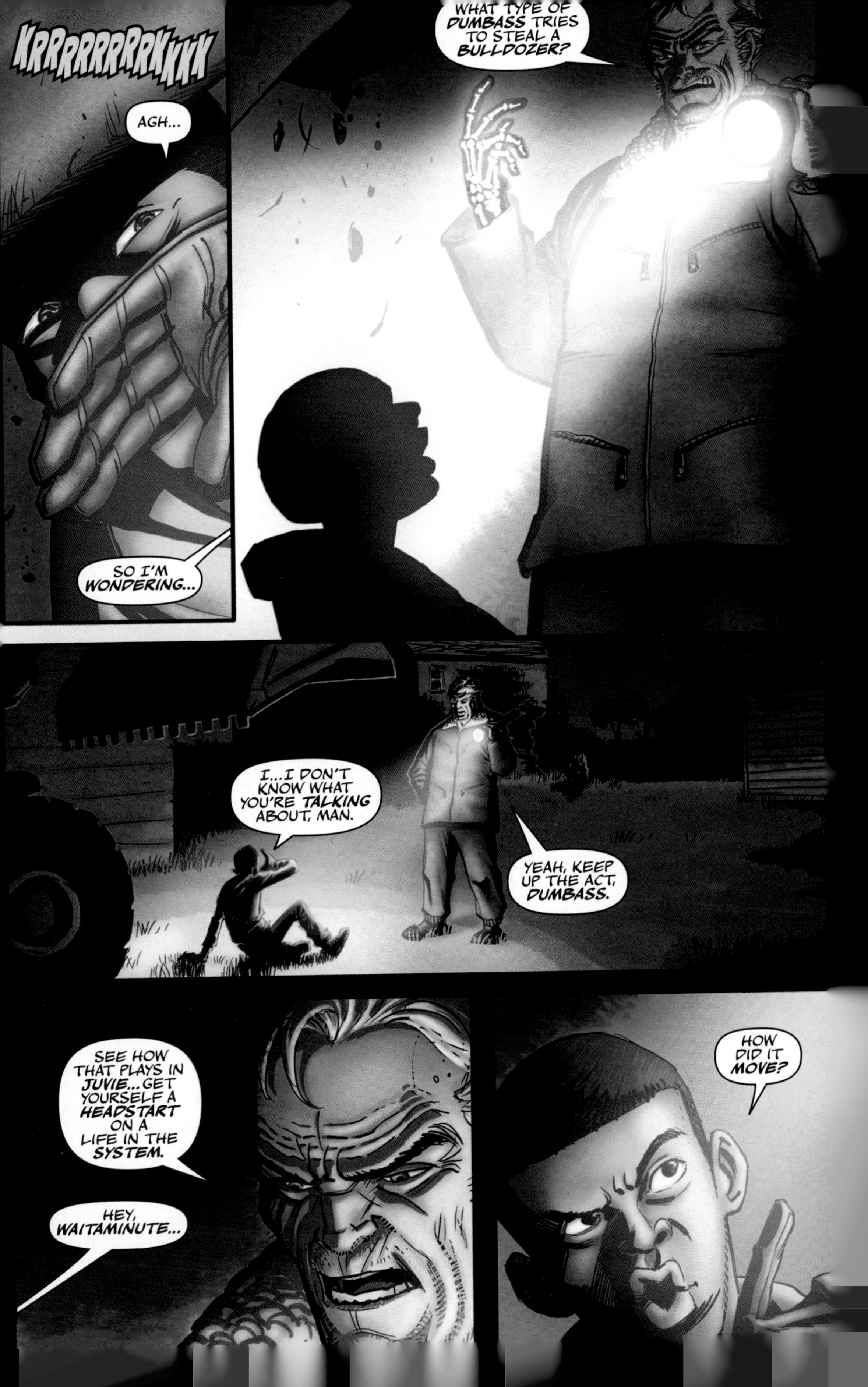
KRRRRRRRRKKKK
AGH...
SO I'M WONDERING...
WHAT TYPE OF DUMBASS TRIES TO STEAL A BULLDOZER?
I...I DON'T KNOW WHAT YOU'RE TALKING ABOUT, MAN.
YEAH, KEEP UP THE ACT, DUMBASS.
SEE HOW THAT PLAYS IN JUVIE...GET YOURSELF A HEADSTART ON A LIFE IN THE SYSTEM.
HEY, WAITAMINUTE...
HOW DID IT MOVE?

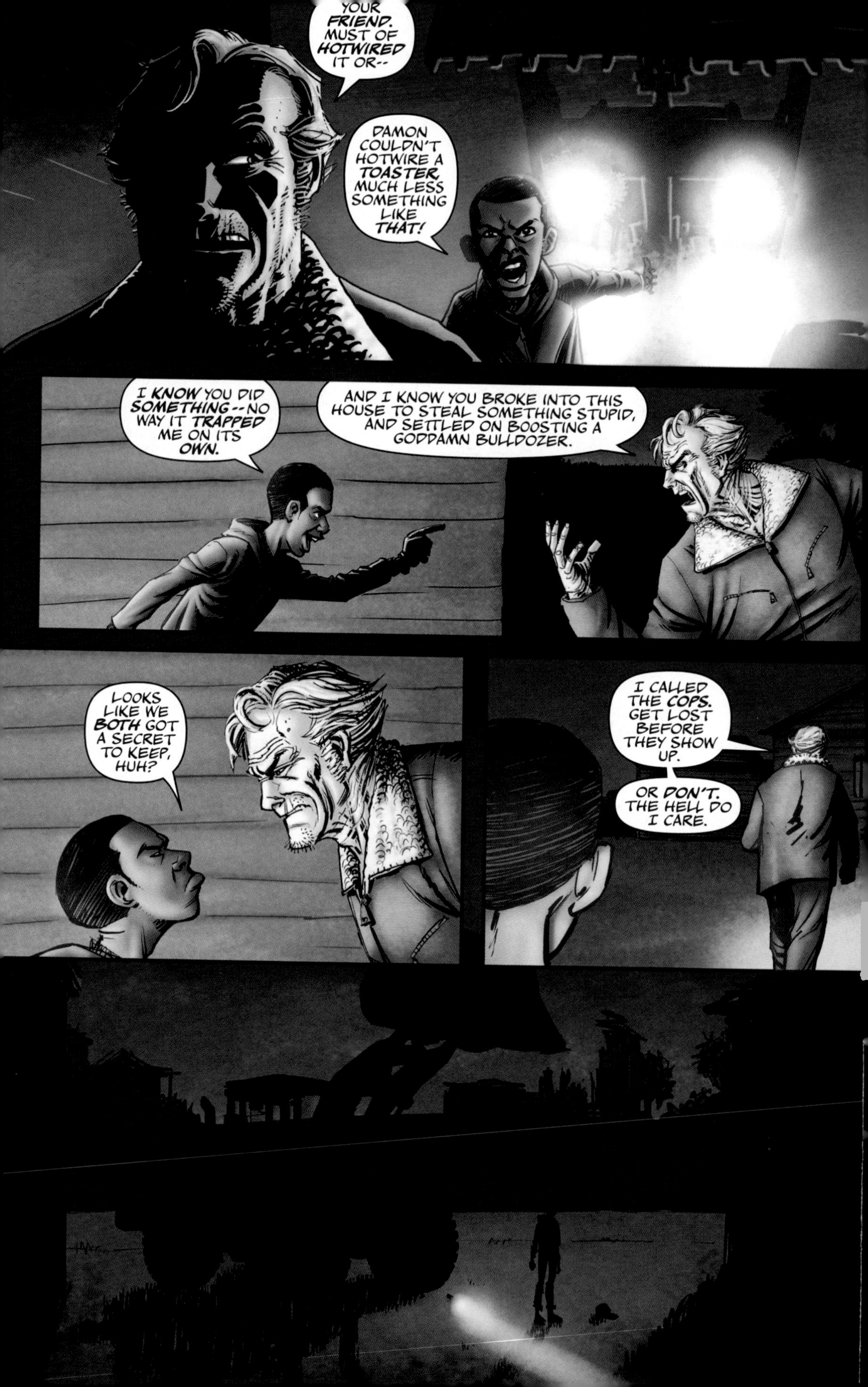
YOUR FRIEND. MUST OF HOTWIRED IT OR--
DAMON COULDN'T HOTWIRE A TOASTER, MUCH LESS SOMETHING LIKE THAT!
I KNOW YOU DID SOMETHING--NO WAY IT TRAPPED ME ON ITS OWN.
AND I KNOW YOU BROKE INTO THIS HOUSE TO STEAL SOMETHING STUPID, AND SETTLED ON BOOSTING A GODDAMN BULLDOZER.
LOOKS LIKE WE BOTH GOT A SECRET TO KEEP, HUH?
I CALLED THE COPS. GET LOST BEFORE THEY SHOW UP.
OR DON'T. THE HELL DO I CARE.

CHAPTER 2

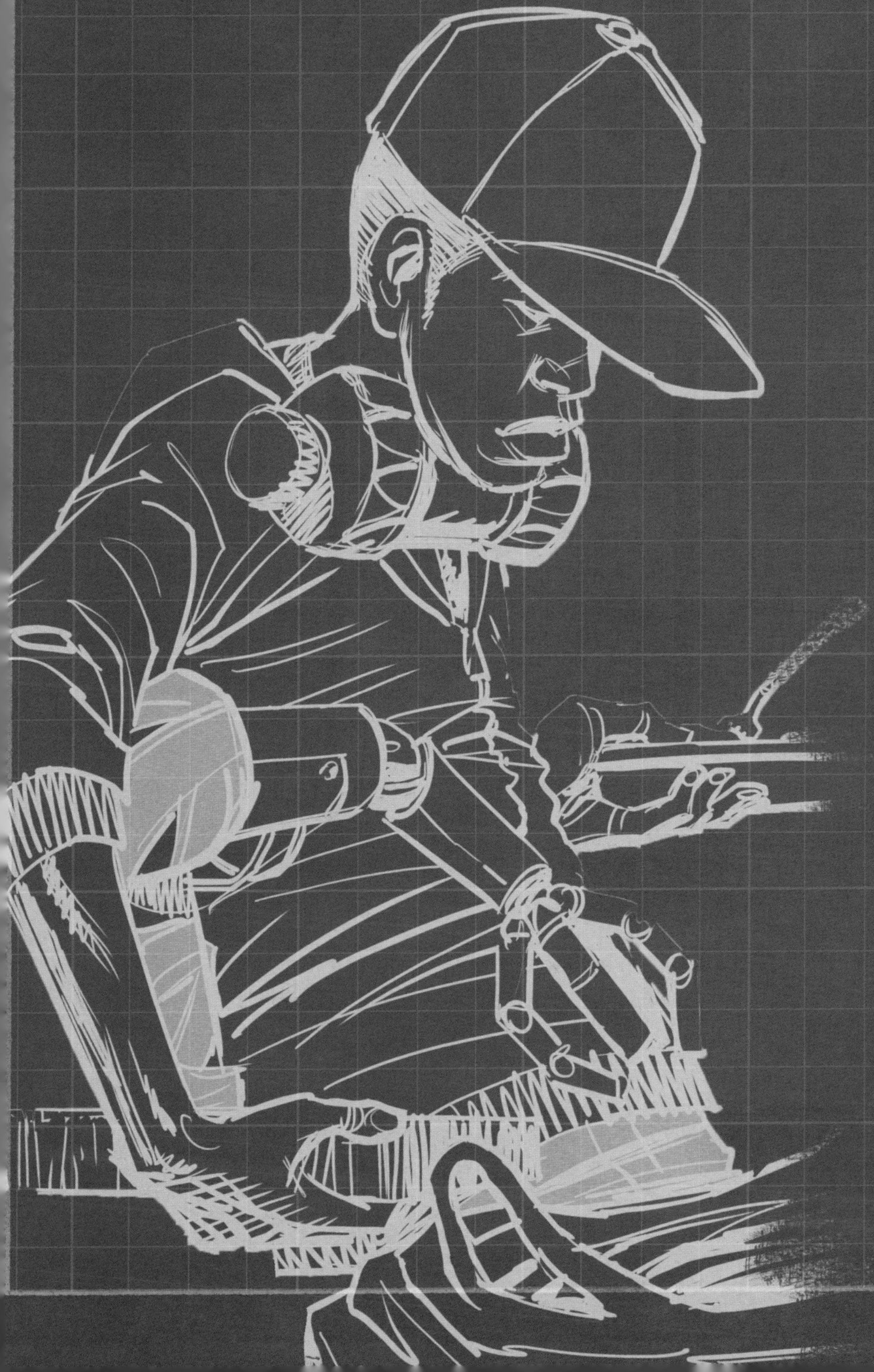

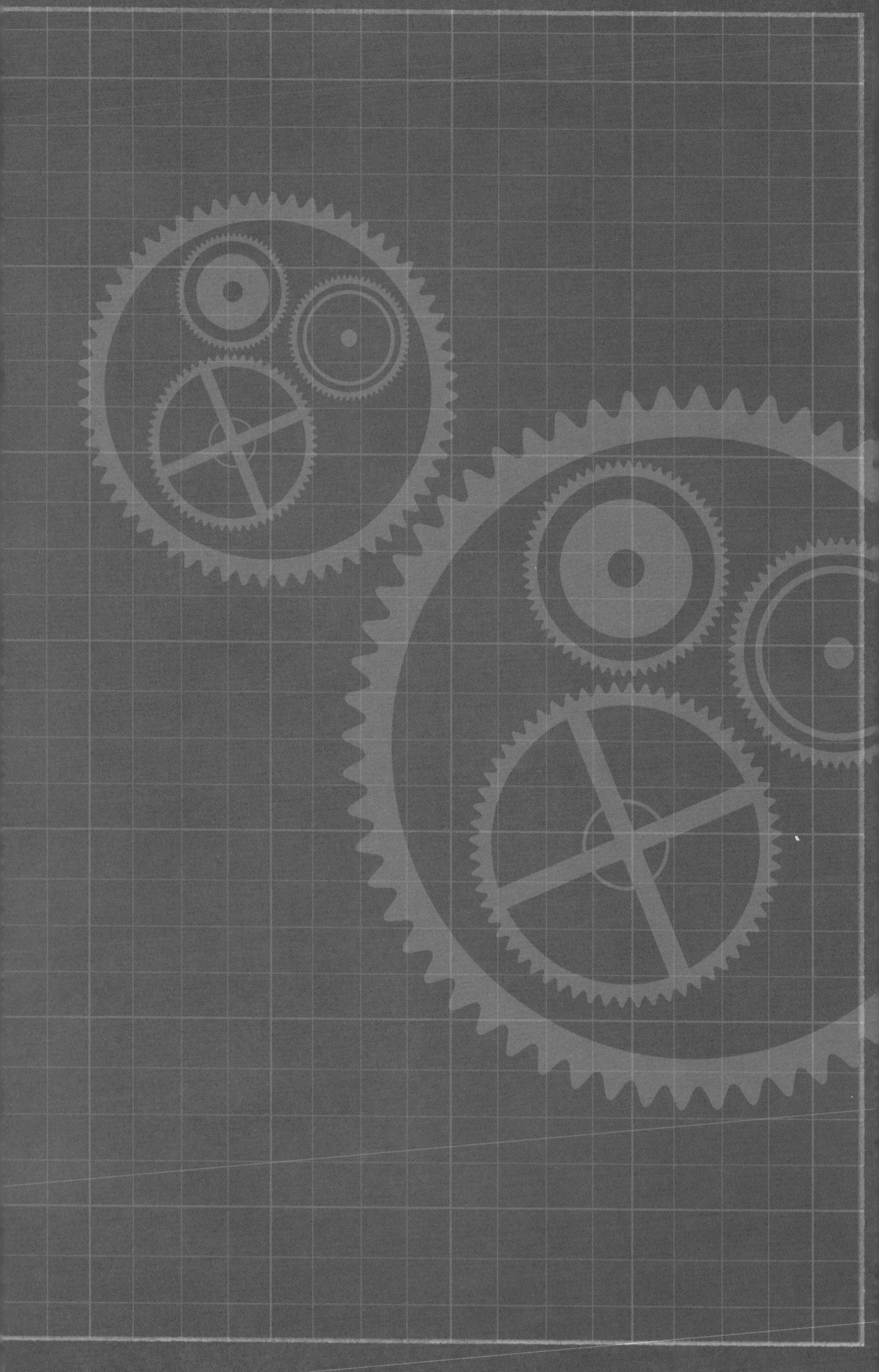

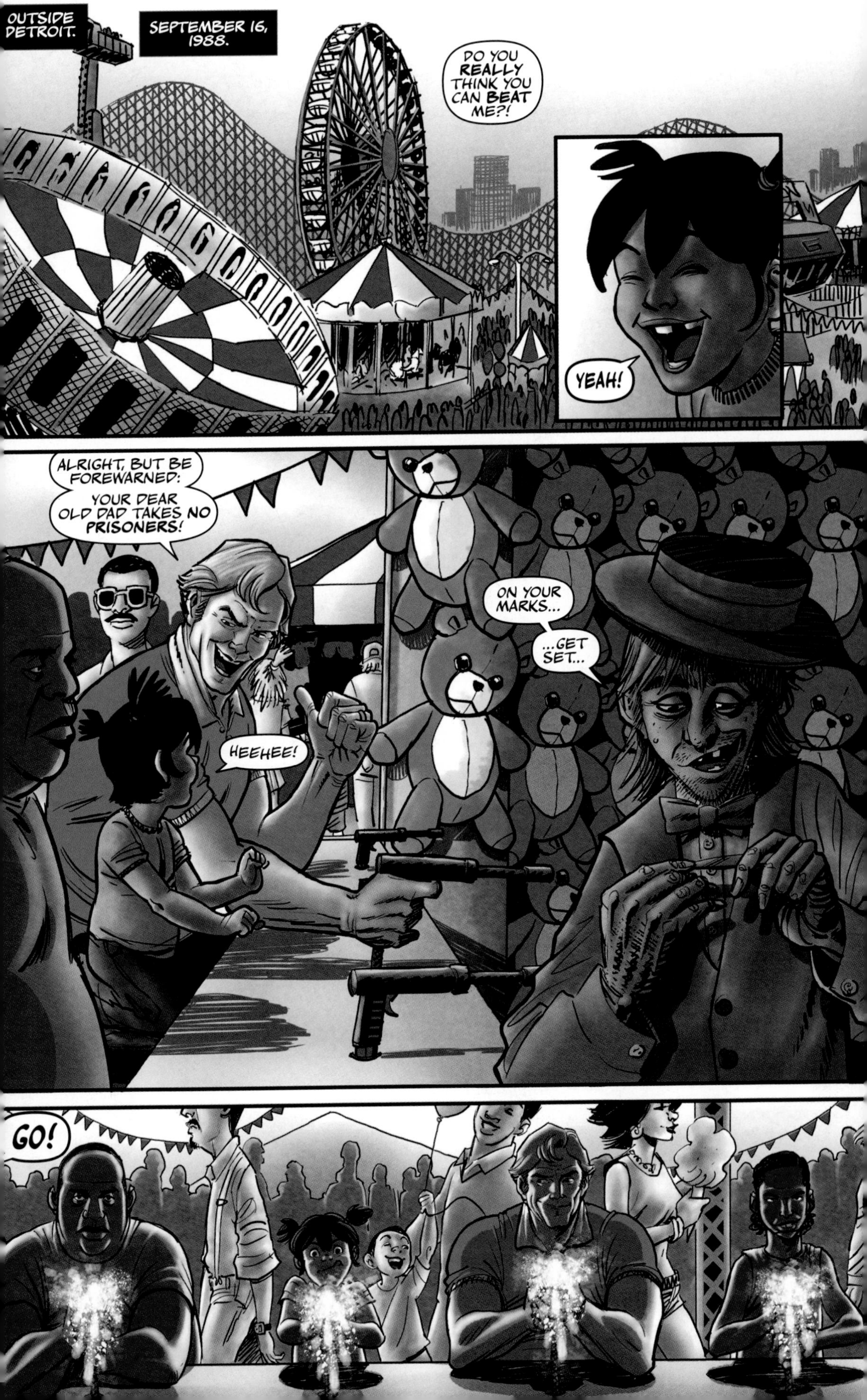
OUTSIDE DETROIT.
SEPTEMBER 16, 1988.
DO YOU REALLY THINK YOU CAN BEAT ME?!
YEAH!
ALRIGHT, BUT BE FOREWARNED: YOUR DEAR OLD DAD TAKES NO PRISONERS!
HEEHEE!
ON YOUR MARKS...
...GET SET...
GO!

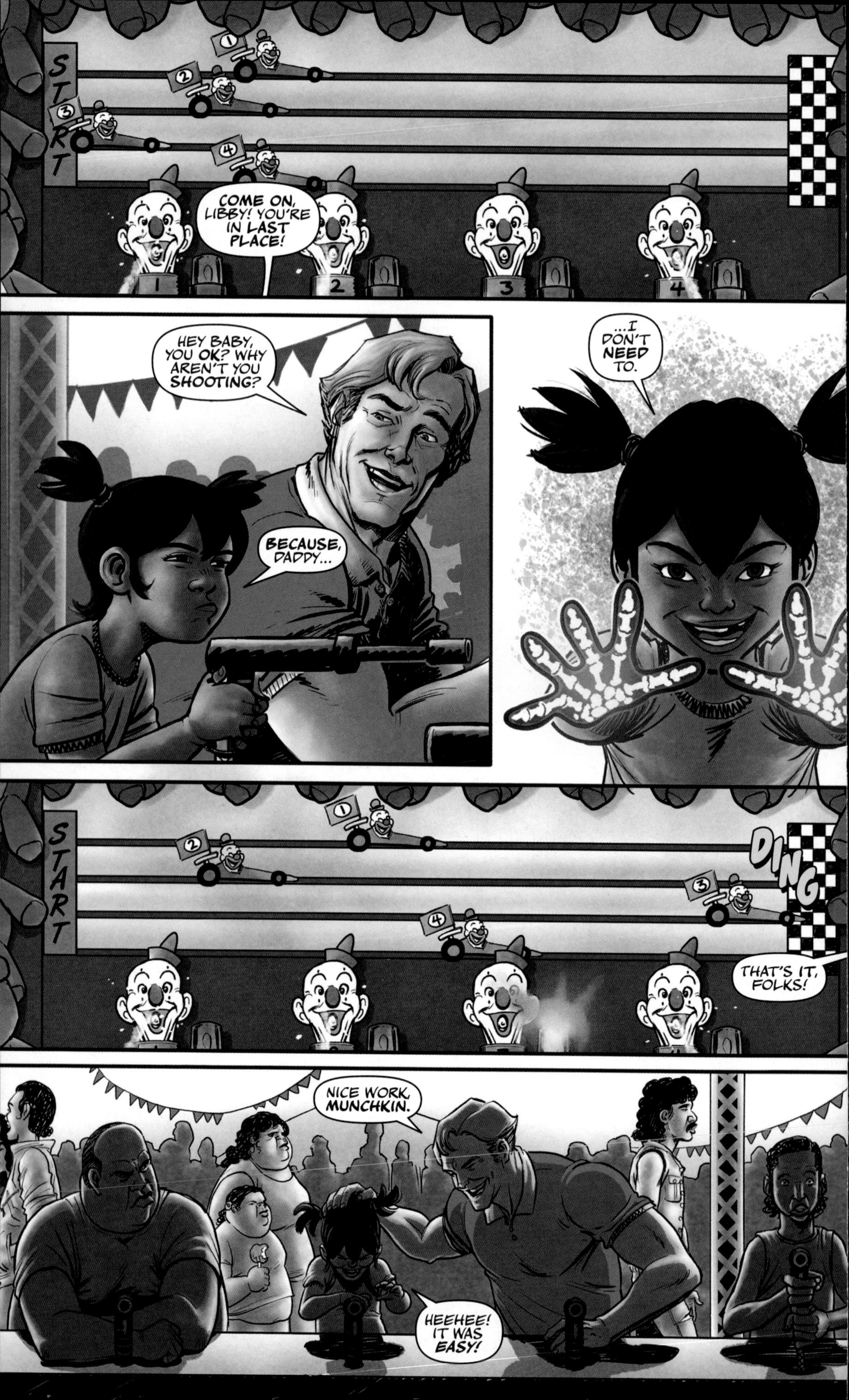
START
COME ON, LIBBY! YOU'RE IN LAST PLACE!
HEY BABY, YOU OK? WHY AREN'T YOU SHOOTING?
BECAUSE, DADDY...
...I DON'T NEED TO.
START
DING
THAT'S IT, FOLKS!
NICE WORK, MUNCHKIN.
HEEHEE! IT WAS EASY!

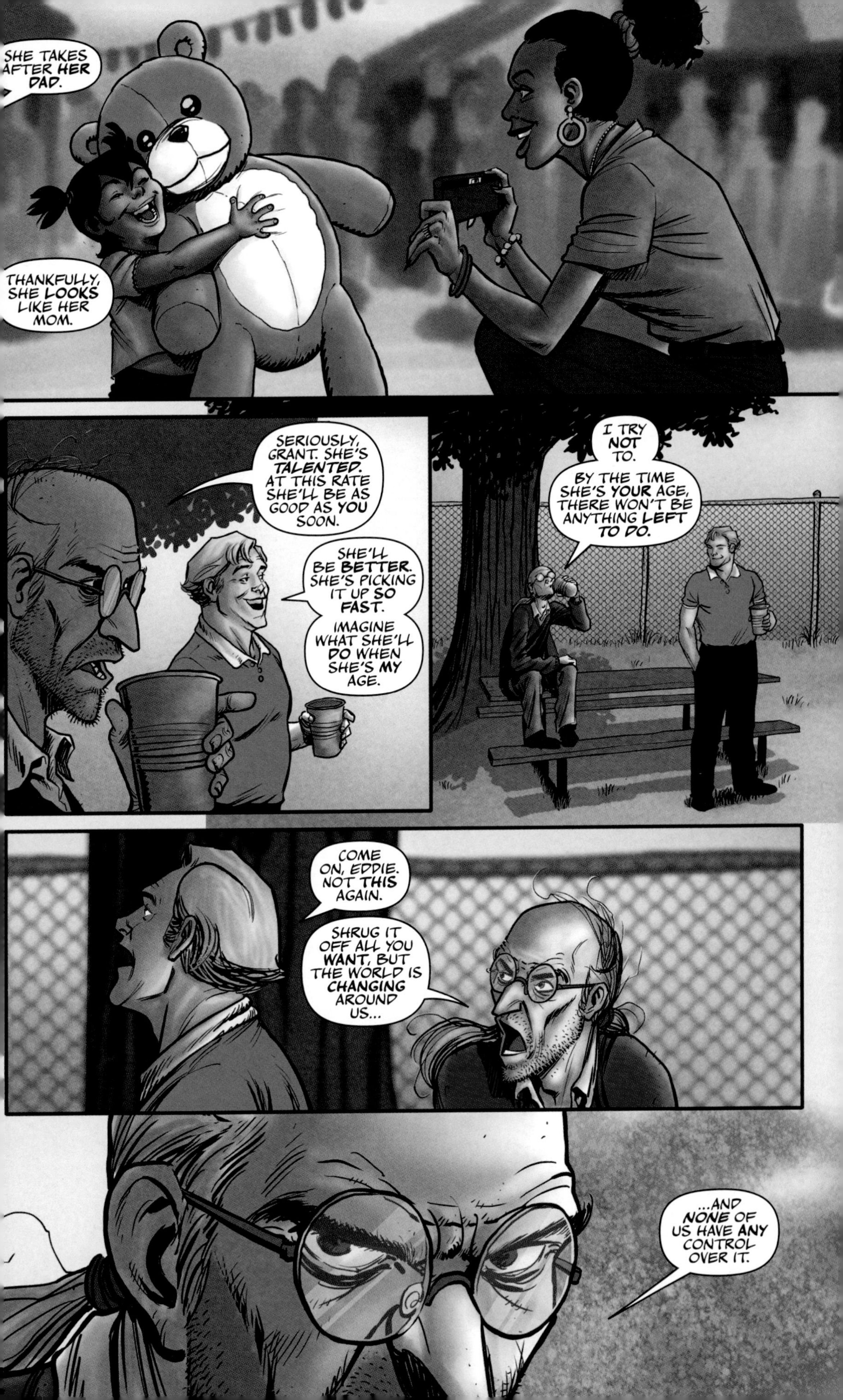

SHE TAKES AFTER HER DAD.
THANKFULLY, SHE LOOKS LIKE HER MOM.
SERIOUSLY, GRANT. SHE'S TALENTED. AT THIS RATE SHE'LL BE AS GOOD AS YOU SOON.
SHE'LL BE BETTER. SHE'S PICKING IT UP SO FAST.
IMAGINE WHAT SHE'LL DO WHEN SHE'S MY AGE.
I TRY NOT TO.
BY THE TIME SHE'S YOUR AGE, THERE WON'T BE ANYTHING LEFT TO DO.
COME ON, EDDIE. NOT THIS AGAIN.
SHRUG IT OFF ALL YOU WANT, BUT THE WORLD IS CHANGING AROUND US...
...AND NONE OF US HAVE ANY CONTROL OVER IT.

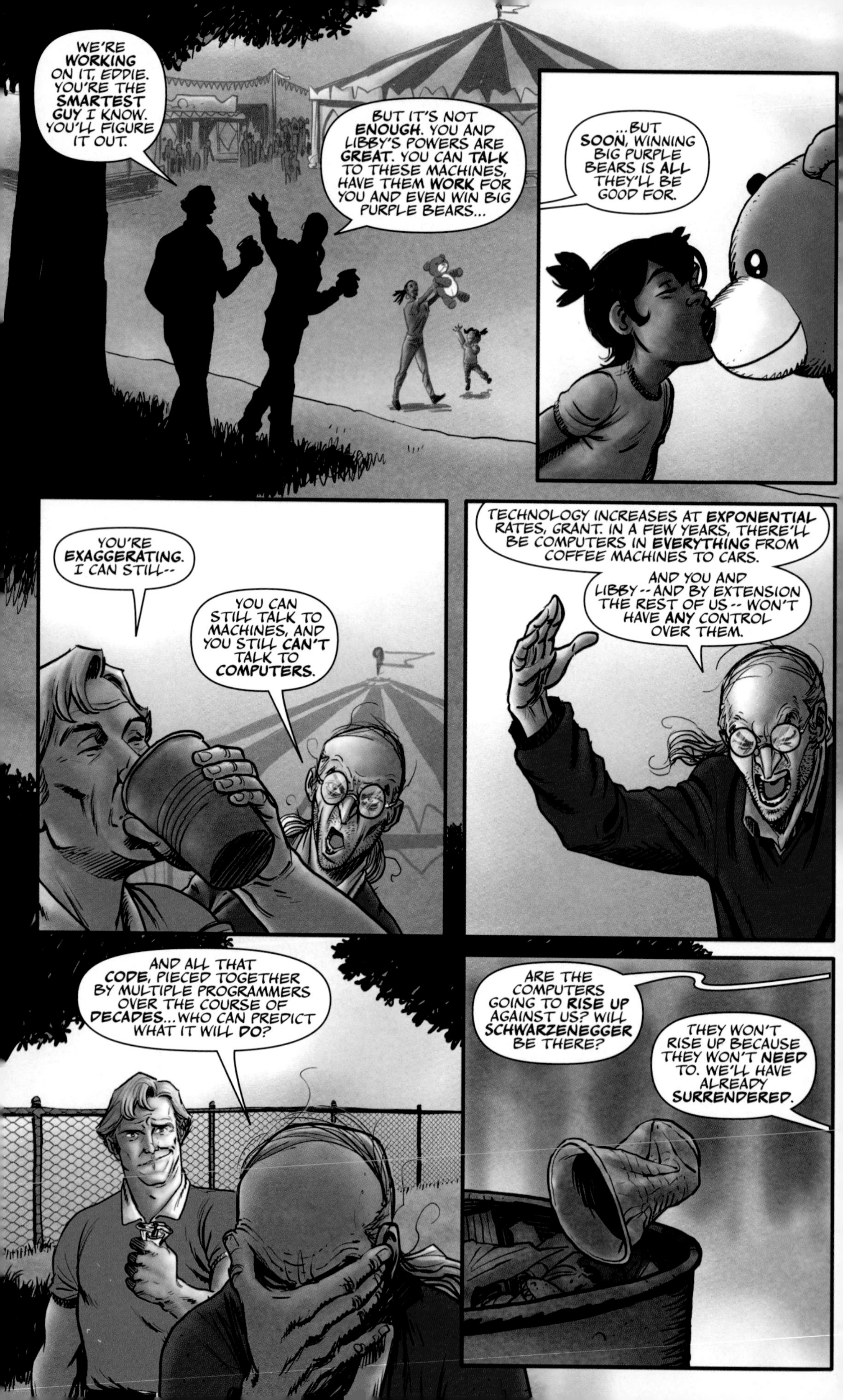
WE'RE WORKING ON IT, EDDIE. YOU'RE THE SMARTEST GUY I KNOW. YOU'LL FIGURE IT OUT.
BUT IT'S NOT ENOUGH. YOU AND LIBBY'S POWERS ARE GREAT. YOU CAN TALK TO THESE MACHINES, HAVE THEM WORK FOR YOU AND EVEN WIN BIG PURPLE BEARS...
...BUT SOON, WINNING BIG PURPLE BEARS IS ALL THEY'LL BE GOOD FOR.
YOU'RE EXAGGERATING. I CAN STILL--
YOU CAN STILL TALK TO MACHINES, AND YOU STILL CAN'T TALK TO COMPUTERS.
TECHNOLOGY INCREASES AT EXPONENTIAL RATES, GRANT. IN A FEW YEARS, THERE'LL BE COMPUTERS IN EVERYTHING FROM COFFEE MACHINES TO CARS.
AND YOU AND LIBBY--AND BY EXTENSION THE REST OF US--WON'T HAVE ANY CONTROL OVER THEM.
AND ALL THAT CODE, PIECED TOGETHER BY MULTIPLE PROGRAMMERS OVER THE COURSE OF DECADES...WHO CAN PREDICT WHAT IT WILL DO?
ARE THE COMPUTERS GOING TO RISE UP AGAINST US? WILL SCHWARZENEGGER BE THERE?
THEY WON'T RISE UP BECAUSE THEY WON'T NEED TO. WE'LL HAVE ALREADY SURRENDERED.

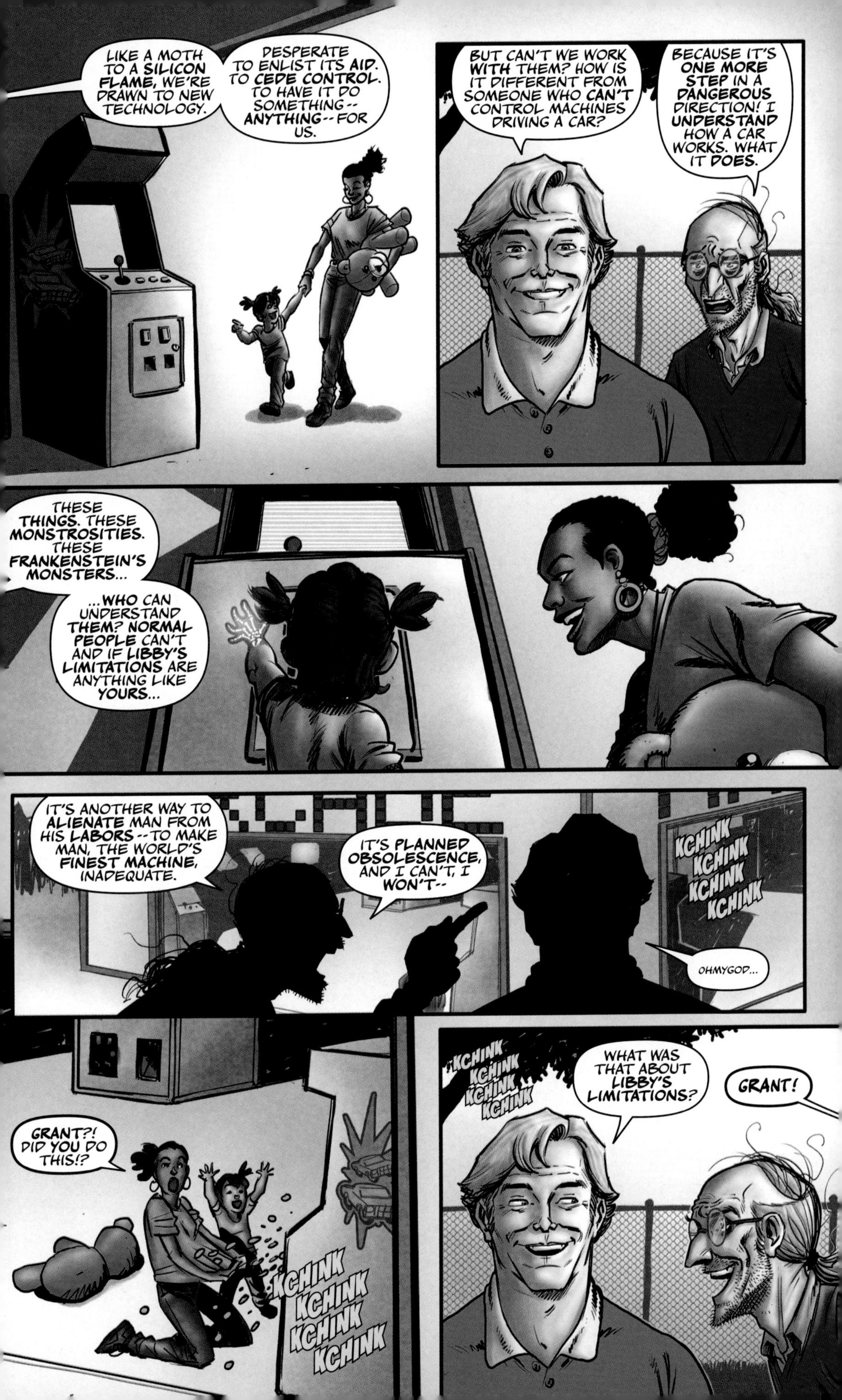
LIKE A MOTH TO A SILICON FLAME, WE'RE DRAWN TO NEW TECHNOLOGY.
DESPERATE TO ENLIST ITS AID. TO CEDE CONTROL. TO HAVE IT DO SOMETHING-- ANYTHING--FOR US.
BUT CAN'T WE WORK WITH THEM? HOW IS IT DIFFERENT FROM SOMEONE WHO CAN'T CONTROL MACHINES DRIVING A CAR?
BECAUSE IT'S ONE MORE STEP IN A DANGEROUS DIRECTION! I UNDERSTAND HOW A CAR WORKS. WHAT IT DOES.
THESE THINGS. THESE MONSTROSITIES. THESE FRANKENSTEIN'S MONSTERS...
...WHO CAN UNDERSTAND THEM? NORMAL PEOPLE CAN'T AND IF LIBBY'S LIMITATIONS ARE ANYTHING LIKE YOURS...
IT'S ANOTHER WAY TO ALIENATE MAN FROM HIS LABORS--TO MAKE MAN, THE WORLD'S FINEST MACHINE, INADEQUATE.
IT'S PLANNED OBSOLESCENCE, AND I CAN'T, I WON'T--
KCHINK KCHINK KCHINK KCHINK
OHMYGOD...
GRANT?! DID YOU DO THIS!?
KCHINK KCHINK KCHINK KCHINK
KCHINK KCHINK KCHINK KCHINK
WHAT WAS THAT ABOUT LIBBY'S LIMITATIONS?
GRANT!

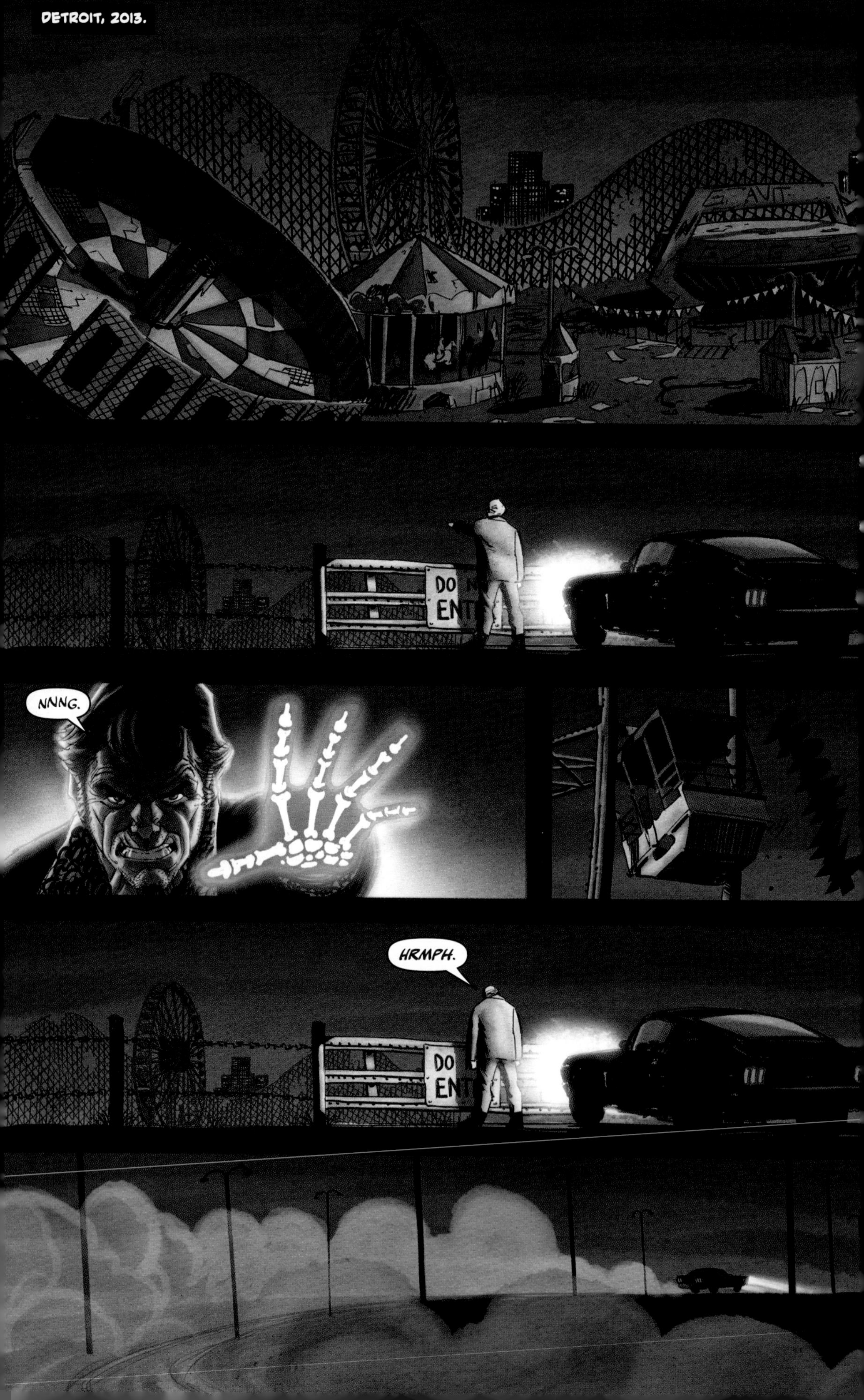
DETROIT, 2013.
NNNG.
HRMPH.

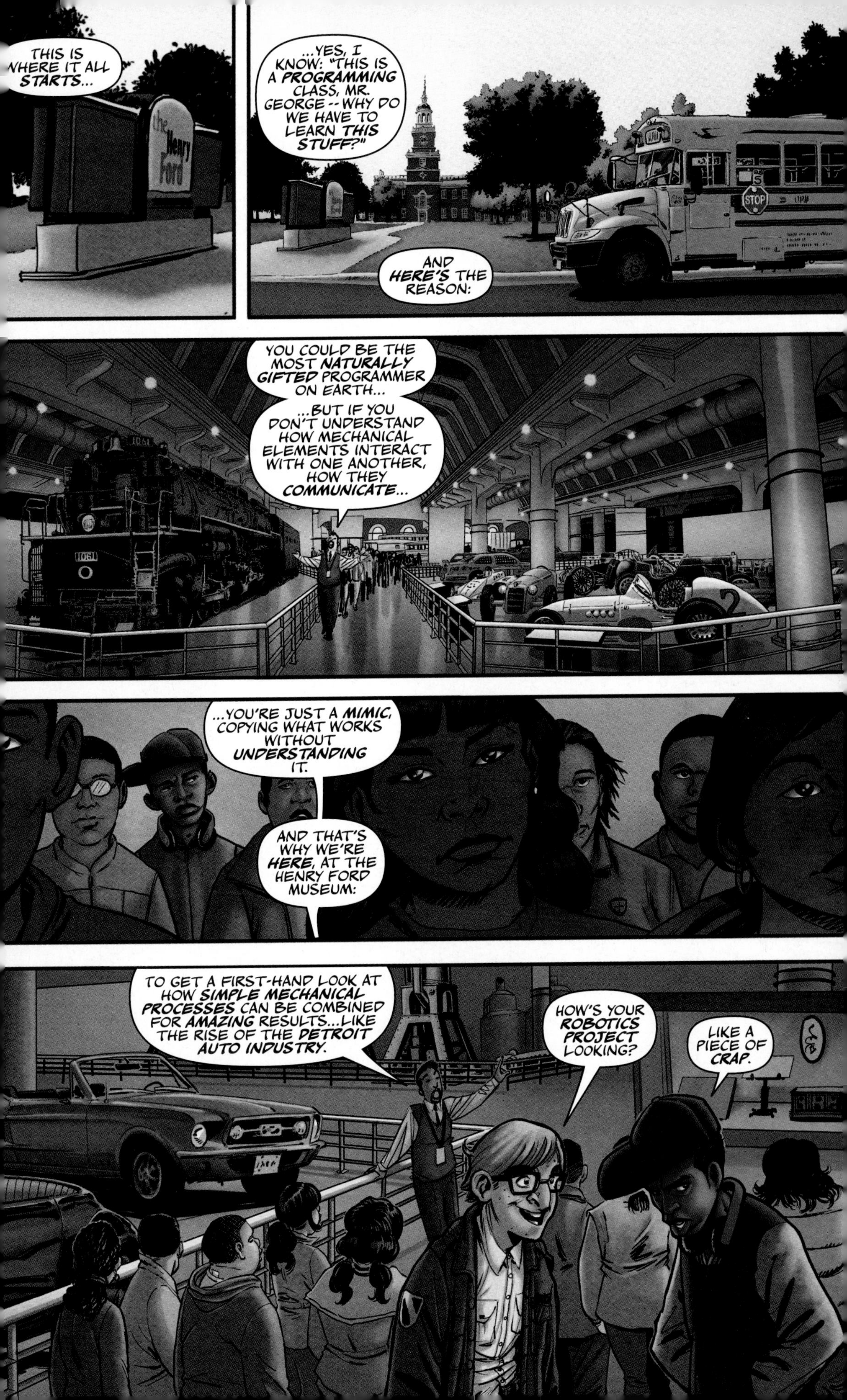
THIS IS WHERE IT ALL STARTS...
...YES, I KNOW: "THIS IS A PROGRAMMING CLASS, MR. GEORGE -- WHY DO WE HAVE TO LEARN THIS STUFF?"
AND HERE'S THE REASON:
YOU COULD BE THE MOST NATURALLY GIFTED PROGRAMMER ON EARTH...
...BUT IF YOU DON'T UNDERSTAND HOW MECHANICAL ELEMENTS INTERACT WITH ONE ANOTHER, HOW THEY COMMUNICATE...
...YOU'RE JUST A MIMIC, COPYING WHAT WORKS WITHOUT UNDERSTANDING IT.
AND THAT'S WHY WE'RE HERE, AT THE HENRY FORD MUSEUM:
TO GET A FIRST-HAND LOOK AT HOW SIMPLE MECHANICAL PROCESSES CAN BE COMBINED FOR AMAZING RESULTS...LIKE THE RISE OF THE DETROIT AUTO INDUSTRY.
HOW'S YOUR ROBOTICS PROJECT LOOKING?
LIKE A PIECE OF CRAP.

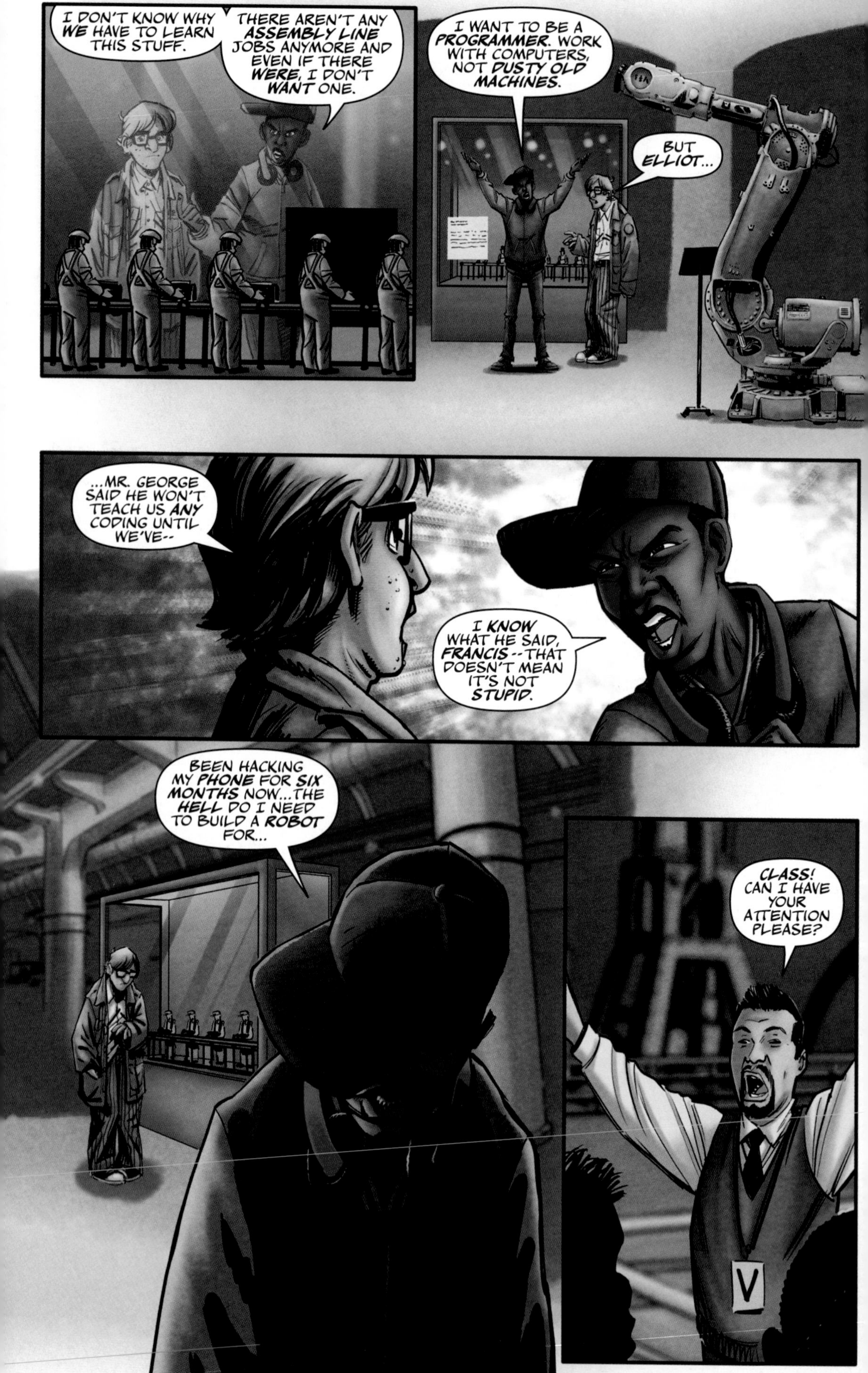

I DON'T KNOW WHY WE HAVE TO LEARN THIS STUFF.
THERE AREN'T ANY ASSEMBLY LINE JOBS ANYMORE AND EVEN IF THERE WERE, I DON'T WANT ONE.
I WANT TO BE A PROGRAMMER. WORK WITH COMPUTERS, NOT DUSTY OLD MACHINES.
BUT ELLIOT...
...MR. GEORGE SAID HE WON'T TEACH US ANY CODING UNTIL WE'VE--
I KNOW WHAT HE SAID, FRANCIS--THAT DOESN'T MEAN IT'S NOT STUPID.
BEEN HACKING MY PHONE FOR SIX MONTHS NOW...THE HELL DO I NEED TO BUILD A ROBOT FOR...
CLASS! CAN I HAVE YOUR ATTENTION PLEASE?

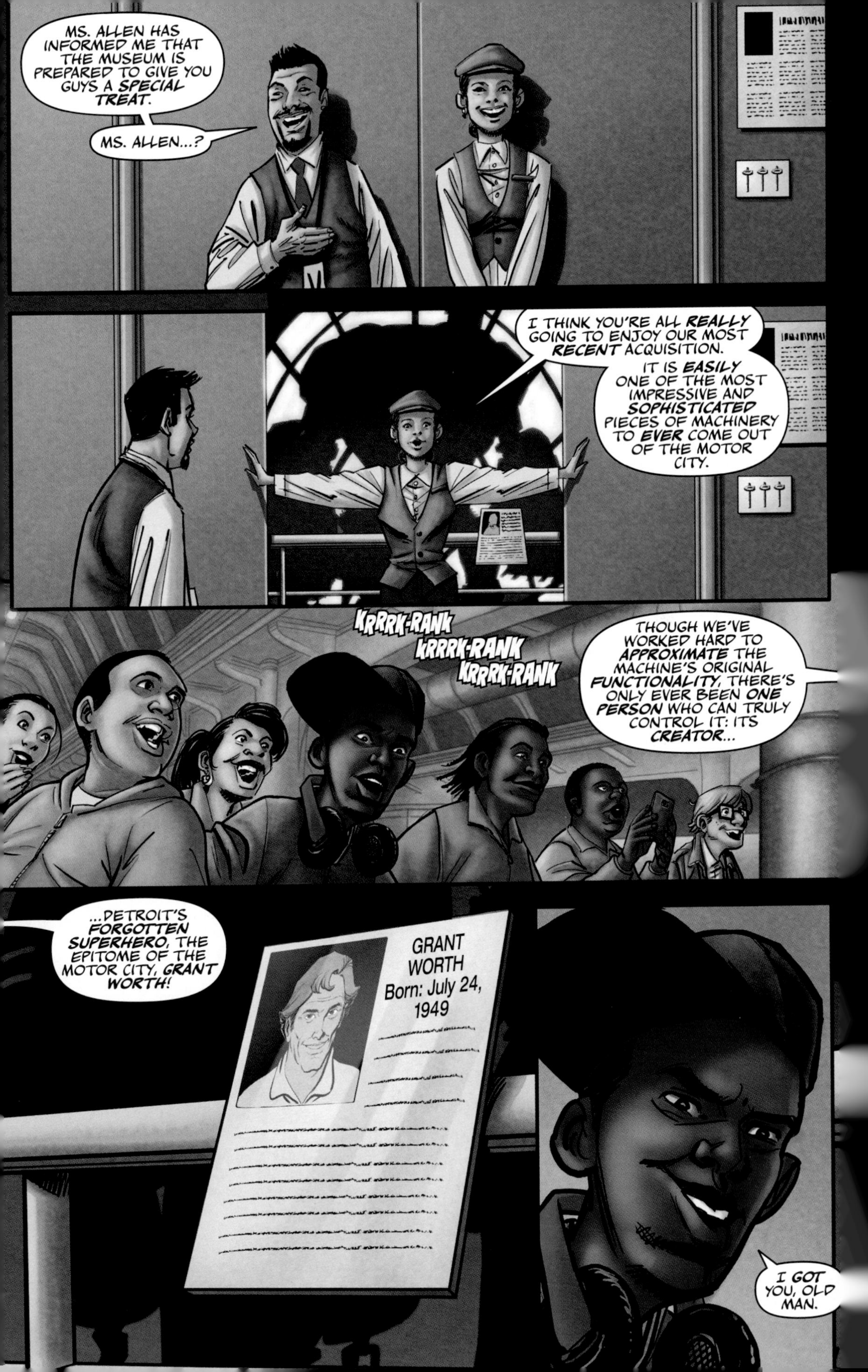
MS. ALLEN HAS INFORMED ME THAT THE MUSEUM IS PREPARED TO GIVE YOU GUYS A SPECIAL TREAT.
MS. ALLEN...?
I THINK YOU'RE ALL REALLY GOING TO ENJOY OUR MOST RECENT ACQUISITION.
IT IS EASILY ONE OF THE MOST IMPRESSIVE AND SOPHISTICATED PIECES OF MACHINERY TO EVER COME OUT OF THE MOTOR CITY.
KRRRK-RANK
KRRRK-RANK
KRRRK-RANK
THOUGH WE'VE WORKED HARD TO APPROXIMATE THE MACHINE'S ORIGINAL FUNCTIONALITY, THERE'S ONLY EVER BEEN ONE PERSON WHO CAN TRULY CONTROL IT: ITS CREATOR...
...DETROIT'S FORGOTTEN SUPERHERO, THE EPITOME OF THE MOTOR CITY, GRANT WORTH!
GRANT WORTH
Born: July 24, 1949
I GOT YOU, OLD MAN.

DING-DONG
DING-DONG
DING—

NOT NOW!

HRMPH...

KNOCK KNOCK
KNOCK KNOCK!

GRAH!

KNOCK KNOCK
KNOCK KNOCK!

ALRIGHTALRIGHT!
I'M COMING!

THE HELL
ARE YOU DOING
HERE? I DON'T
WANT ANY CANDY
BARS.

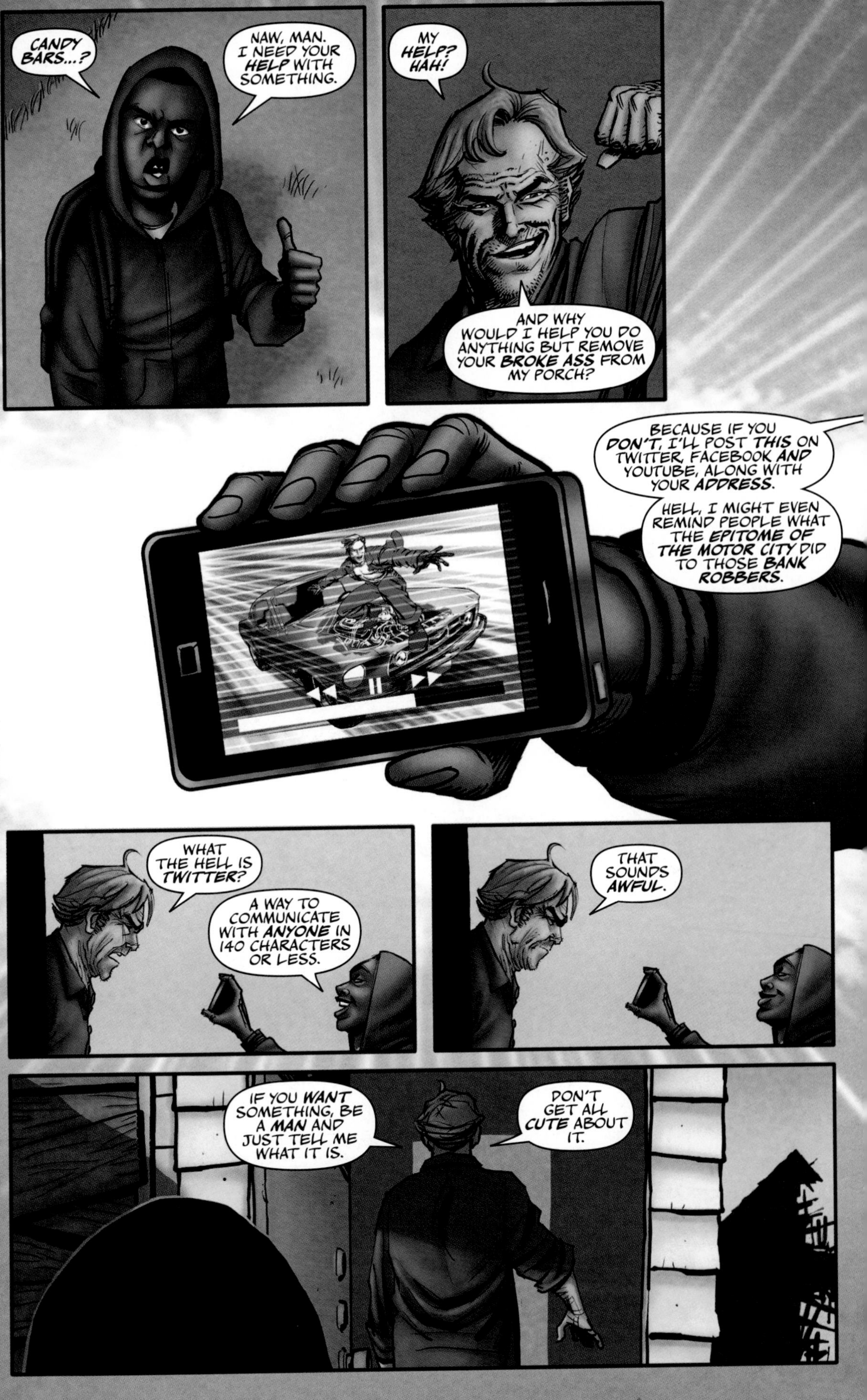
CANDY BARS...?
NAW, MAN. I NEED YOUR HELP WITH SOMETHING.
MY HELP? HAH!
AND WHY WOULD I HELP YOU DO ANYTHING BUT REMOVE YOUR BROKE ASS FROM MY PORCH?
BECAUSE IF YOU DON'T, I'LL POST THIS ON TWITTER, FACEBOOK AND YOUTUBE, ALONG WITH YOUR ADDRESS.
HELL, I MIGHT EVEN REMIND PEOPLE WHAT THE EPITOME OF THE MOTOR CITY DID TO THOSE BANK ROBBERS.
WHAT THE HELL IS TWITTER?
A WAY TO COMMUNICATE WITH ANYONE IN 140 CHARACTERS OR LESS.
THAT SOUNDS AWFUL.
IF YOU WANT SOMETHING, BE A MAN AND JUST TELL ME WHAT IT IS.
DON'T GET ALL CUTE ABOUT IT.

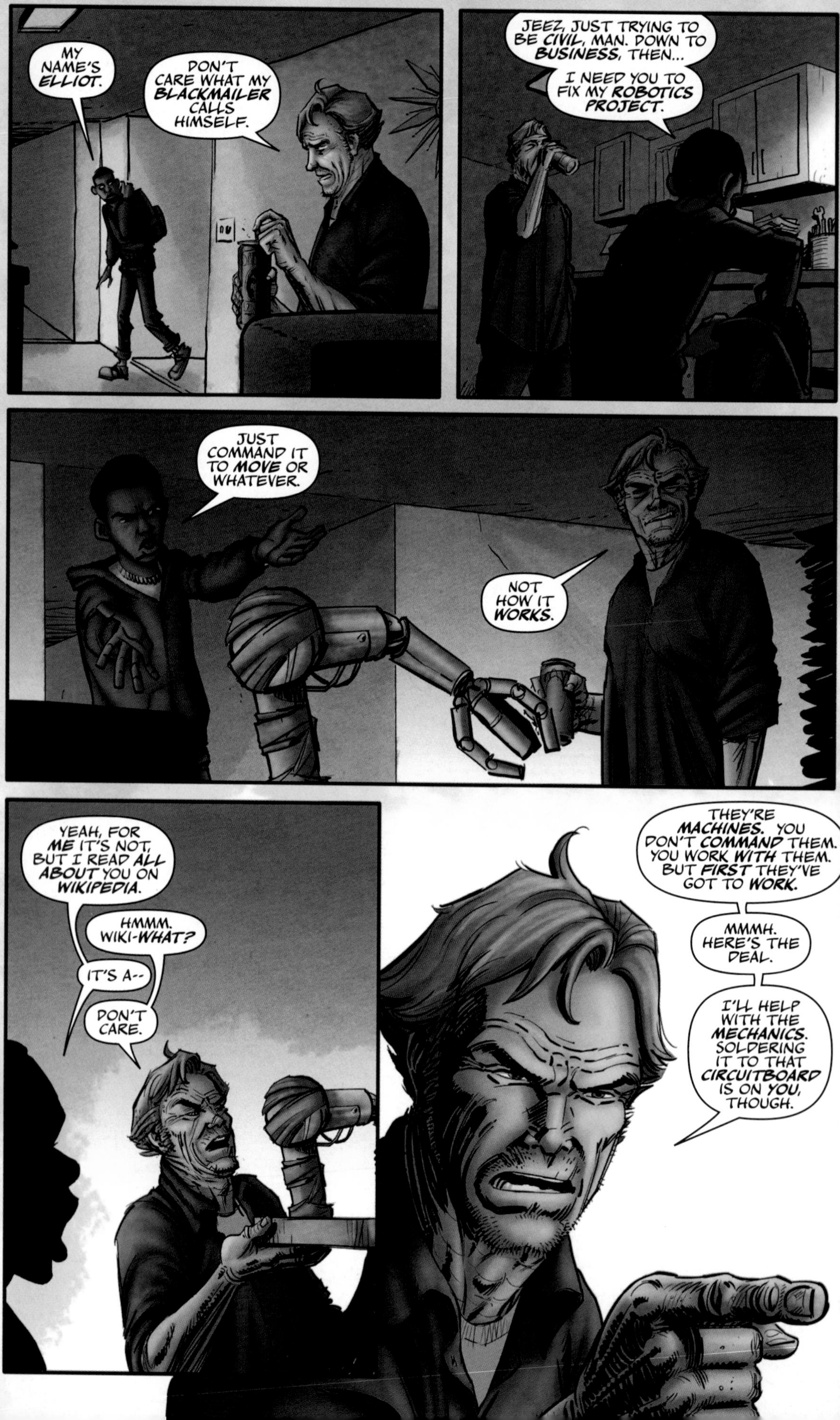
MY NAME'S ELLIOT.
DON'T CARE WHAT MY BLACKMAILER CALLS HIMSELF.
JEEZ, JUST TRYING TO BE CIVIL, MAN. DOWN TO BUSINESS, THEN...
I NEED YOU TO FIX MY ROBOTICS PROJECT.
JUST COMMAND IT TO MOVE OR WHATEVER.
NOT HOW IT WORKS.
YEAH, FOR ME IT'S NOT, BUT I READ ALL ABOUT YOU ON WIKIPEDIA.
HMMM. WIKI-WHAT?
IT'S A--
DON'T CARE.
THEY'RE MACHINES. YOU DON'T COMMAND THEM. YOU WORK WITH THEM. BUT FIRST THEY'VE GOT TO WORK.
MMMH. HERE'S THE DEAL.
I'LL HELP WITH THE MECHANICS. SOLDERING IT TO THAT CIRCUITBOARD IS ON YOU, THOUGH.

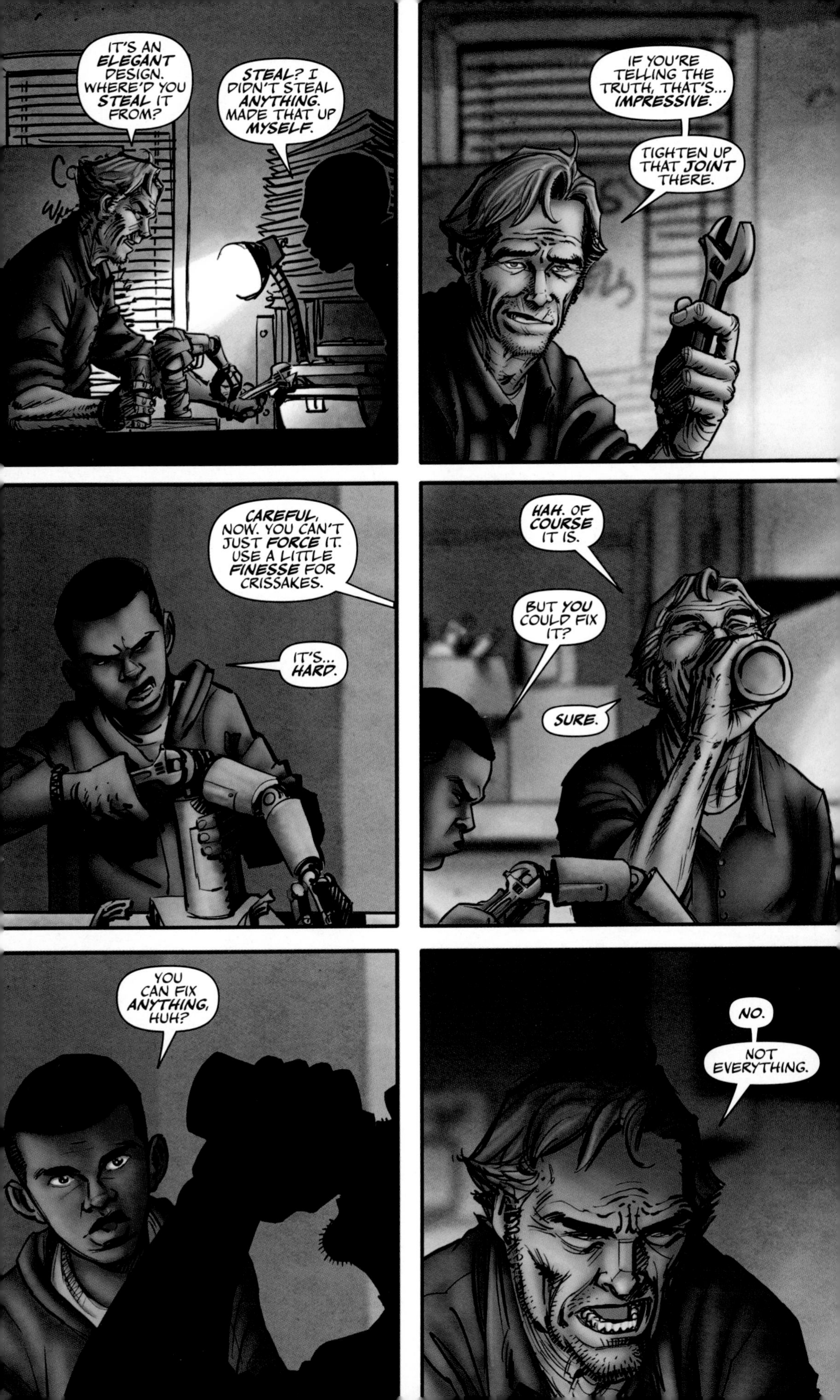
IT'S AN ELEGANT DESIGN. WHERE'D YOU STEAL IT FROM?
STEAL? I DIDN'T STEAL ANYTHING. MADE THAT UP MYSELF.
IF YOU'RE TELLING THE TRUTH, THAT'S... IMPRESSIVE.
TIGHTEN UP THAT JOINT THERE.
CAREFUL, NOW. YOU CAN'T JUST FORCE IT. USE A LITTLE FINESSE FOR CRISSAKES.
IT'S... HARD.
HAH. OF COURSE IT IS.
BUT YOU COULD FIX IT?
SURE.
YOU CAN FIX ANYTHING, HUH?
NO.
NOT EVERYTHING.

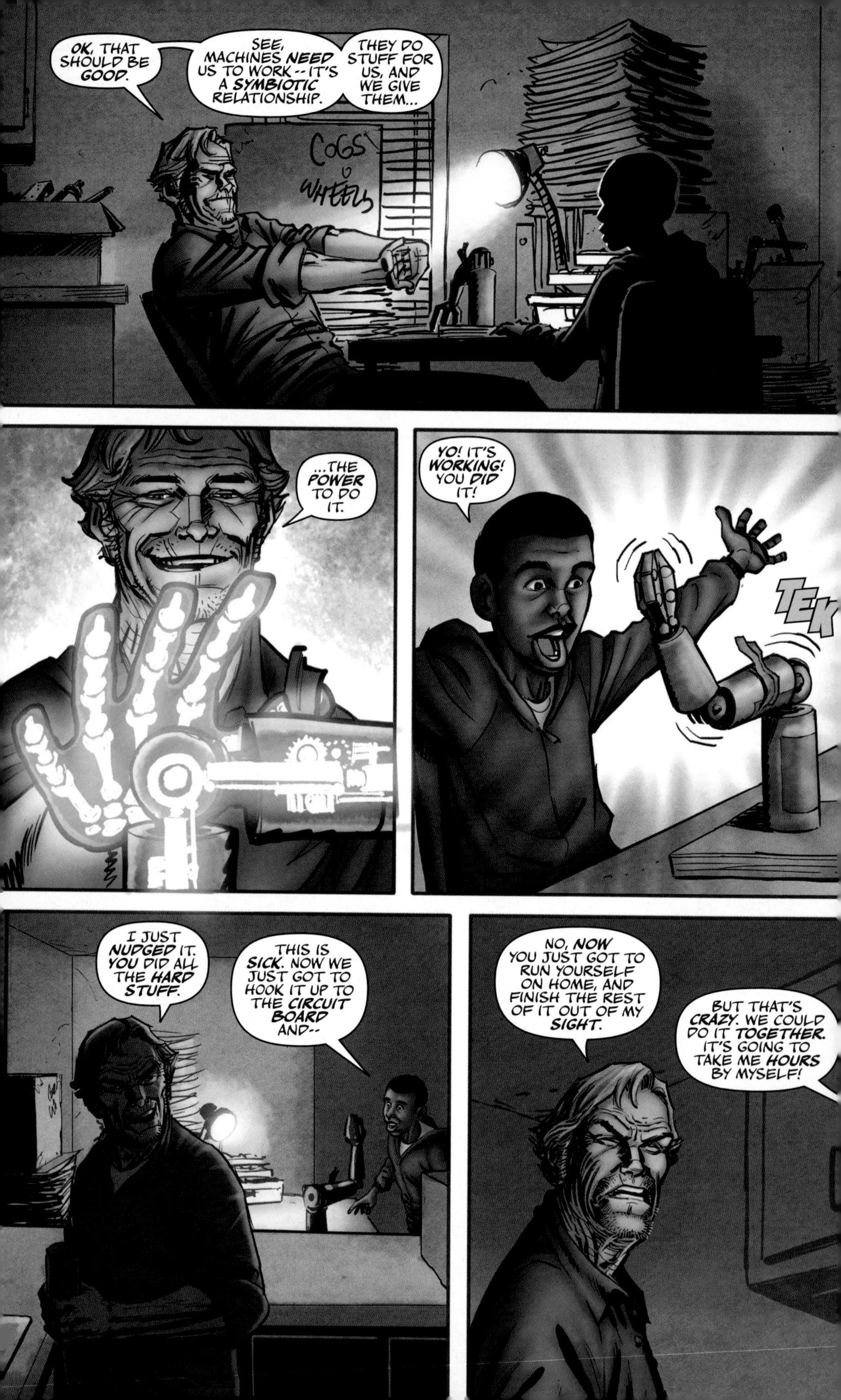

OK, THAT SHOULD BE GOOD.
SEE, MACHINES NEED US TO WORK--IT'S A SYMBIOTIC RELATIONSHIP.
THEY DO STUFF FOR US, AND WE GIVE THEM...
COGS ♡ WHEELS
...THE POWER TO DO IT.
YO! IT'S WORKING! YOU DID IT!
TEK
I JUST NUDGED IT. YOU DID ALL THE HARD STUFF.
THIS IS SICK. NOW WE JUST GOT TO HOOK IT UP TO THE CIRCUIT BOARD AND--
NO, NOW YOU JUST GOT TO RUN YOURSELF ON HOME, AND FINISH THE REST OF IT OUT OF MY SIGHT.
BUT THAT'S CRAZY. WE COULD DO IT TOGETHER. IT'S GOING TO TAKE ME HOURS BY MYSELF!

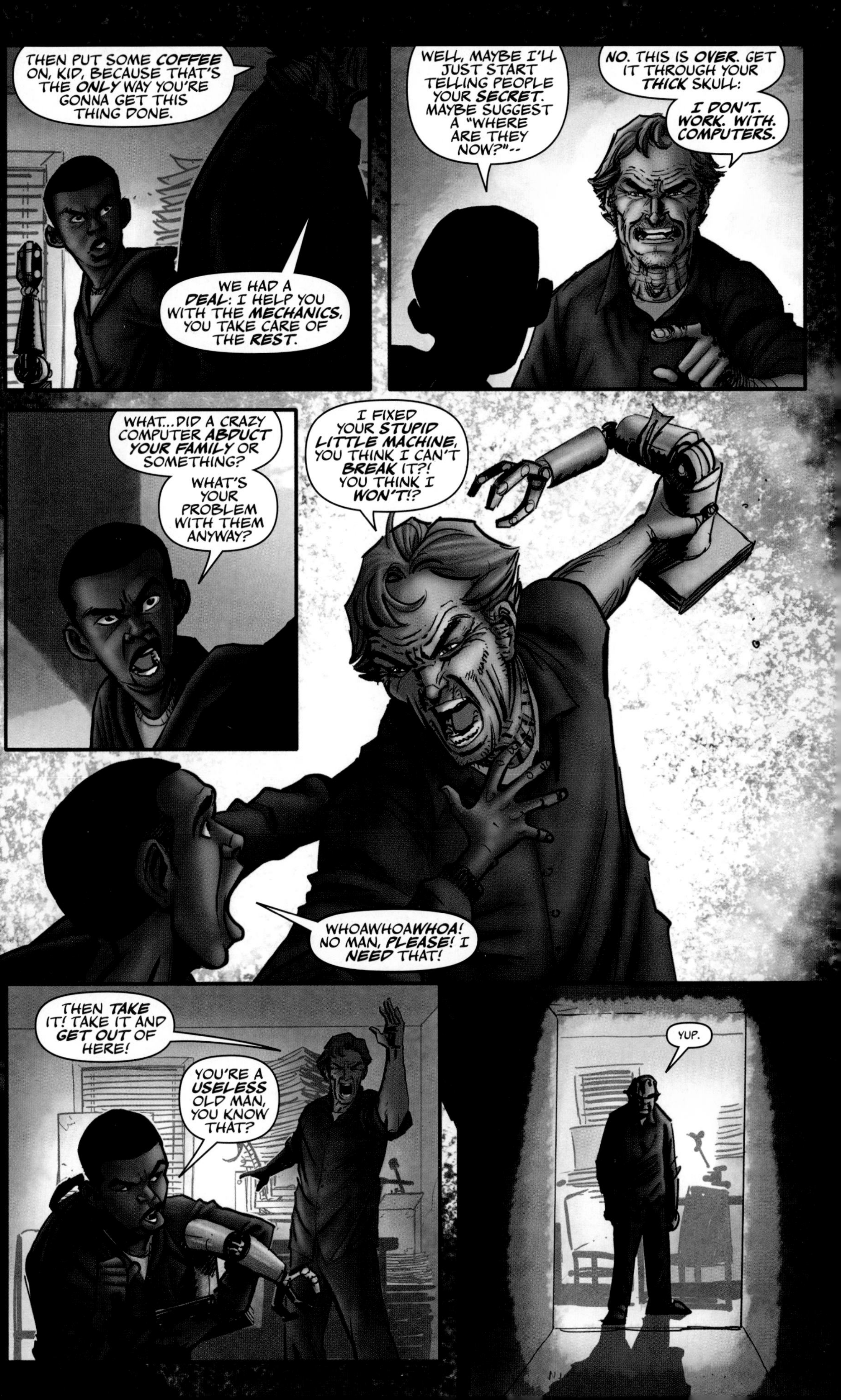
THEN PUT SOME COFFEE ON, KID, BECAUSE THAT'S THE ONLY WAY YOU'RE GONNA GET THIS THING DONE.
WE HAD A DEAL: I HELP YOU WITH THE MECHANICS, YOU TAKE CARE OF THE REST.
WELL, MAYBE I'LL JUST START TELLING PEOPLE YOUR SECRET. MAYBE SUGGEST A "WHERE ARE THEY NOW?"--
NO. THIS IS OVER. GET IT THROUGH YOUR THICK SKULL:
I DON'T. WORK. WITH. COMPUTERS.
WHAT...DID A CRAZY COMPUTER ABDUCT YOUR FAMILY OR SOMETHING?
WHAT'S YOUR PROBLEM WITH THEM ANYWAY?
I FIXED YOUR STUPID LITTLE MACHINE, YOU THINK I CAN'T BREAK IT?! YOU THINK I WON'T!?
WHOAWHOAWHOA! NO MAN, PLEASE! I NEED THAT!
THEN TAKE IT! TAKE IT AND GET OUT OF HERE!
YOU'RE A USELESS OLD MAN, YOU KNOW THAT?
YUP.

CHAPTER 3

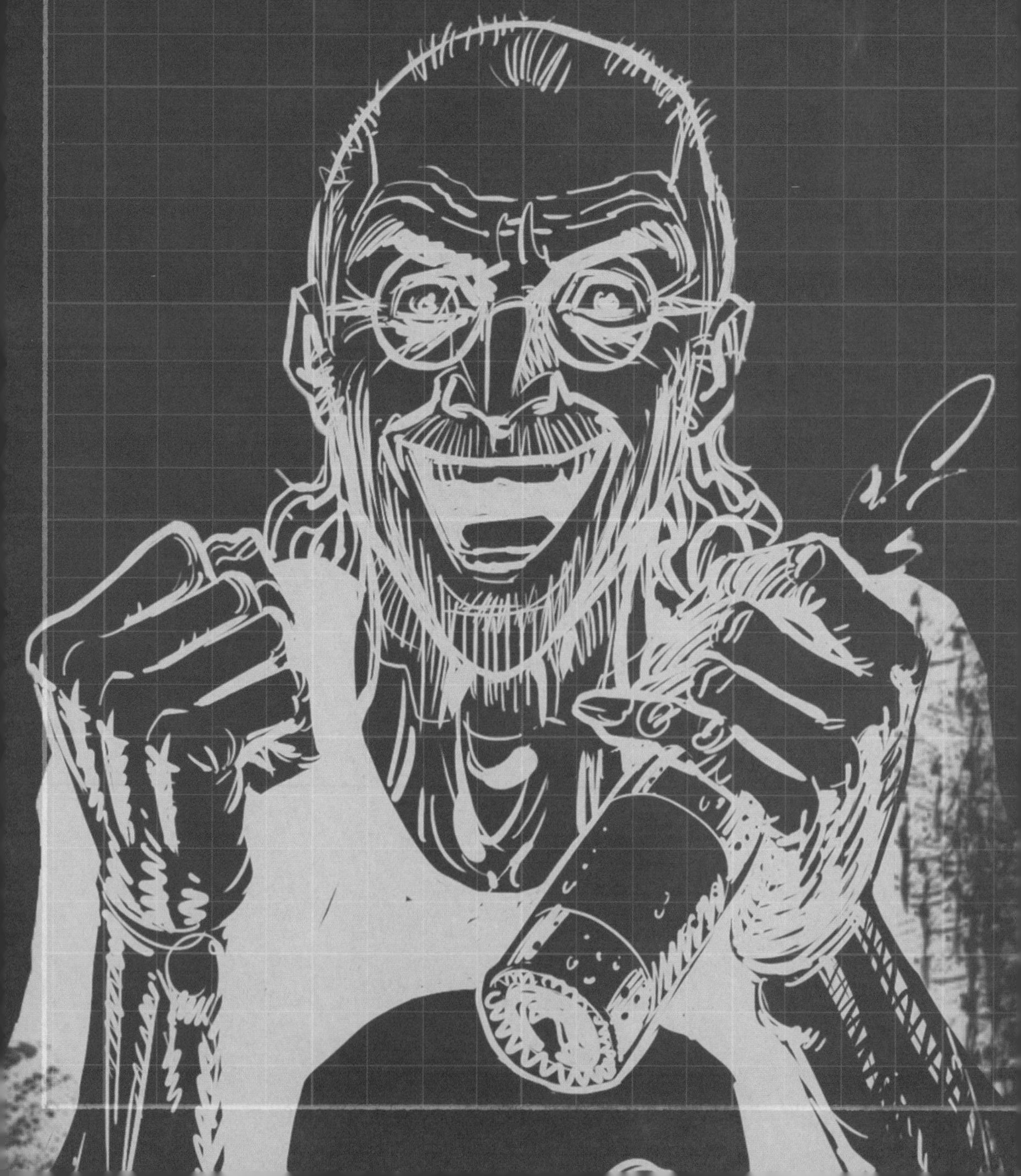

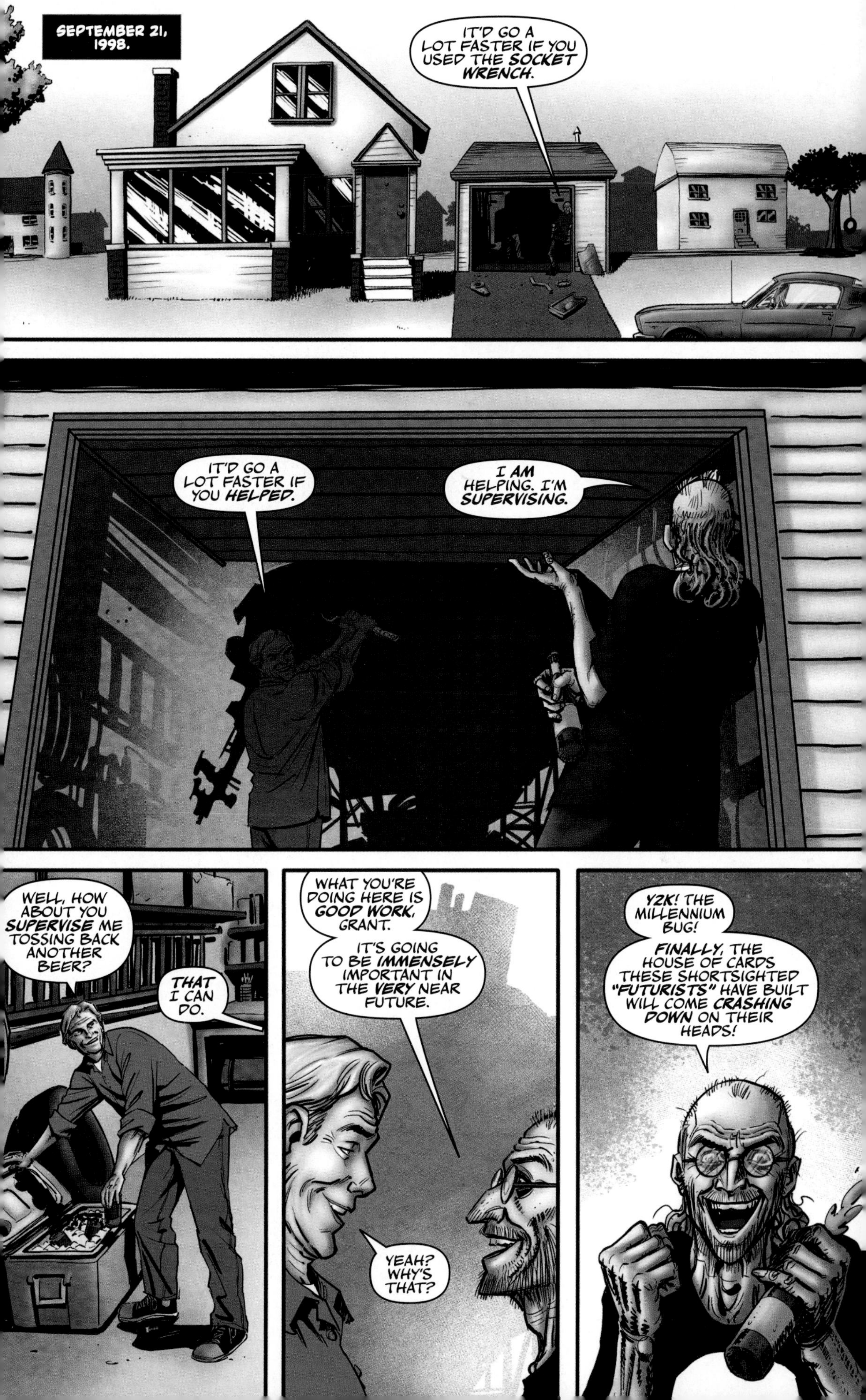
SEPTEMBER 21, 1998.
IT'D GO A LOT FASTER IF YOU USED THE SOCKET WRENCH.
IT'D GO A LOT FASTER IF YOU HELPED.
I AM HELPING. I'M SUPERVISING.
WELL, HOW ABOUT YOU SUPERVISE ME TOSSING BACK ANOTHER BEER?
THAT I CAN DO.
WHAT YOU'RE DOING HERE IS GOOD WORK, GRANT.
IT'S GOING TO BE IMMENSELY IMPORTANT IN THE VERY NEAR FUTURE.
YEAH? WHY'S THAT?
Y2K! THE MILLENNIUM BUG!
FINALLY, THE HOUSE OF CARDS THESE SHORTSIGHTED "FUTURISTS" HAVE BUILT WILL COME CRASHING DOWN ON THEIR HEADS!

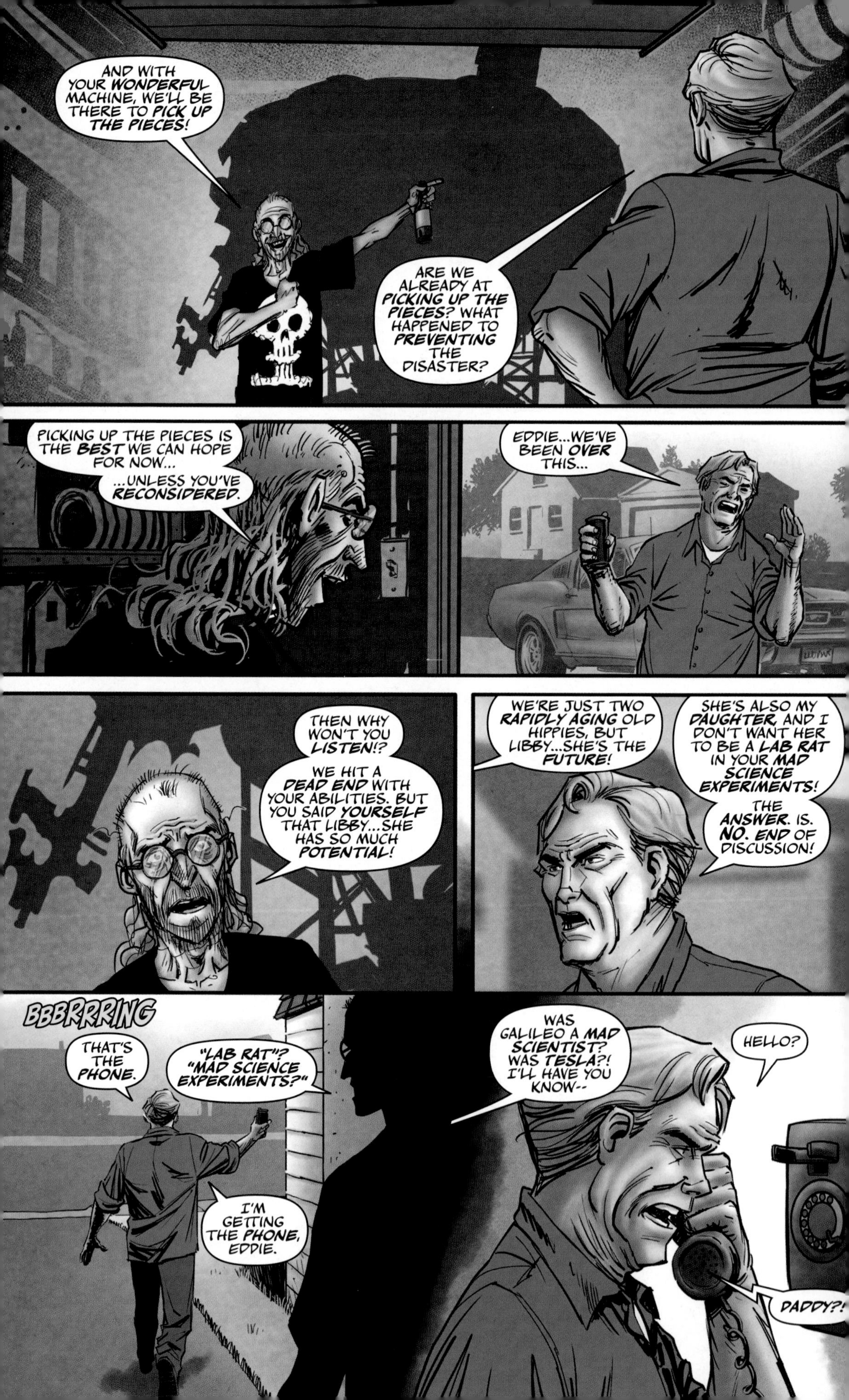
AND WITH YOUR WONDERFUL MACHINE, WE'LL BE THERE TO PICK UP THE PIECES!
ARE WE ALREADY AT PICKING UP THE PIECES? WHAT HAPPENED TO PREVENTING THE DISASTER?
PICKING UP THE PIECES IS THE BEST WE CAN HOPE FOR NOW...
...UNLESS YOU'VE RECONSIDERED.
EDDIE...WE'VE BEEN OVER THIS...
THEN WHY WON'T YOU LISTEN!?
WE HIT A DEAD END WITH YOUR ABILITIES. BUT YOU SAID YOURSELF THAT LIBBY...SHE HAS SO MUCH POTENTIAL!
WE'RE JUST TWO RAPIDLY AGING OLD HIPPIES, BUT LIBBY...SHE'S THE FUTURE!
SHE'S ALSO MY DAUGHTER, AND I DON'T WANT HER TO BE A LAB RAT IN YOUR MAD SCIENCE EXPERIMENTS!
THE ANSWER. IS. NO. END OF DISCUSSION!
BBBRRRING
THAT'S THE PHONE.
"LAB RAT"? "MAD SCIENCE EXPERIMENTS?"
I'M GETTING THE PHONE, EDDIE.
WAS GALILEO A MAD SCIENTIST? WAS TESLA?! I'LL HAVE YOU KNOW--
HELLO?
DADDY?!

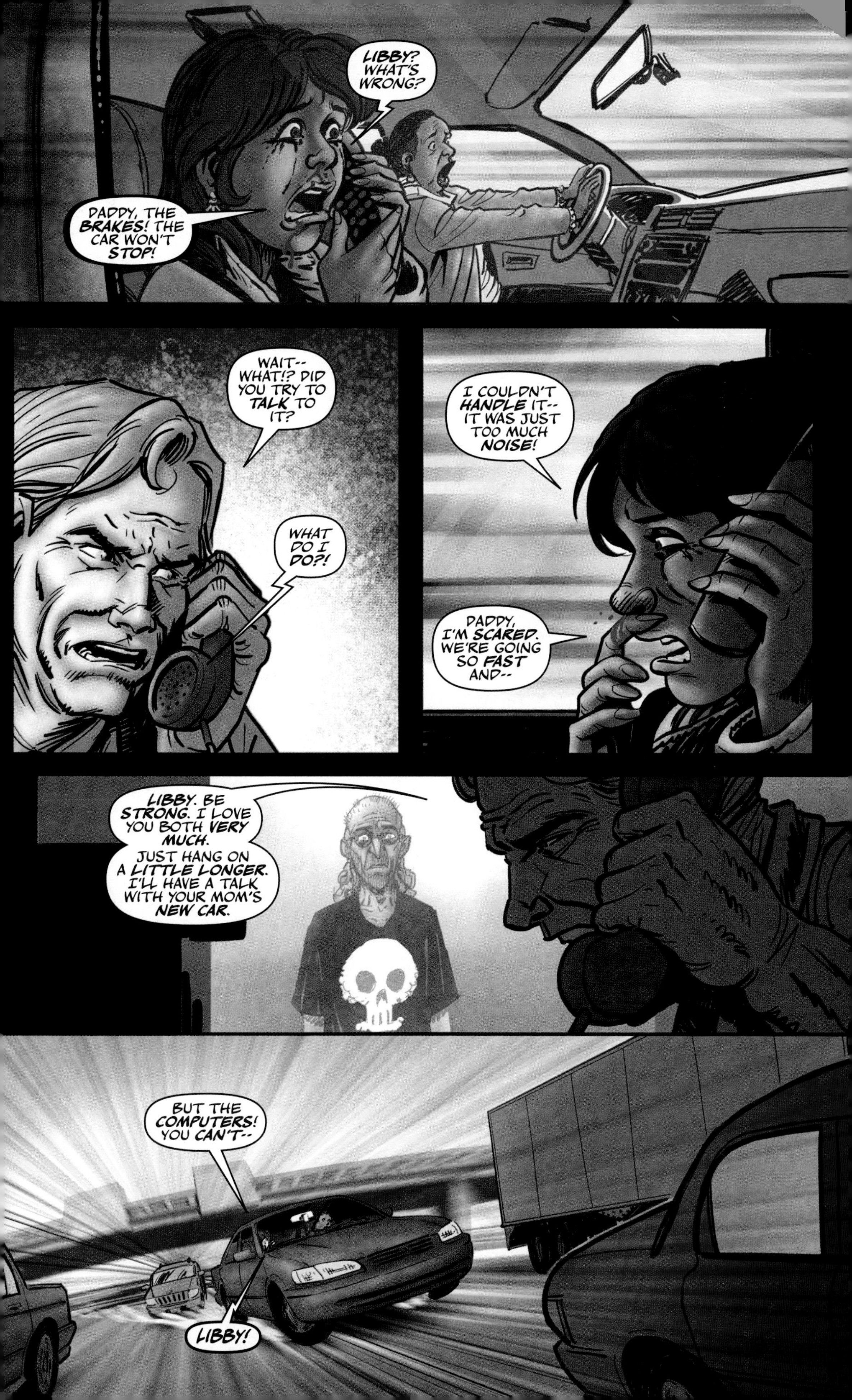
LIBBY? WHAT'S WRONG?
DADDY, THE BRAKES! THE CAR WON'T STOP!
WAIT-- WHAT!? DID YOU TRY TO TALK TO IT?
WHAT DO I DO?!
I COULDN'T HANDLE IT-- IT WAS JUST TOO MUCH NOISE!
DADDY, I'M SCARED. WE'RE GOING SO FAST AND--
LIBBY. BE STRONG. I LOVE YOU BOTH VERY MUCH.
JUST HANG ON A LITTLE LONGER. I'LL HAVE A TALK WITH YOUR MOM'S NEW CAR.
BUT THE COMPUTERS! YOU CAN'T--
LIBBY!

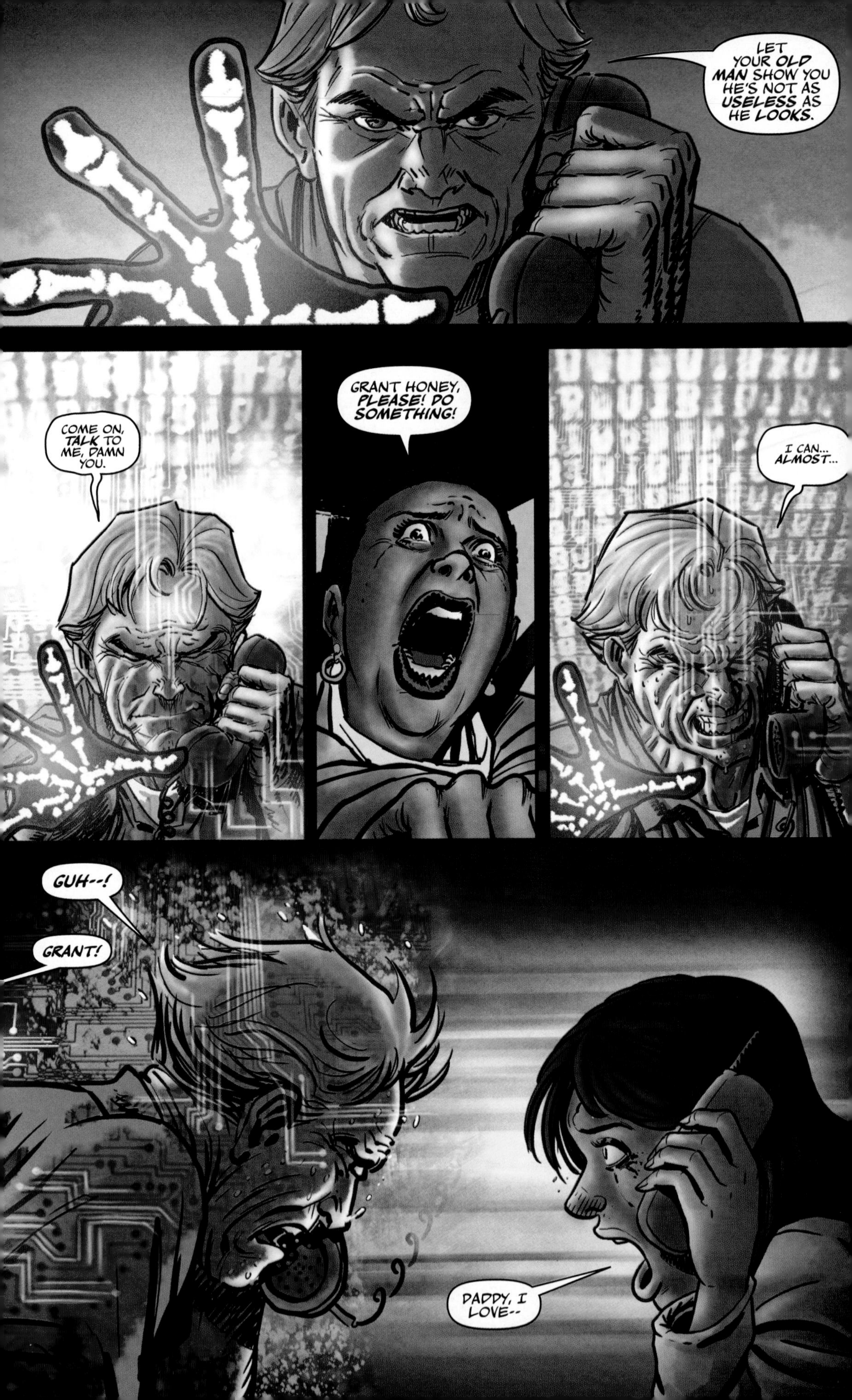
LET YOUR OLD MAN SHOW YOU HE'S NOT AS USELESS AS HE LOOKS.
COME ON, TALK TO ME, DAMN YOU.
GRANT HONEY, PLEASE! DO SOMETHING!
I CAN... ALMOST...
GUH--!
GRANT!
DADDY, I LOVE--

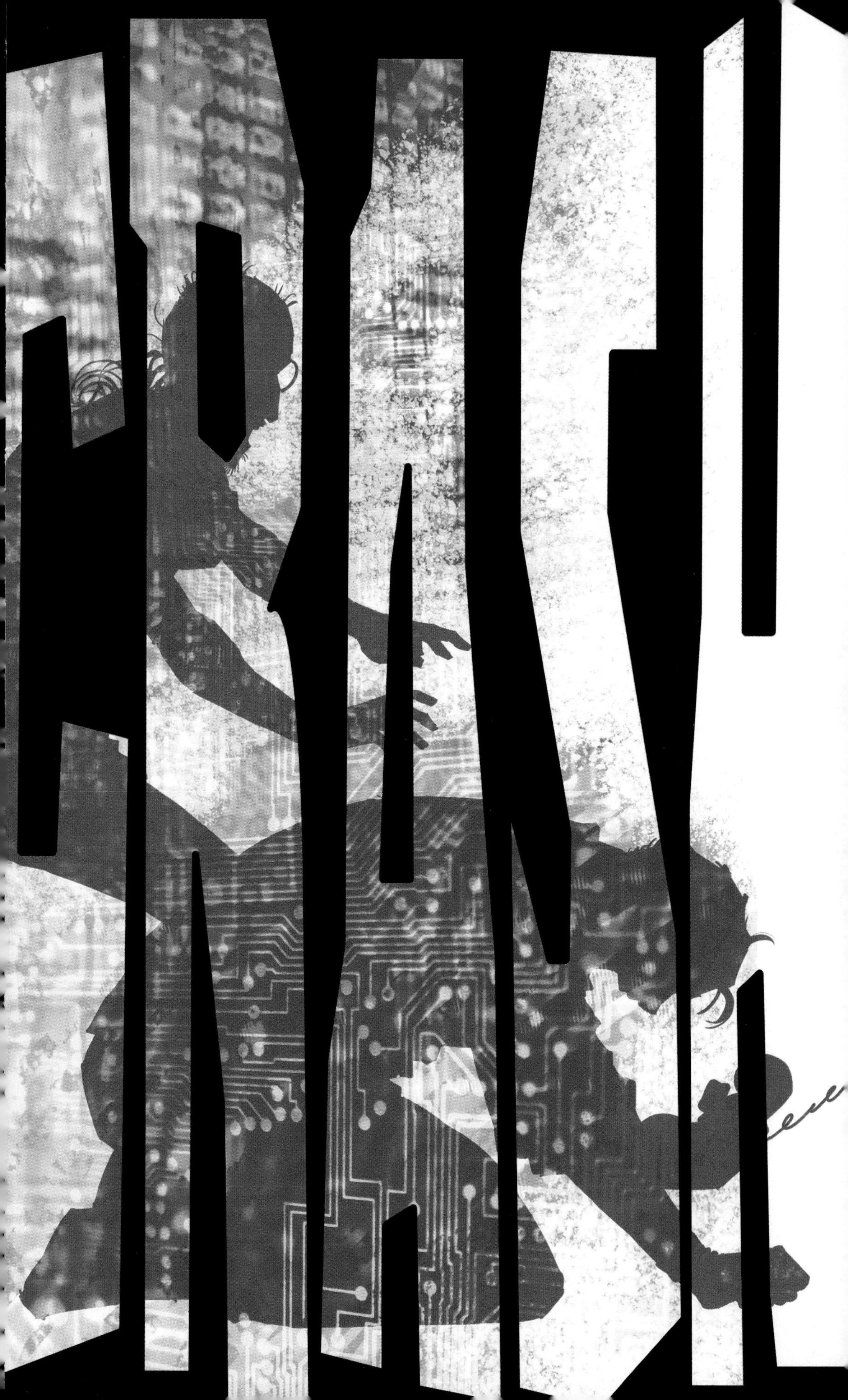

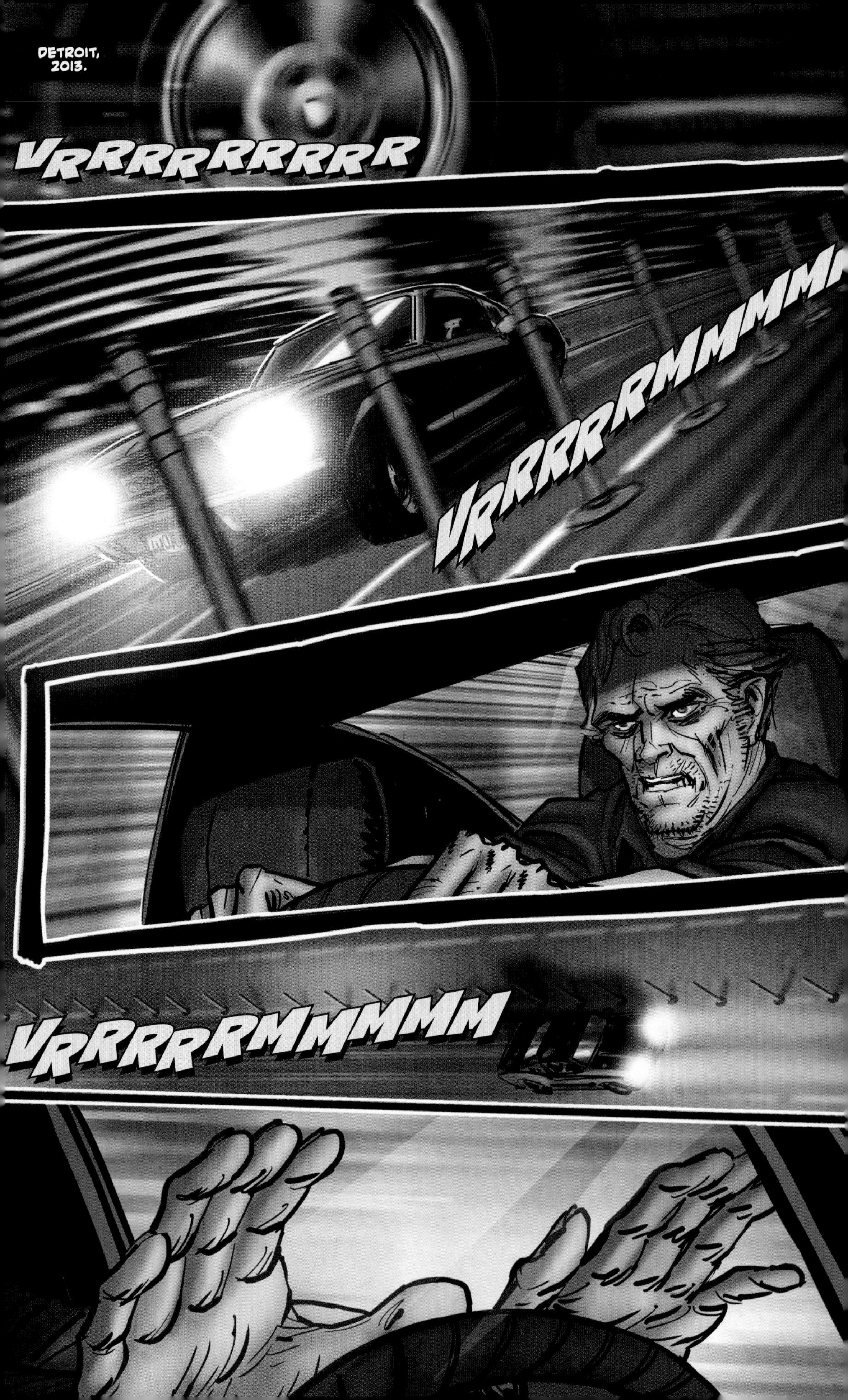
DETROIT, 2013.
VRRRRRRRRRR
VRRRRRMMMMM
VRRRRRMMMMMM

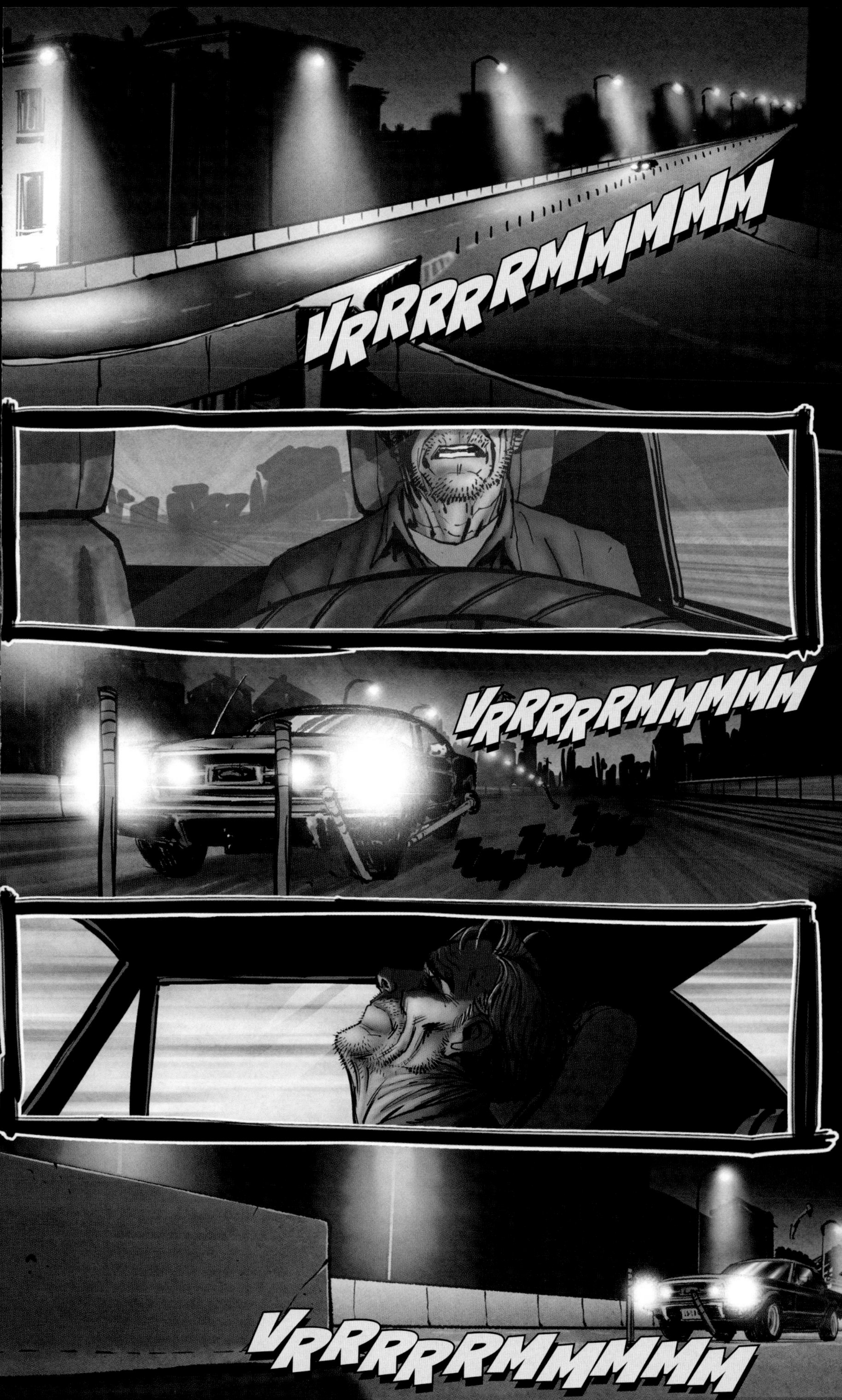

VRRRRRMMMMMM
VRRRRRMMMMMM
VRRRRRMMMMMM

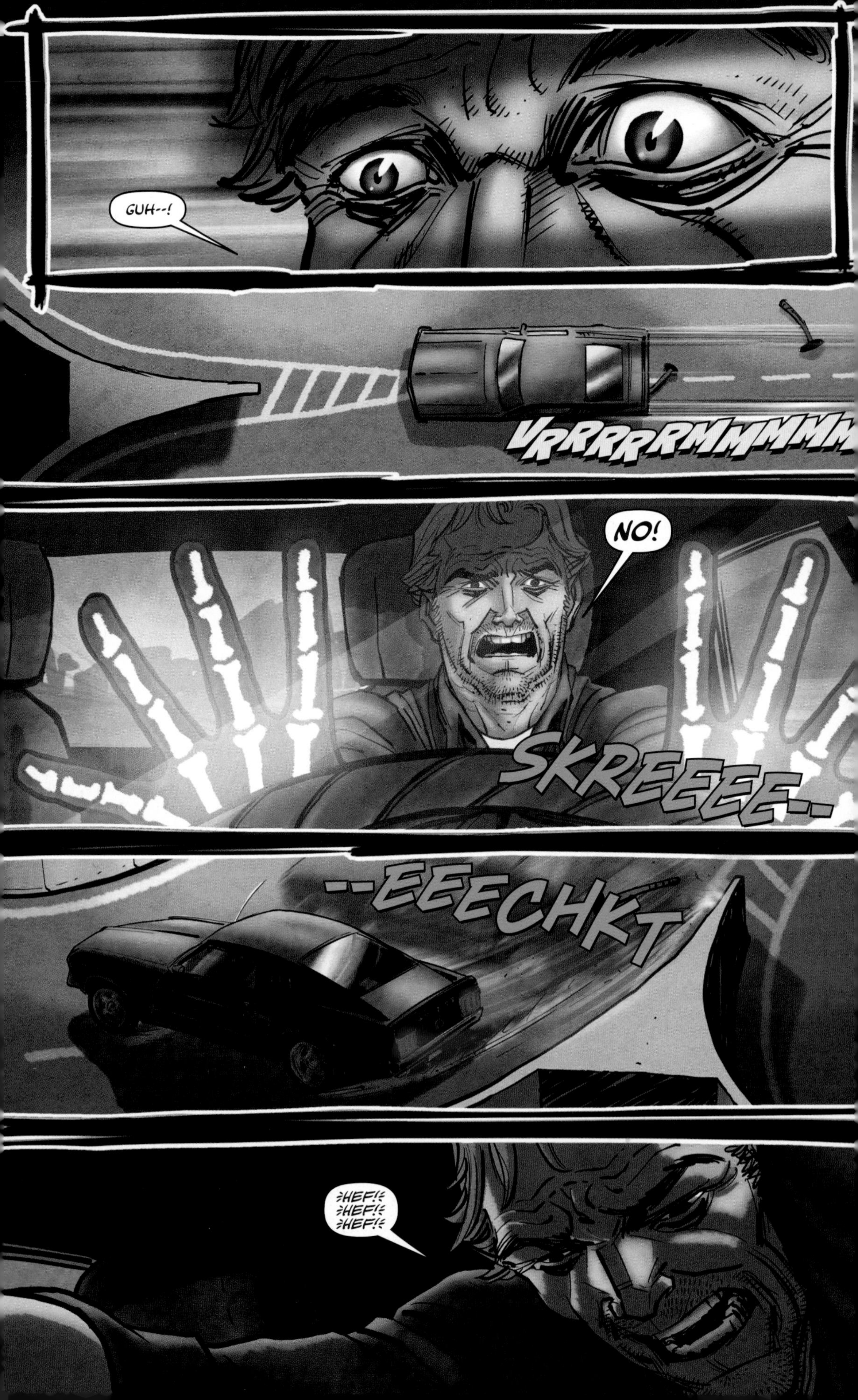
GUH--!
VRRRRRMMMMM
NO!
SKREEEEE--
--EEECHKT
HEF!
HEF!
HEF!

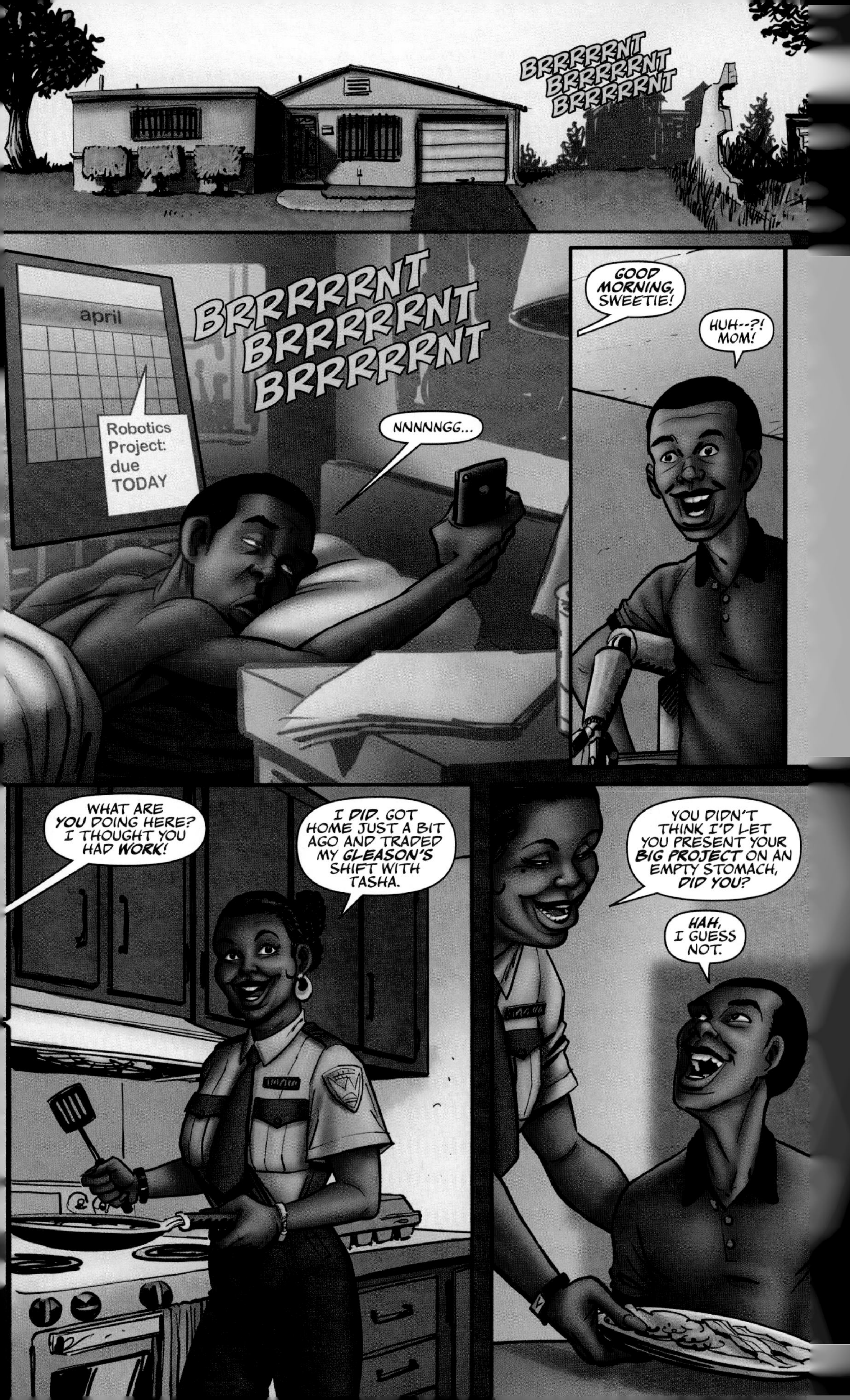
BRRRRRNT BRRRRRNT BRRRRRNT
april
Robotics Project: due TODAY
BRRRRRNT BRRRRRNT BRRRRRNT
NNNNNGG...
GOOD MORNING, SWEETIE!
HUH--?! MOM!
WHAT ARE YOU DOING HERE? I THOUGHT YOU HAD WORK!
I DID. GOT HOME JUST A BIT AGO AND TRADED MY GLEASON'S SHIFT WITH TASHA.
YOU DIDN'T THINK I'D LET YOU PRESENT YOUR BIG PROJECT ON AN EMPTY STOMACH, DID YOU?
HAH, I GUESS NOT.

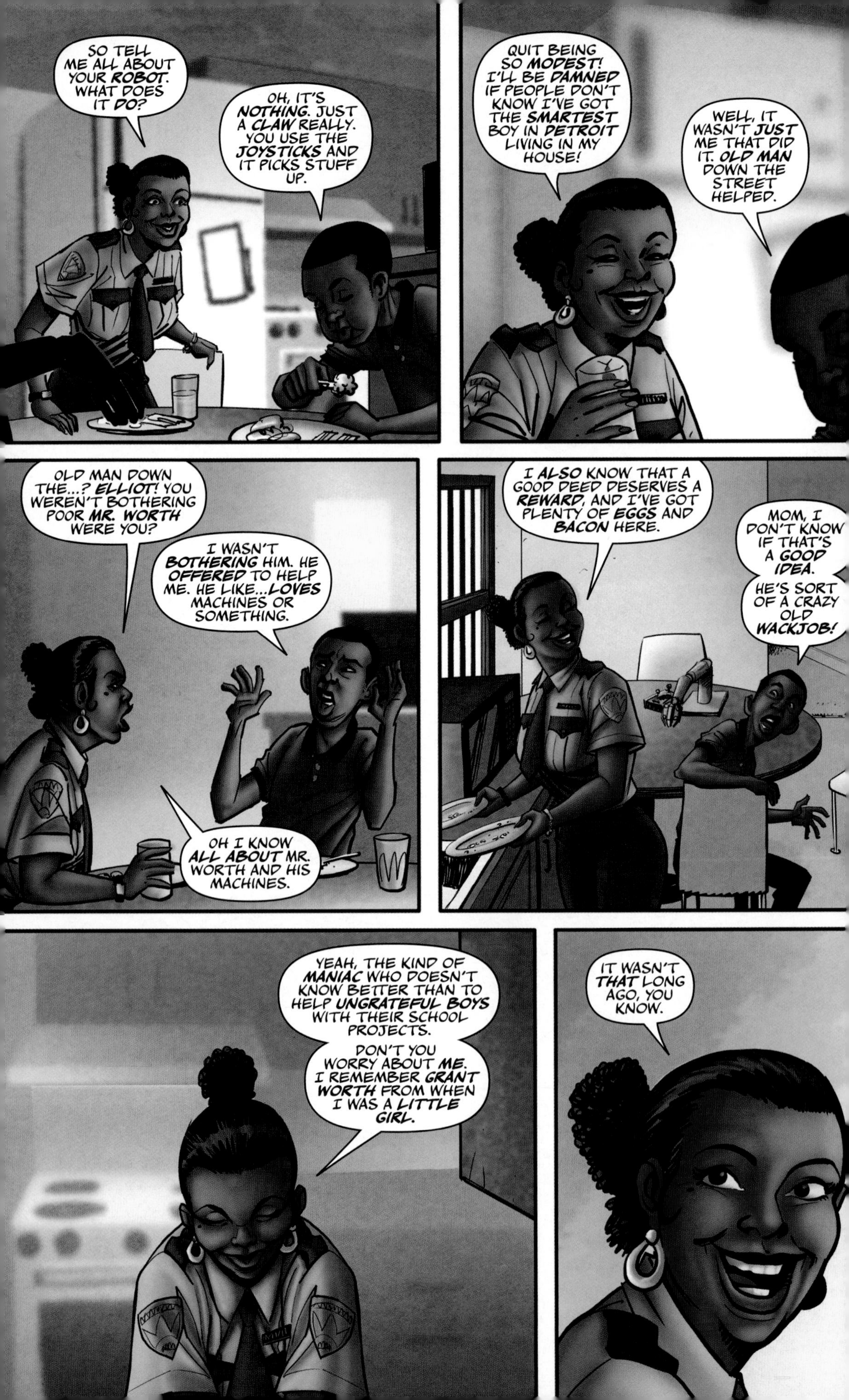
SO TELL ME ALL ABOUT YOUR ROBOT. WHAT DOES IT DO?
OH, IT'S NOTHING. JUST A CLAW REALLY. YOU USE THE JOYSTICKS AND IT PICKS STUFF UP.
QUIT BEING SO MODEST! I'LL BE DAMNED IF PEOPLE DON'T KNOW I'VE GOT THE SMARTEST BOY IN DETROIT LIVING IN MY HOUSE!
WELL, IT WASN'T JUST ME THAT DID IT. OLD MAN DOWN THE STREET HELPED.
OLD MAN DOWN THE...? ELLIOT! YOU WEREN'T BOTHERING POOR MR. WORTH WERE YOU?
I WASN'T BOTHERING HIM. HE OFFERED TO HELP ME. HE LIKE...LOVES MACHINES OR SOMETHING.
OH I KNOW ALL ABOUT MR. WORTH AND HIS MACHINES.
I ALSO KNOW THAT A GOOD DEED DESERVES A REWARD, AND I'VE GOT PLENTY OF EGGS AND BACON HERE.
MOM, I DON'T KNOW IF THAT'S A GOOD IDEA.
HE'S SORT OF A CRAZY OLD WACKJOB!
YEAH, THE KIND OF MANIAC WHO DOESN'T KNOW BETTER THAN TO HELP UNGRATEFUL BOYS WITH THEIR SCHOOL PROJECTS.
DON'T YOU WORRY ABOUT ME. I REMEMBER GRANT WORTH FROM WHEN I WAS A LITTLE GIRL.
IT WASN'T THAT LONG AGO, YOU KNOW.

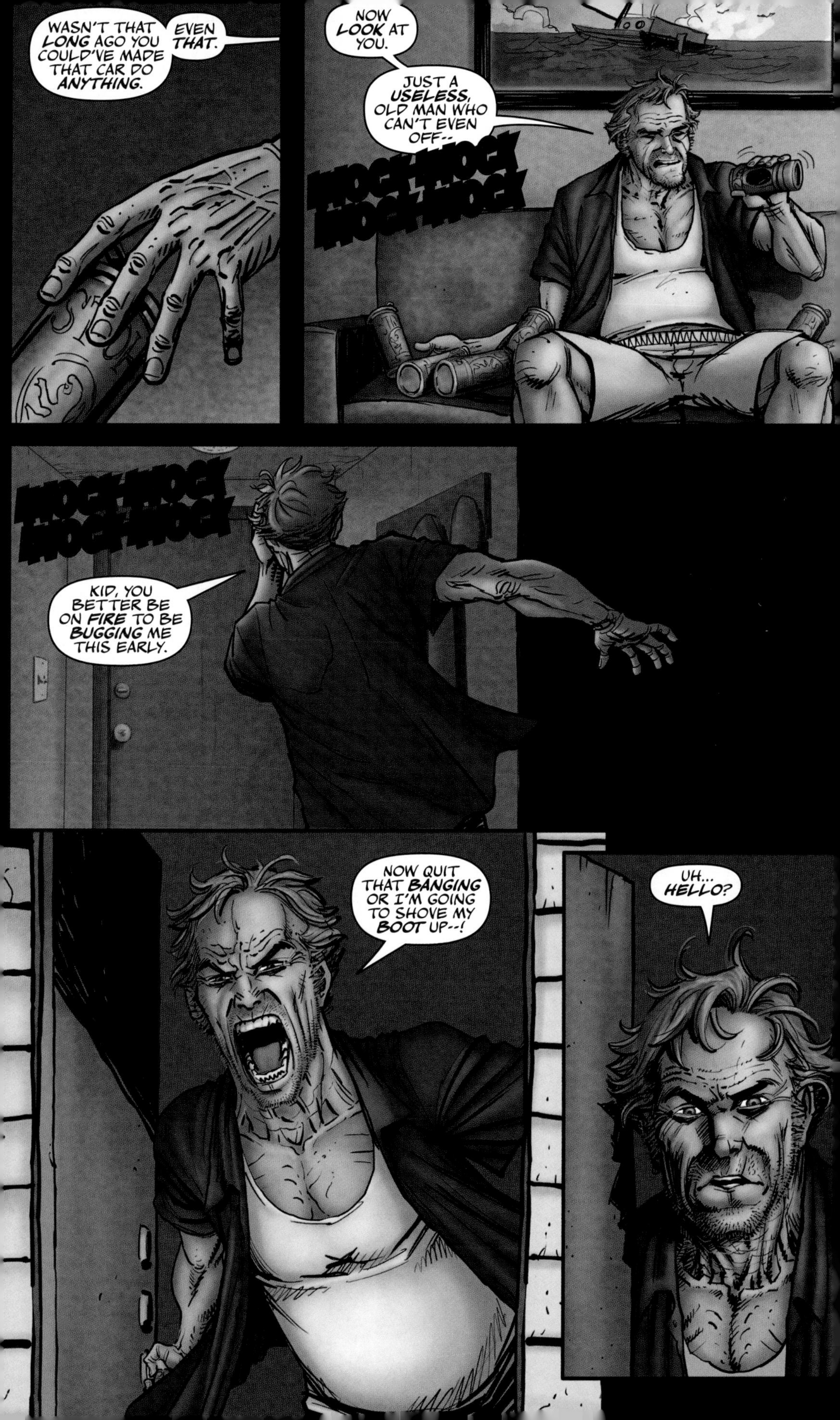
WASN'T THAT LONG AGO YOU COULD'VE MADE THAT CAR DO ANYTHING.
EVEN THAT.
NOW LOOK AT YOU.
JUST A USELESS, OLD MAN WHO CAN'T EVEN OFF--
KNOCK KNOCK KNOCK KNOCK
KNOCK KNOCK KNOCK KNOCK
KID, YOU BETTER BE ON FIRE TO BE BUGGING ME THIS EARLY.
NOW QUIT THAT BANGING OR I'M GOING TO SHOVE MY BOOT UP--!
UH... HELLO?

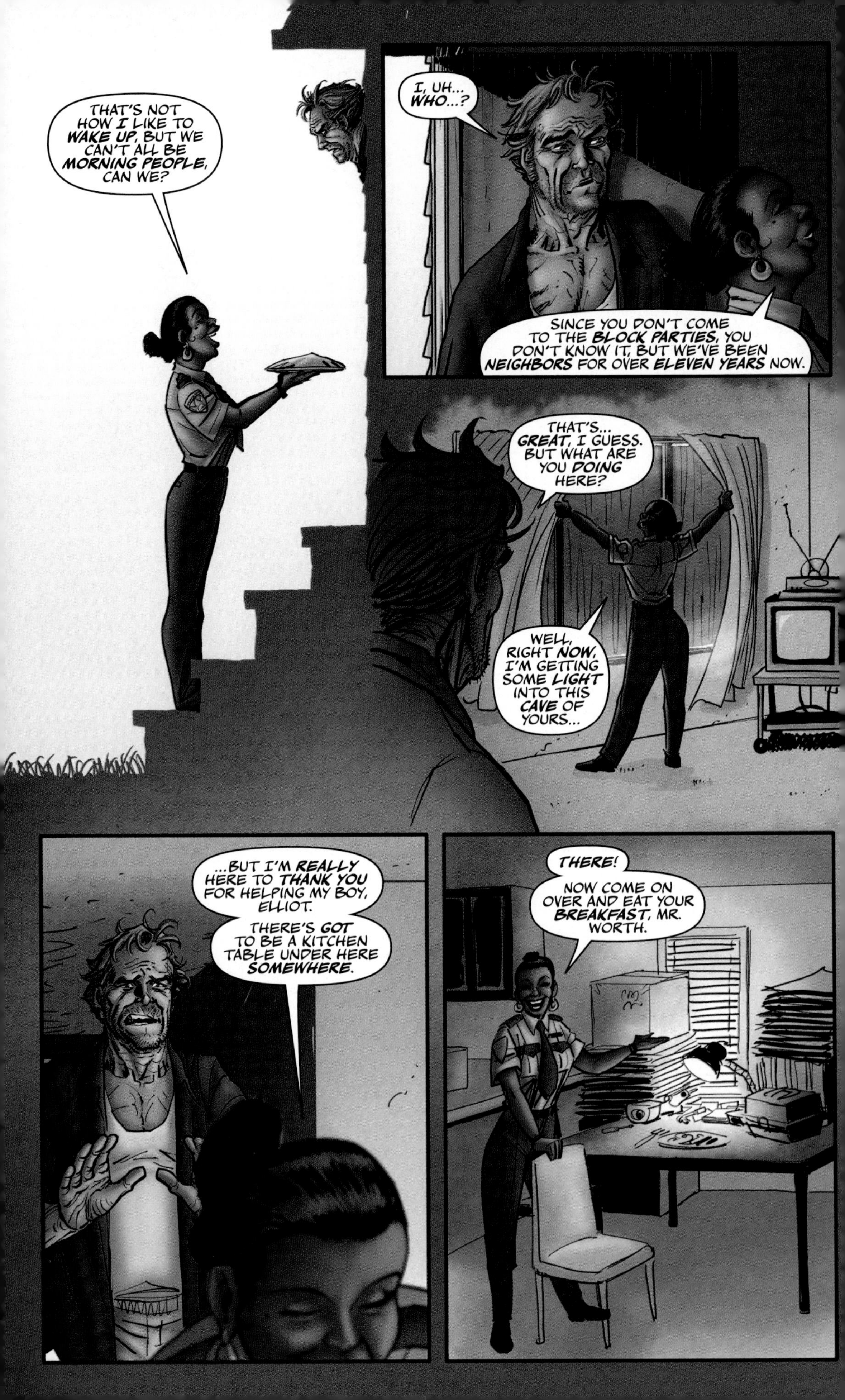
THAT'S NOT HOW I LIKE TO WAKE UP, BUT WE CAN'T ALL BE MORNING PEOPLE, CAN WE?
I, UH... WHO...?
SINCE YOU DON'T COME TO THE BLOCK PARTIES, YOU DON'T KNOW IT, BUT WE'VE BEEN NEIGHBORS FOR OVER ELEVEN YEARS NOW.
THAT'S... GREAT, I GUESS. BUT WHAT ARE YOU DOING HERE?
WELL, RIGHT NOW, I'M GETTING SOME LIGHT INTO THIS CAVE OF YOURS...
...BUT I'M REALLY HERE TO THANK YOU FOR HELPING MY BOY, ELLIOT.
THERE'S GOT TO BE A KITCHEN TABLE UNDER HERE SOMEWHERE.
THERE!
NOW COME ON OVER AND EAT YOUR BREAKFAST, MR. WORTH.

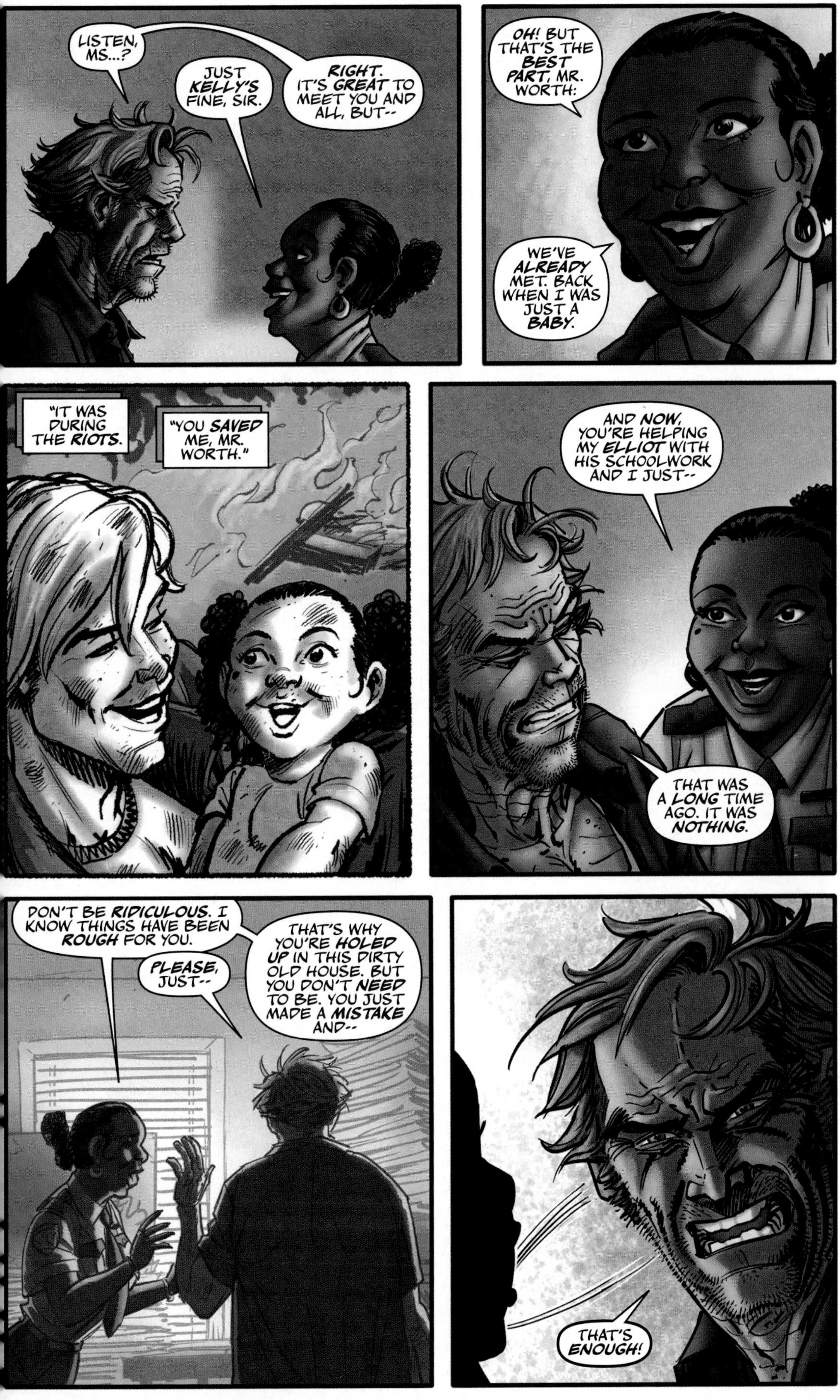
LISTEN, MS...?
JUST KELLY'S FINE, SIR.
RIGHT. IT'S GREAT TO MEET YOU AND ALL, BUT--
OH! BUT THAT'S THE BEST PART, MR. WORTH:
WE'VE ALREADY MET. BACK WHEN I WAS JUST A BABY.
"IT WAS DURING THE RIOTS.
"YOU SAVED ME, MR. WORTH."
AND NOW, YOU'RE HELPING MY ELLIOT WITH HIS SCHOOLWORK AND I JUST--
THAT WAS A LONG TIME AGO. IT WAS NOTHING.
DON'T BE RIDICULOUS. I KNOW THINGS HAVE BEEN ROUGH FOR YOU.
PLEASE, JUST--
THAT'S WHY YOU'RE HOLED UP IN THIS DIRTY OLD HOUSE. BUT YOU DON'T NEED TO BE. YOU JUST MADE A MISTAKE AND--
THAT'S ENOUGH!

YOU *BARGE* YOUR WAY IN HERE *UNINVITED*, LIKE WE'RE...WE'RE... *FRIENDS* OR SOMETHING.

PLEASE... WHERE'S *ALL* THIS--?

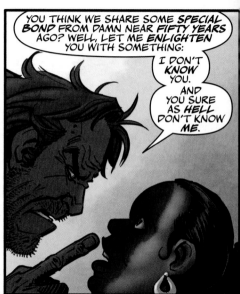

YOU THINK WE SHARE SOME *SPECIAL BOND* FROM DAMN NEAR *FIFTY YEARS* AGO? WELL, LET ME *ENLIGHTEN* YOU WITH SOMETHING:

I DON'T *KNOW* YOU.

AND YOU SURE AS *HELL* DON'T KNOW ME.

YOU DON'T KNOW ANYTHING *ABOUT* ME.

YEAH...I *GOT* IT. BUT NOW, LET ME TELL *YOU* SOMETHING, MR. WORTH.

WHAT HAPPENED TO YOU WAS AWFUL. TRULY *AWFUL.* BUT IT'S *NO REASON* TO BE SO *NASTY.* ESPECIALLY TO PEOPLE WHO WANT TO *HELP,* OR GOD FORBID, BE YOUR *FRIEND.*

YOU *USED TO BE* SOMETHING SPECIAL. I *LOOKED* UP TO YOU. HELL, *EVERYONE* IN THIS CITY DID.

BUT? *NOW?* NOW YOU'RE JUST A *SAD OLD MAN.*

LEAVE THE *PLATE* ON YOUR *PORCH* WHEN YOU'RE DONE.

SLAM

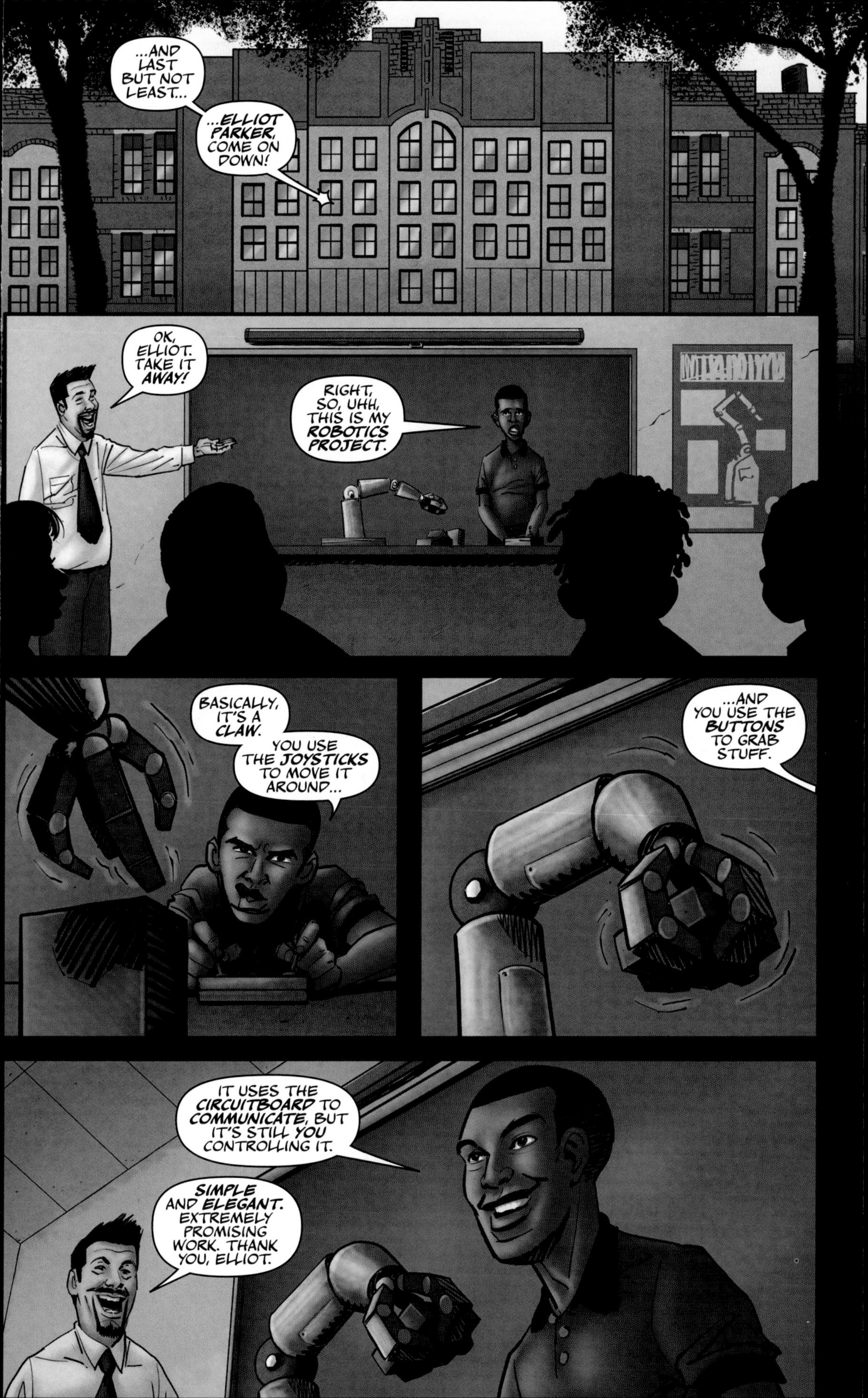
...AND LAST BUT NOT LEAST...
...ELLIOT PARKER, COME ON DOWN!
OK, ELLIOT. TAKE IT AWAY!
RIGHT, SO, UHH, THIS IS MY ROBOTICS PROJECT.
BASICALLY, IT'S A CLAW.
YOU USE THE JOYSTICKS TO MOVE IT AROUND...
...AND YOU USE THE BUTTONS TO GRAB STUFF.
IT USES THE CIRCUITBOARD TO COMMUNICATE, BUT IT'S STILL YOU CONTROLLING IT.
SIMPLE AND ELEGANT. EXTREMELY PROMISING WORK. THANK YOU, ELLIOT.

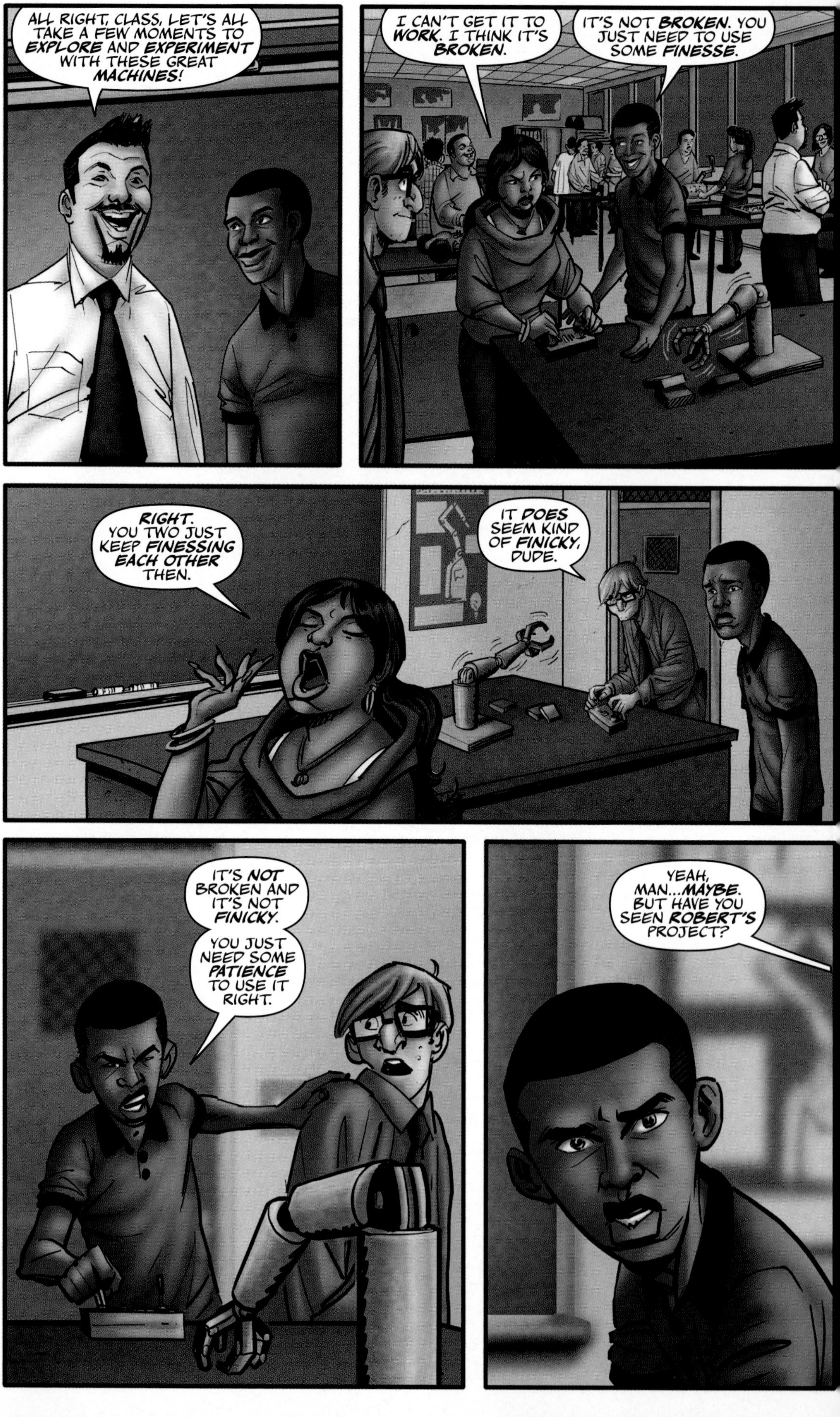
ALL RIGHT, CLASS, LET'S ALL TAKE A FEW MOMENTS TO EXPLORE AND EXPERIMENT WITH THESE GREAT MACHINES!
I CAN'T GET IT TO WORK. I THINK IT'S BROKEN.
IT'S NOT BROKEN. YOU JUST NEED TO USE SOME FINESSE.
RIGHT. YOU TWO JUST KEEP FINESSING EACH OTHER THEN.
IT DOES SEEM KIND OF FINICKY, DUDE.
IT'S NOT BROKEN AND IT'S NOT FINICKY.
YOU JUST NEED SOME PATIENCE TO USE IT RIGHT.
YEAH, MAN...MAYBE. BUT HAVE YOU SEEN ROBERT'S PROJECT?

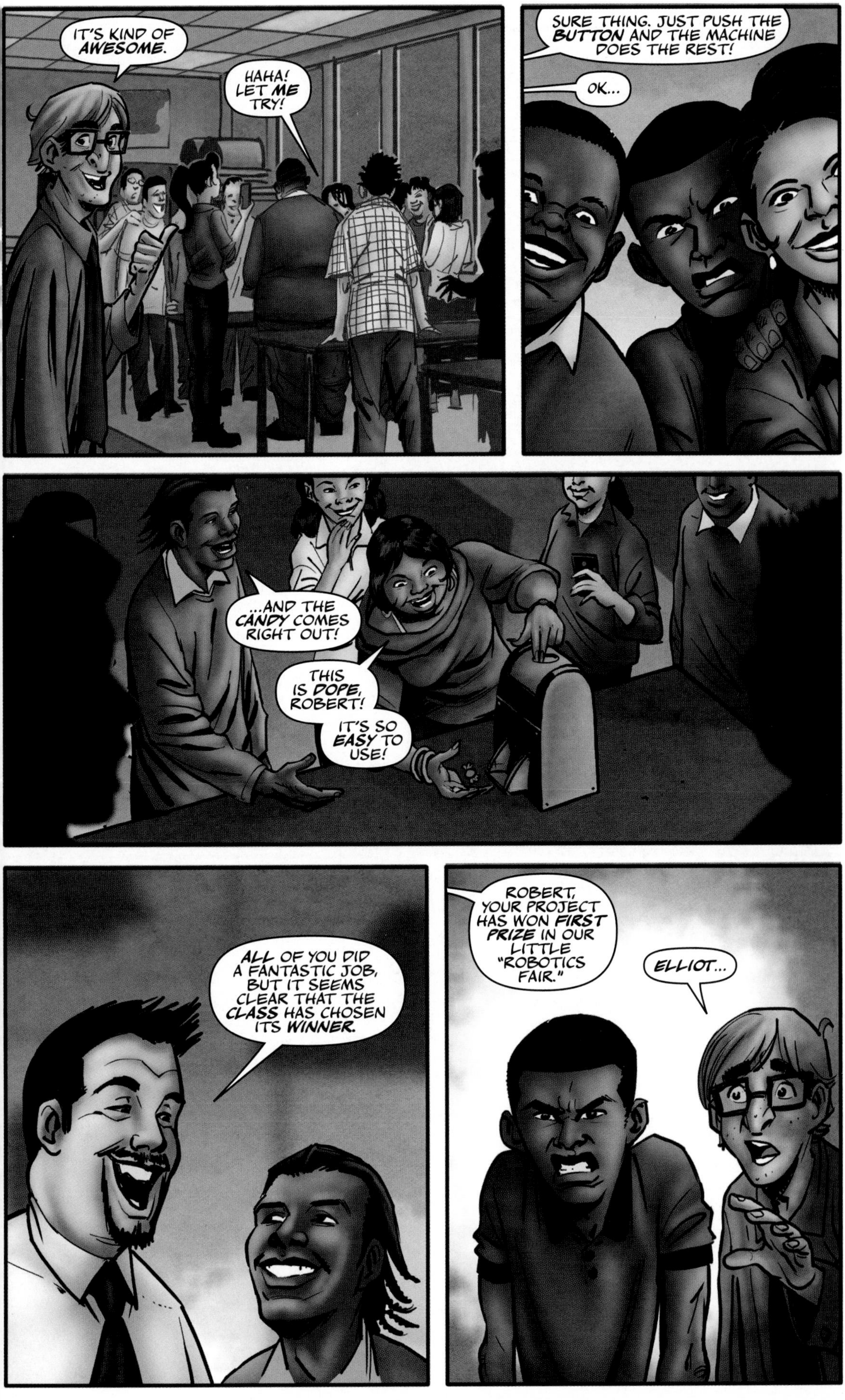
IT'S KIND OF AWESOME.
HAHA! LET ME TRY!
SURE THING. JUST PUSH THE BUTTON AND THE MACHINE DOES THE REST!
OK...
...AND THE CANDY COMES RIGHT OUT!
THIS IS DOPE, ROBERT!
IT'S SO EASY TO USE!
ALL OF YOU DID A FANTASTIC JOB, BUT IT SEEMS CLEAR THAT THE CLASS HAS CHOSEN ITS WINNER.
ROBERT, YOUR PROJECT HAS WON FIRST PRIZE IN OUR LITTLE "ROBOTICS FAIR."
ELLIOT...

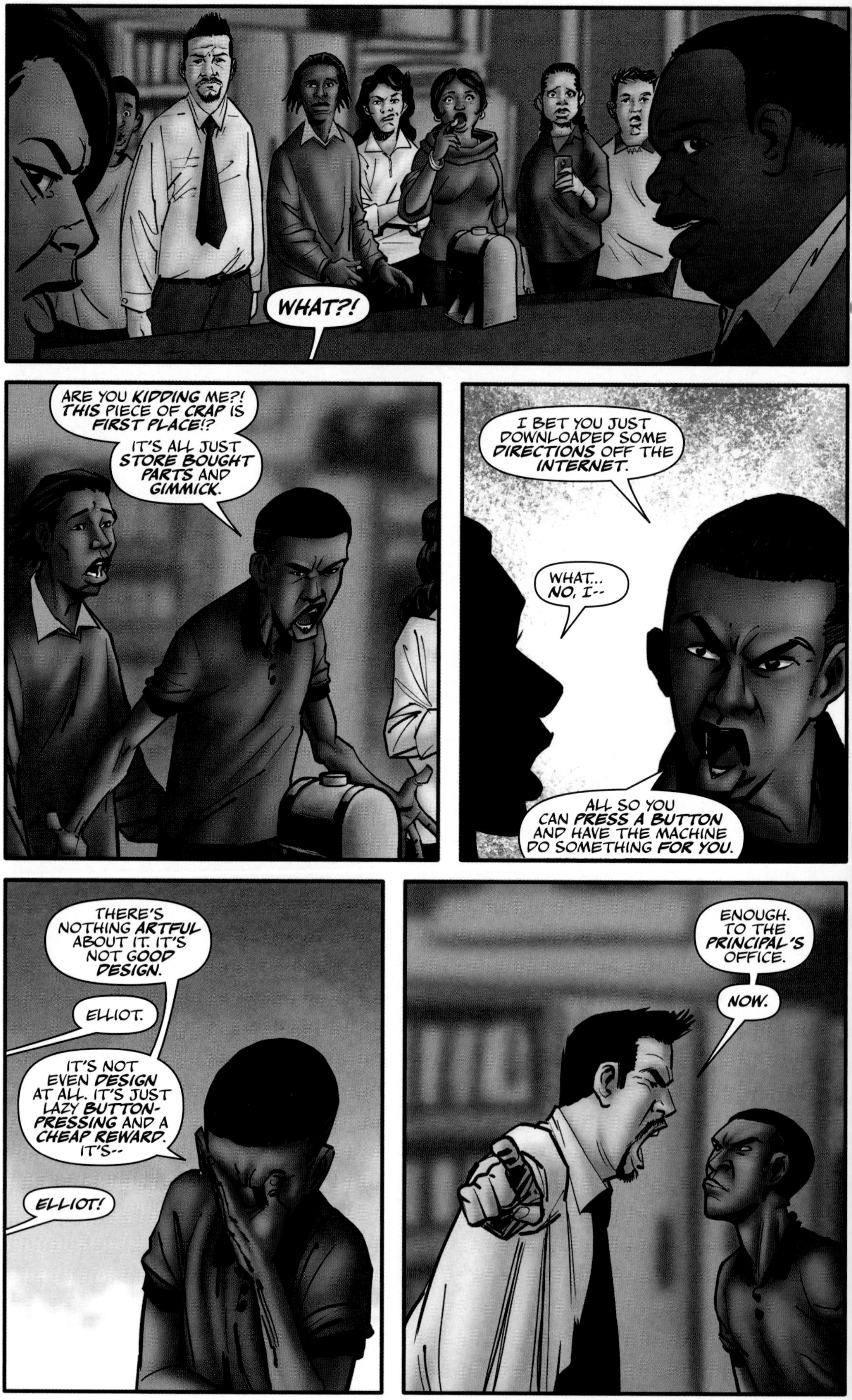

WHAT?!
ARE YOU KIDDING ME?! THIS PIECE OF CRAP IS FIRST PLACE!?
IT'S ALL JUST STORE BOUGHT PARTS AND GIMMICK.
I BET YOU JUST DOWNLOADED SOME DIRECTIONS OFF THE INTERNET.
WHAT... NO, I--
ALL SO YOU CAN PRESS A BUTTON AND HAVE THE MACHINE DO SOMETHING FOR YOU.
THERE'S NOTHING ARTFUL ABOUT IT. IT'S NOT GOOD DESIGN.
ELLIOT.
IT'S NOT EVEN DESIGN AT ALL. IT'S JUST LAZY BUTTON-PRESSING AND A CHEAP REWARD. IT'S--
ELLIOT!
ENOUGH. TO THE PRINCIPAL'S OFFICE.
NOW.

YOU WORTHLESS...

OLD...

BASTARD...

CAN'T EVEN GET THIS PIECE OF JUNK IN WORKING ORDER--

KNOCK KNOCK KNOCK KNOCK

ARE YOU KIDDING ME?!

KNOCK KNOCK KNOCK KNOCK

KNOCK KNOCK KNOCK KNOCK

I'VE BEEN LIVING HERE FOR YEARS, WITHOUT A SINGLE PROBLEM.

NOW, IN THE SPAN OF A WEEK, I'M SOME KIND OF NEIGHBORHOOD PROJECT!?

I SWEAR, YOU DAMN PEOPLE SHOW UP ON MY PORCH ONE MORE TIME AND I'LL--

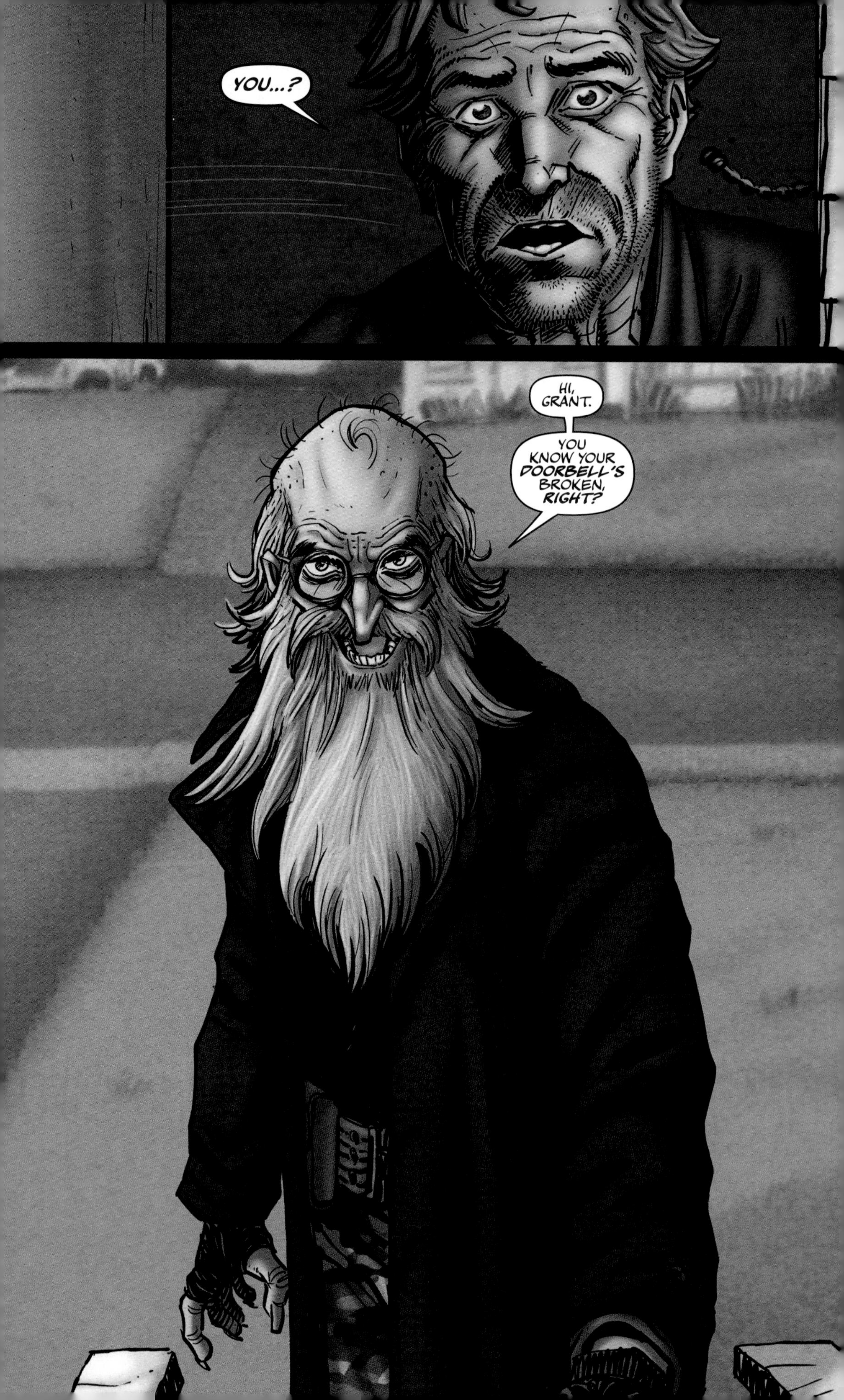
YOU...?
HI, GRANT.
YOU KNOW YOUR DOORBELL'S BROKEN, RIGHT?

CHAPTER 4

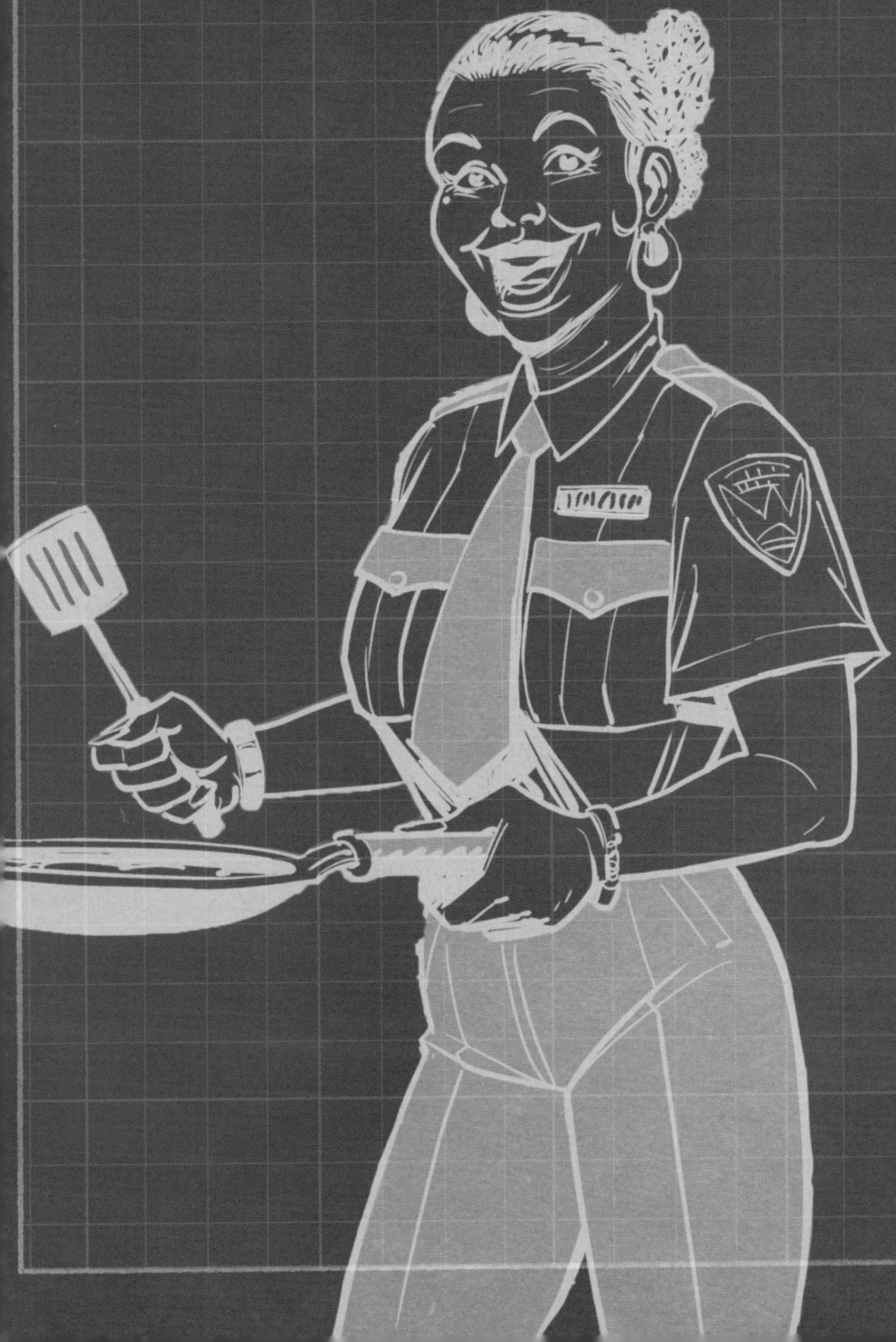

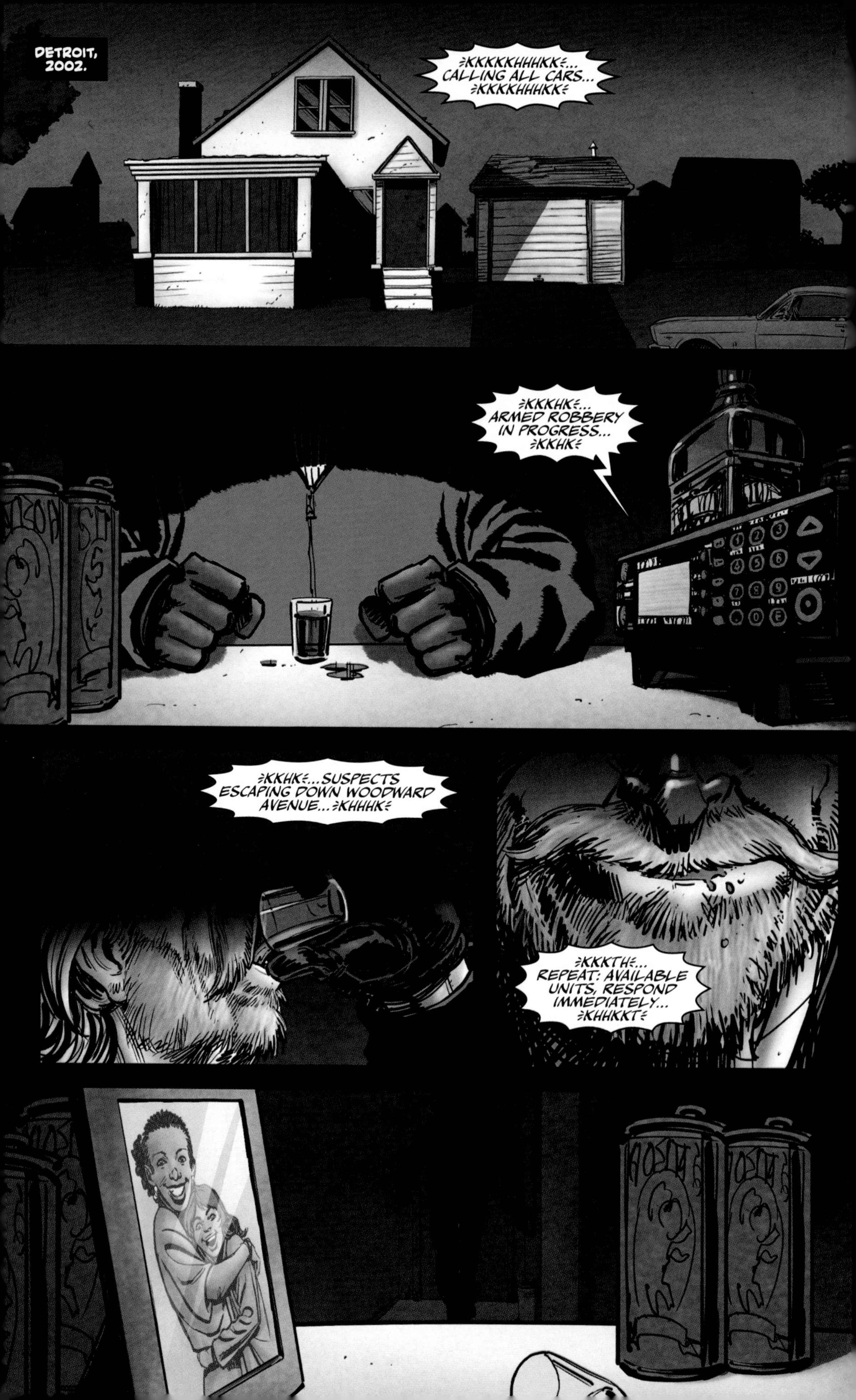
DETROIT, 2002.
KKKKKHHHKK... CALLING ALL CARS... KKKKHHHKK
KKKHK... ARMED ROBBERY IN PROGRESS... KKHK
KKHK...SUSPECTS ESCAPING DOWN WOODWARD AVENUE... KHHHK
KKKTH... REPEAT: AVAILABLE UNITS, RESPOND IMMEDIATELY... KHHKKT

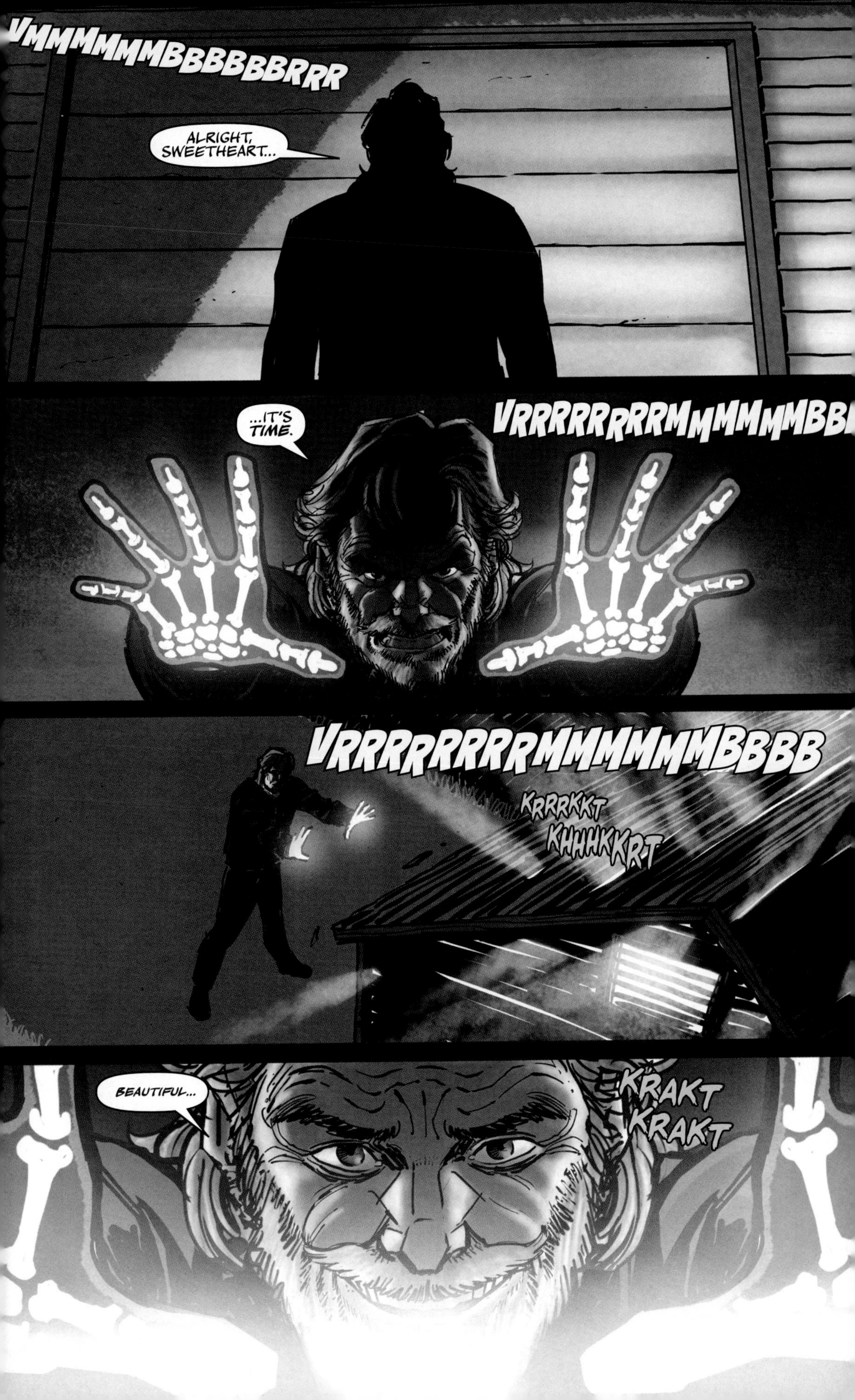
VMMMMMMMBBBBBBRRRR
ALRIGHT, SWEETHEART...
...IT'S TIME.
VRRRRRRRRMMMMMMBB
VRRRRRRRRMMMMMMBBBB
KRRRKKT
KHHHKKRT
BEAUTIFUL...
KRAKT
KRAKT

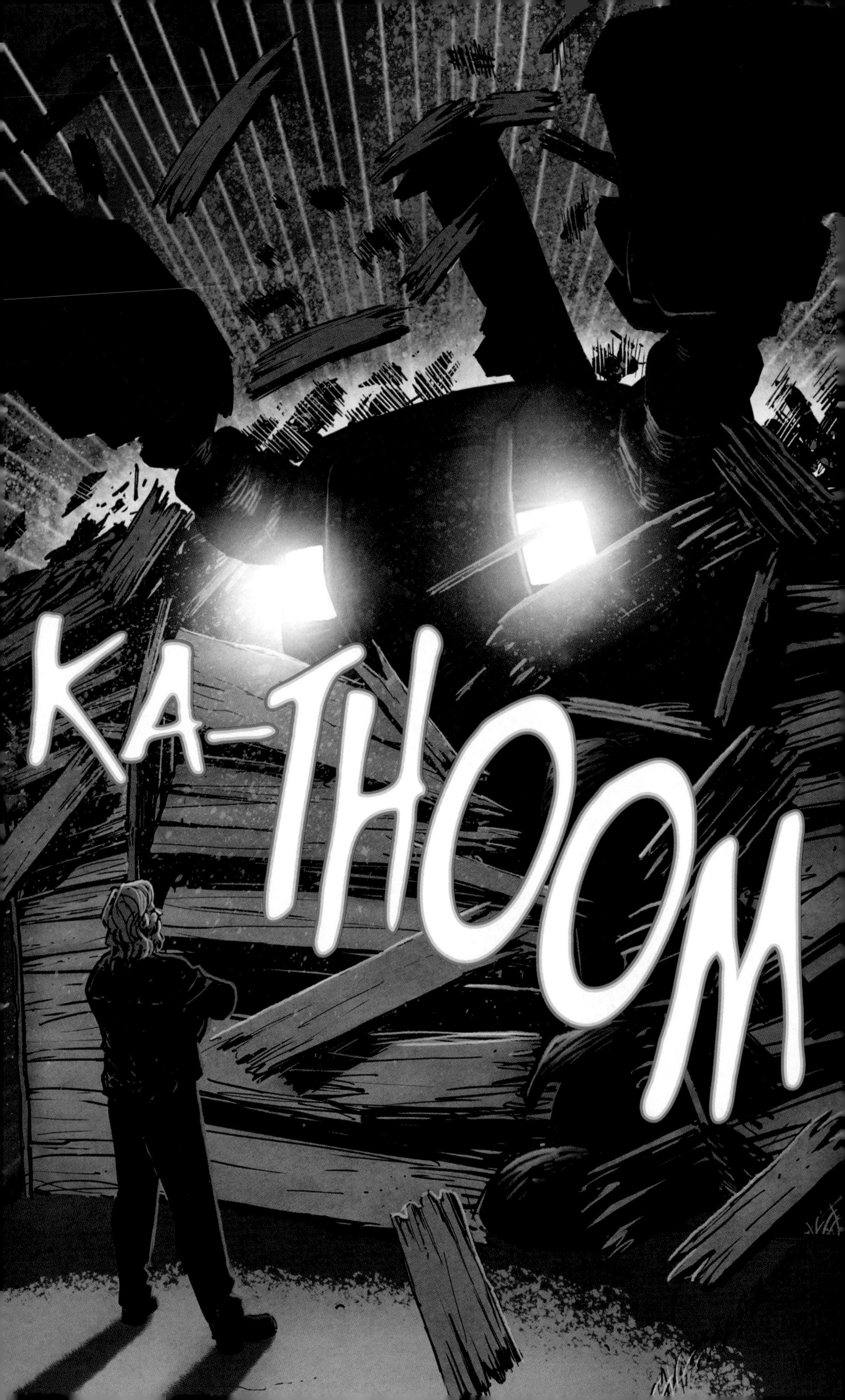
KA-THOOM

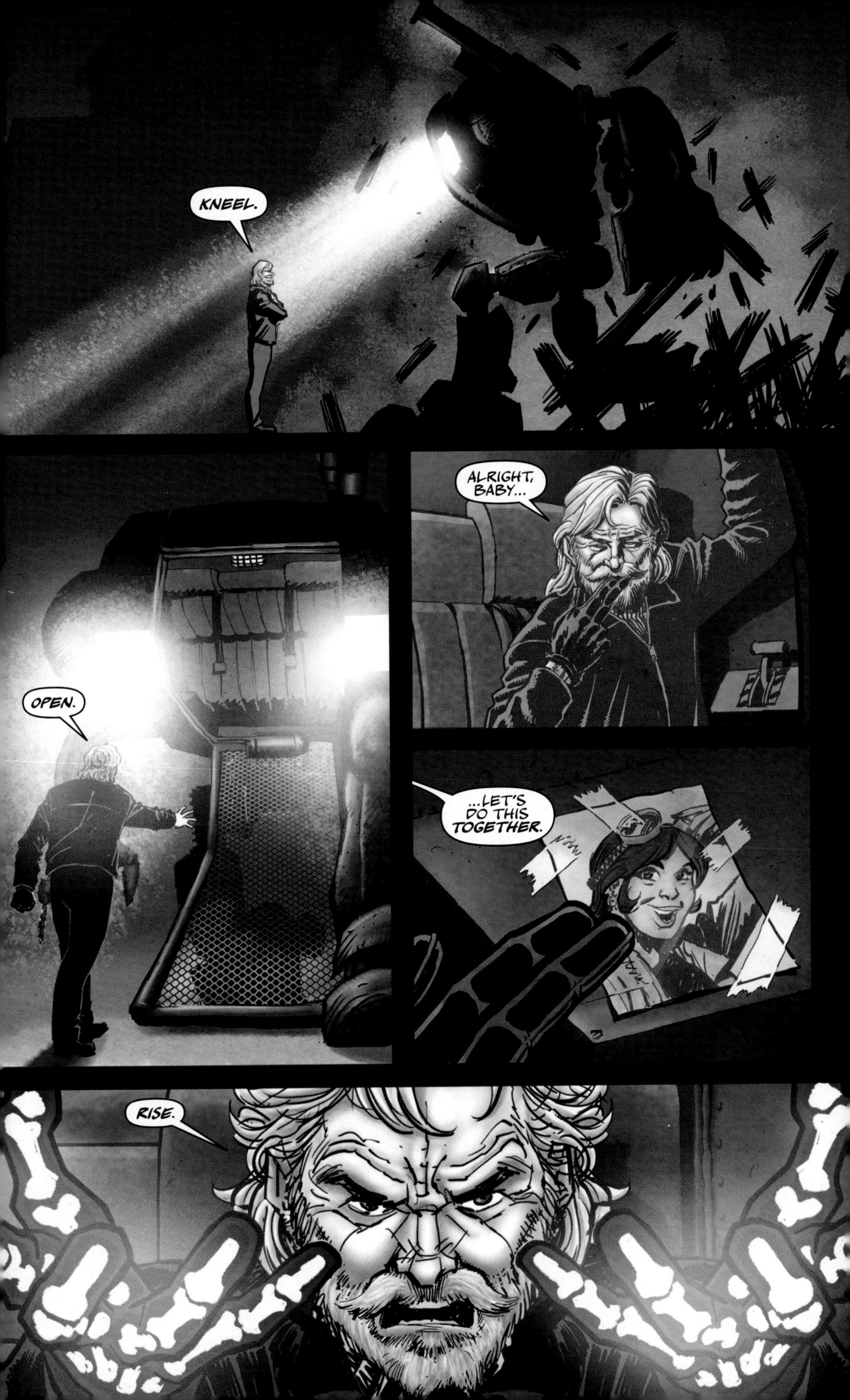
KNEEL.
OPEN.
ALRIGHT, BABY...
...LET'S DO THIS TOGETHER.
RISE.

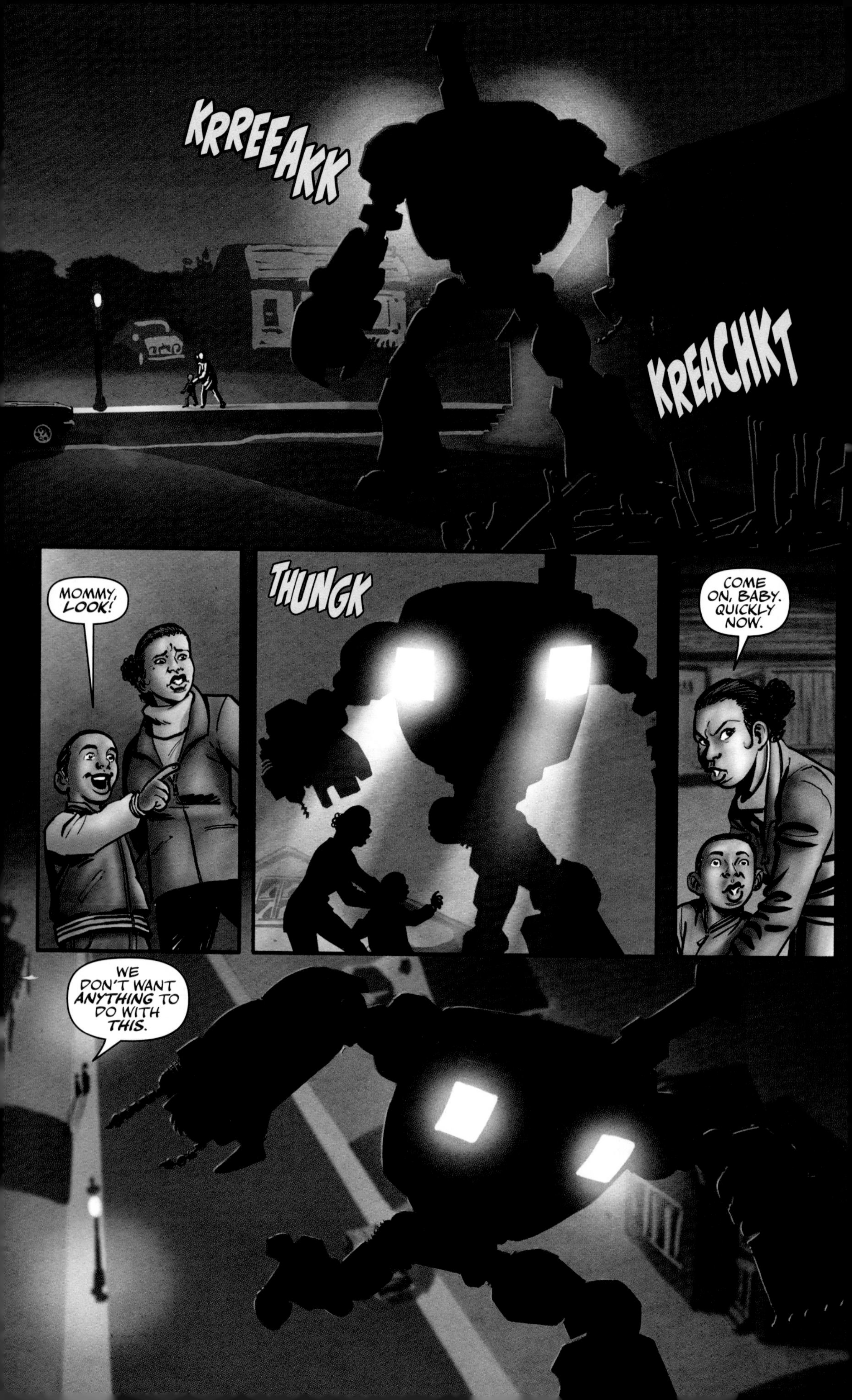
KRREEAKK
KREACHKT
MOMMY, LOOK!
THUNGK
COME ON, BABY. QUICKLY NOW.
WE DON'T WANT ANYTHING TO DO WITH THIS.

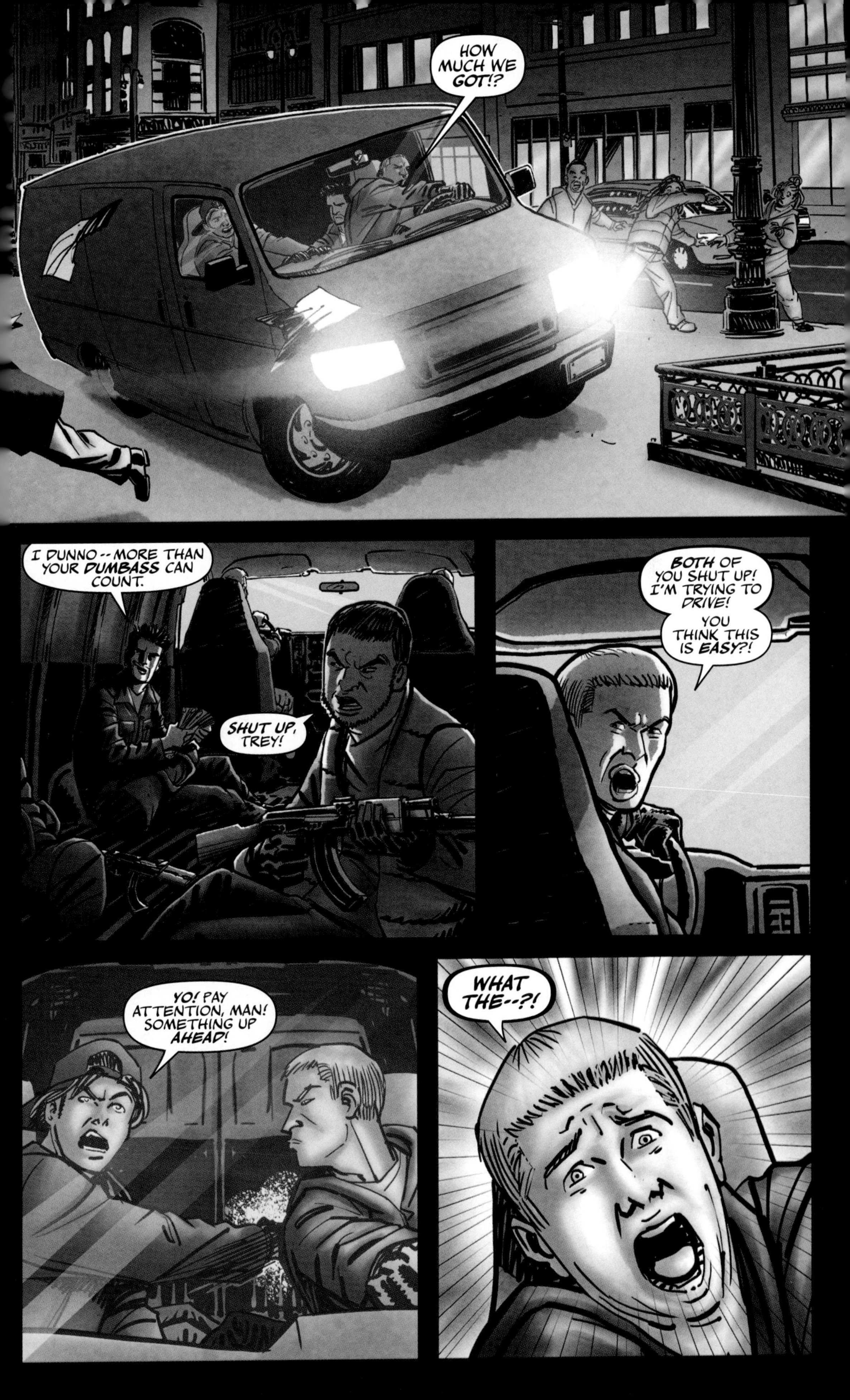
HOW MUCH WE GOT!?
I DUNNO -- MORE THAN YOUR DUMBASS CAN COUNT.
SHUT UP, TREY!
BOTH OF YOU SHUT UP! I'M TRYING TO DRIVE!
YOU THINK THIS IS EASY?!
YO! PAY ATTENTION, MAN! SOMETHING UP AHEAD!
WHAT THE--?!

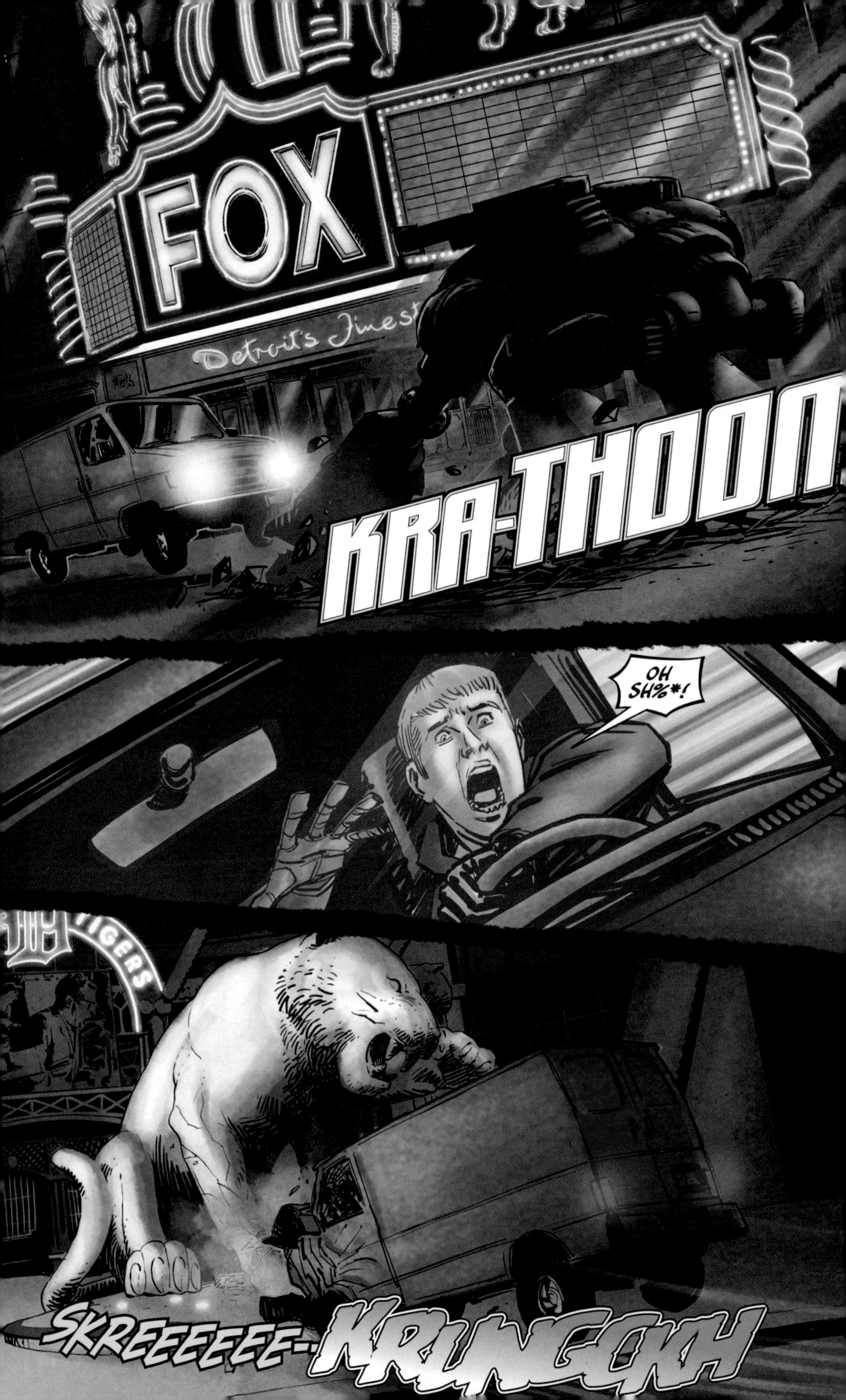
FOX
Detroit's Finest
KRA-THOOM
OH SH%*!
TIGERS
SKREEEEEEE-KRUNCKKH

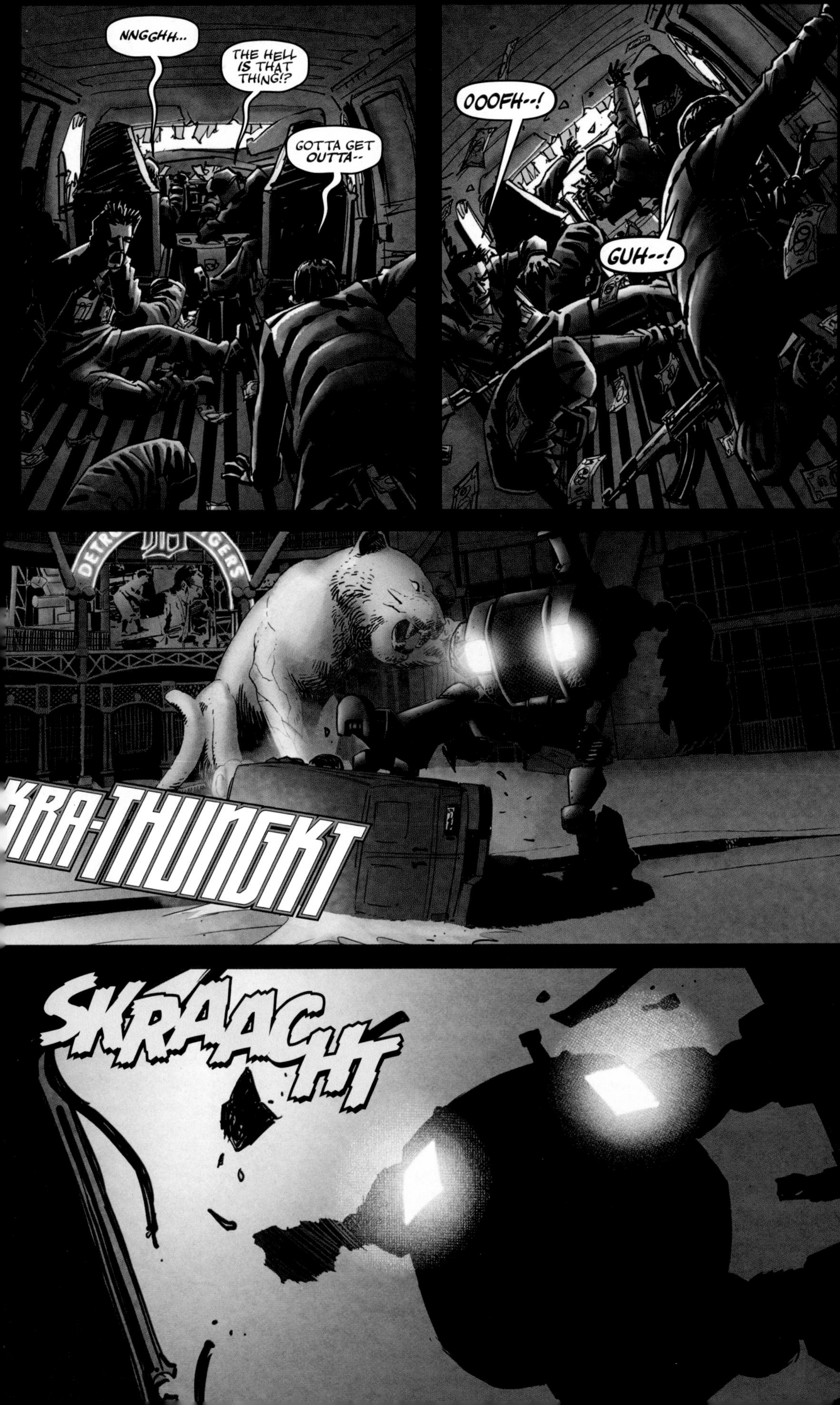
NNGGHH...
THE HELL IS THAT THING!?
GOTTA GET OUTTA--
OOOFH--!
GUH--!
KRA-THUNGKT
SKRAACH

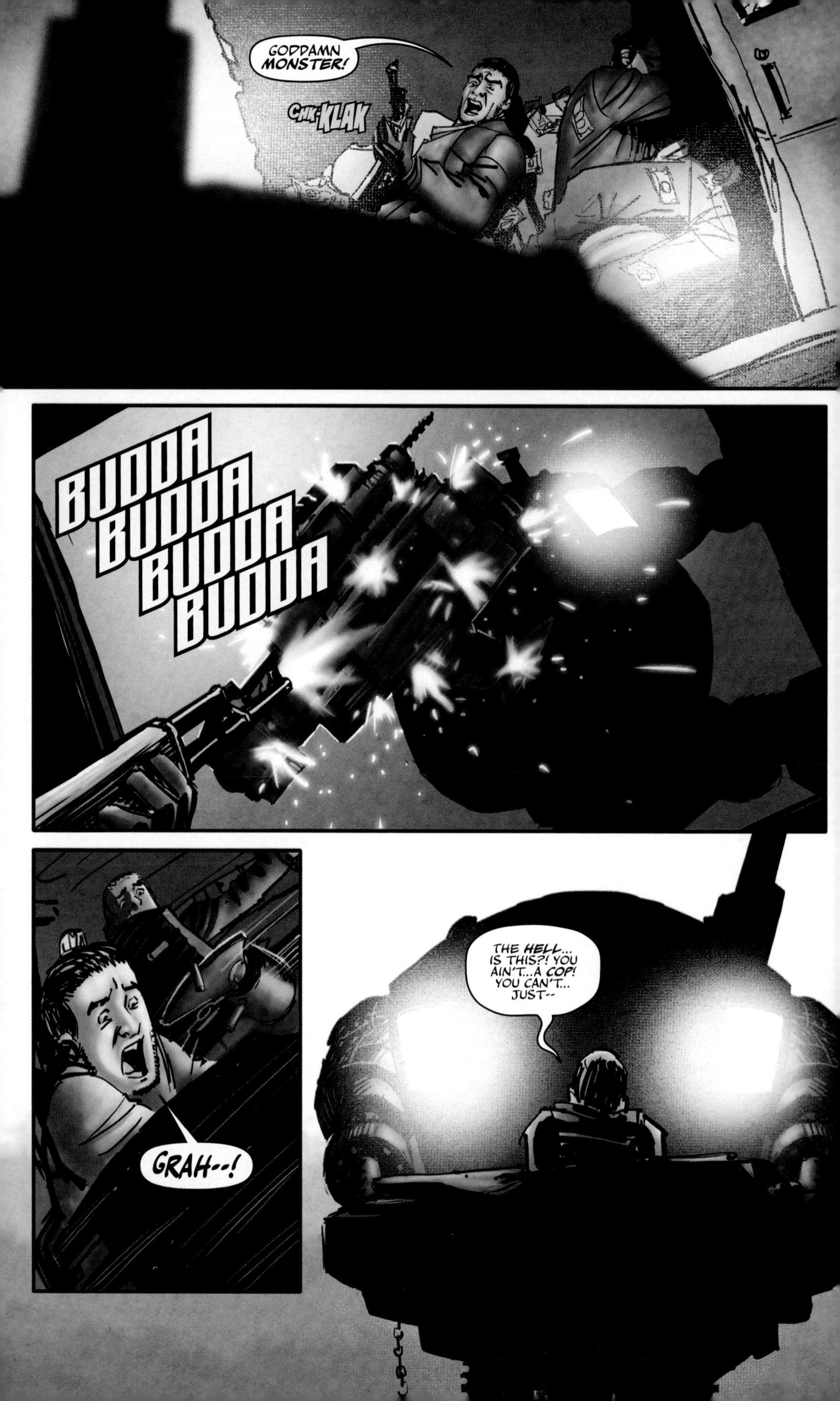
GODDAMN MONSTER!
CHK-KLAK
BUDDA BUDDA BUDDA BUDDA
GRAH--!
THE HELL... IS THIS?! YOU AIN'T...A COP! YOU CAN'T... JUST--

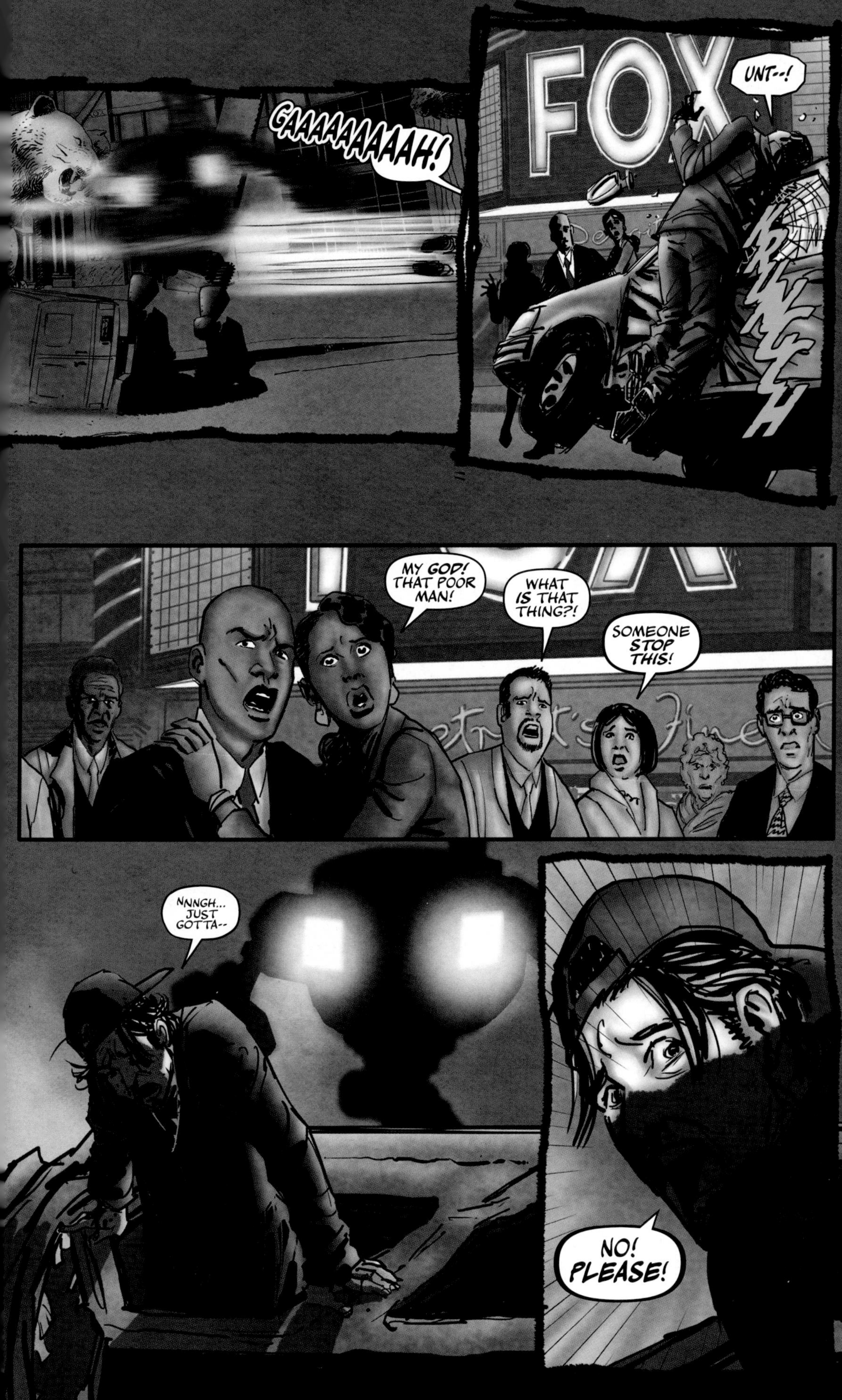

GAAAAAAAAAH!
UNT--!
KRUNCH
MY GOD! THAT POOR MAN!
WHAT IS THAT THING?!
SOMEONE STOP THIS!
NNNGH... JUST GOTTA--
NO! PLEASE!

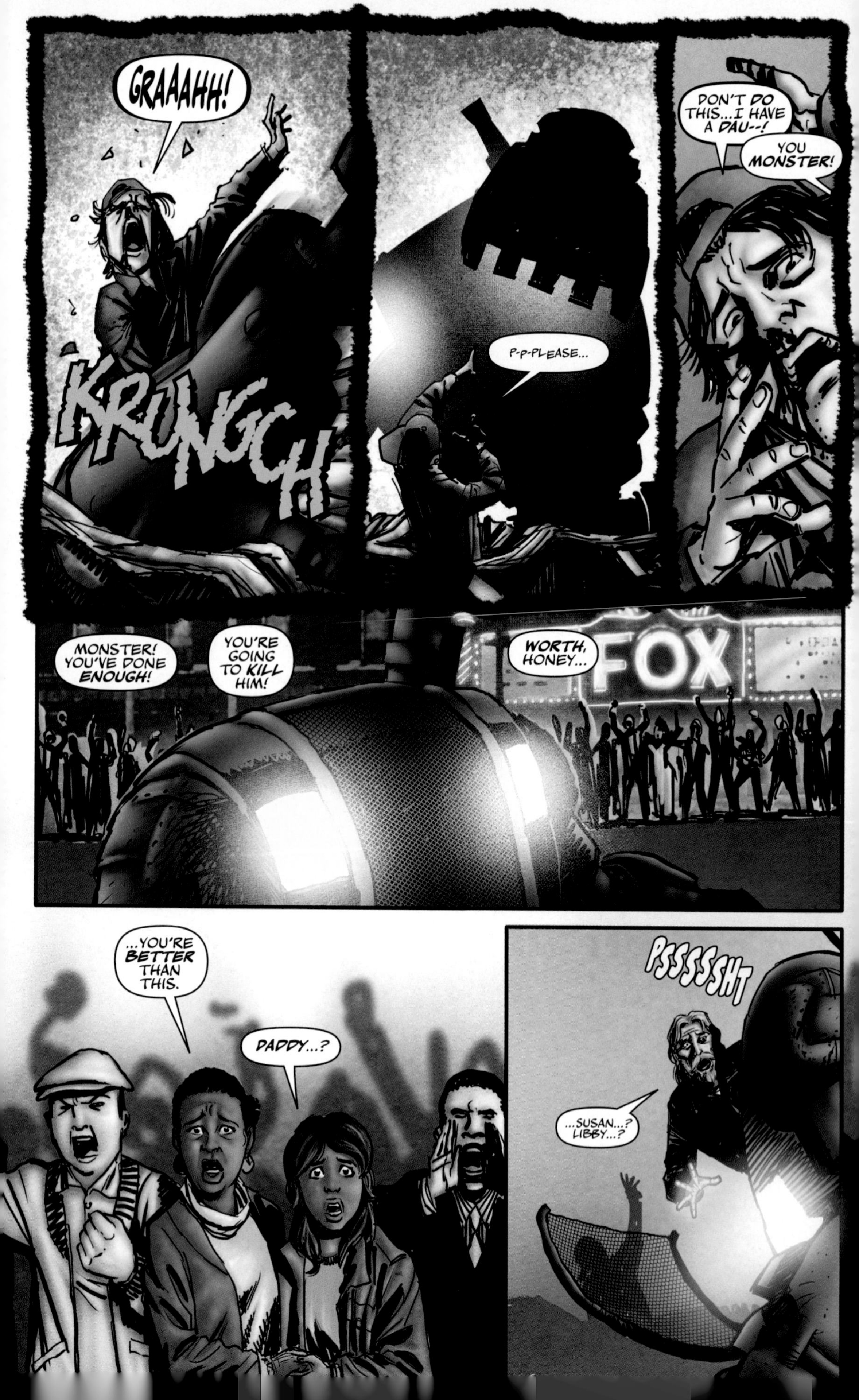
GRAAAHH!
KRUNGCH
P-P-PLEASE...
DON'T DO THIS...I HAVE A DAU--!
YOU MONSTER!
MONSTER! YOU'VE DONE ENOUGH!
YOU'RE GOING TO KILL HIM!
WORTH, HONEY...
FOX
...YOU'RE BETTER THAN THIS.
DADDY...?
PSSSSSHT
...SUSAN...? LIBBY...?

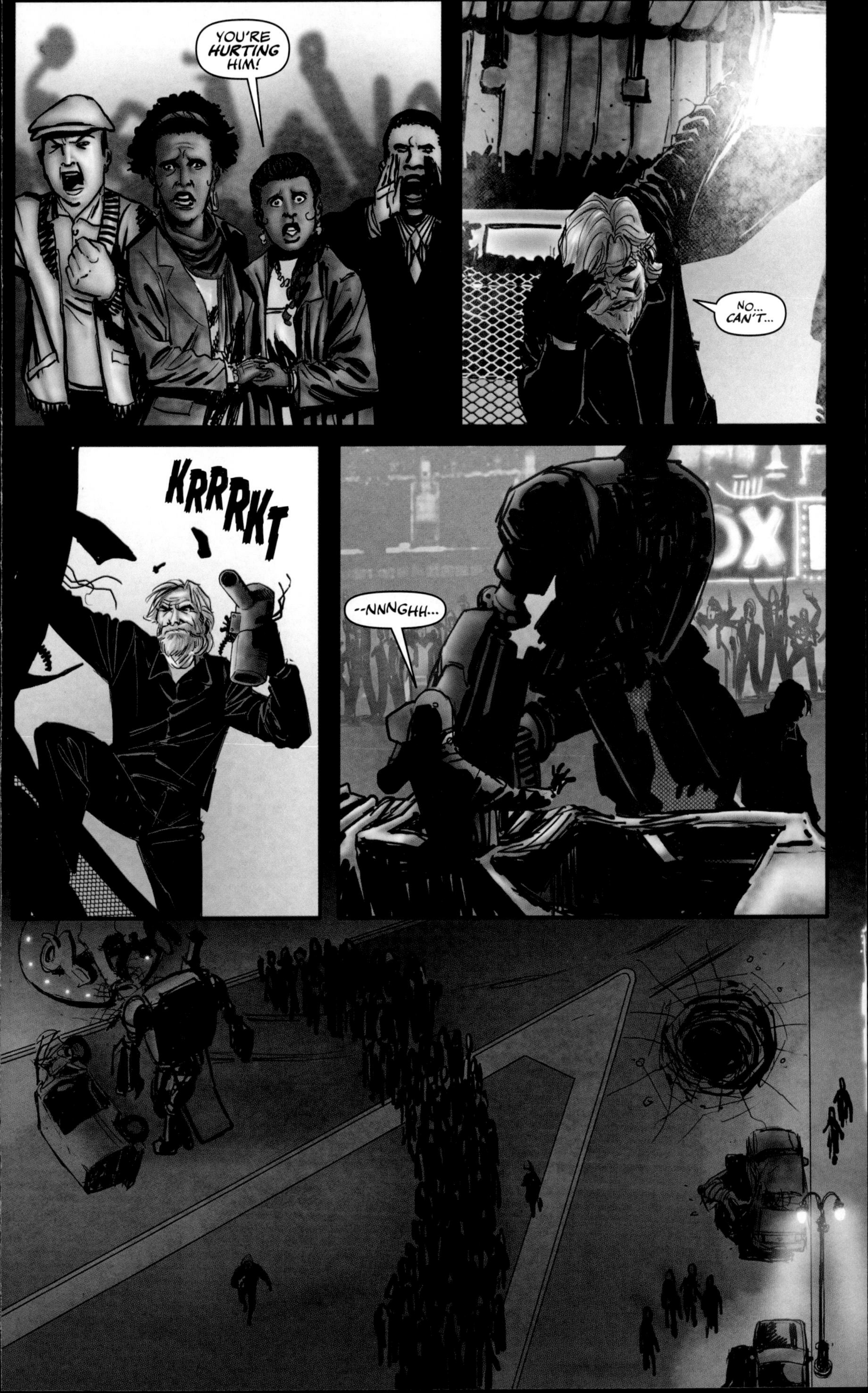
YOU'RE HURTING HIM!
NO... CAN'T...
KRRRKT
--NNNGHH...

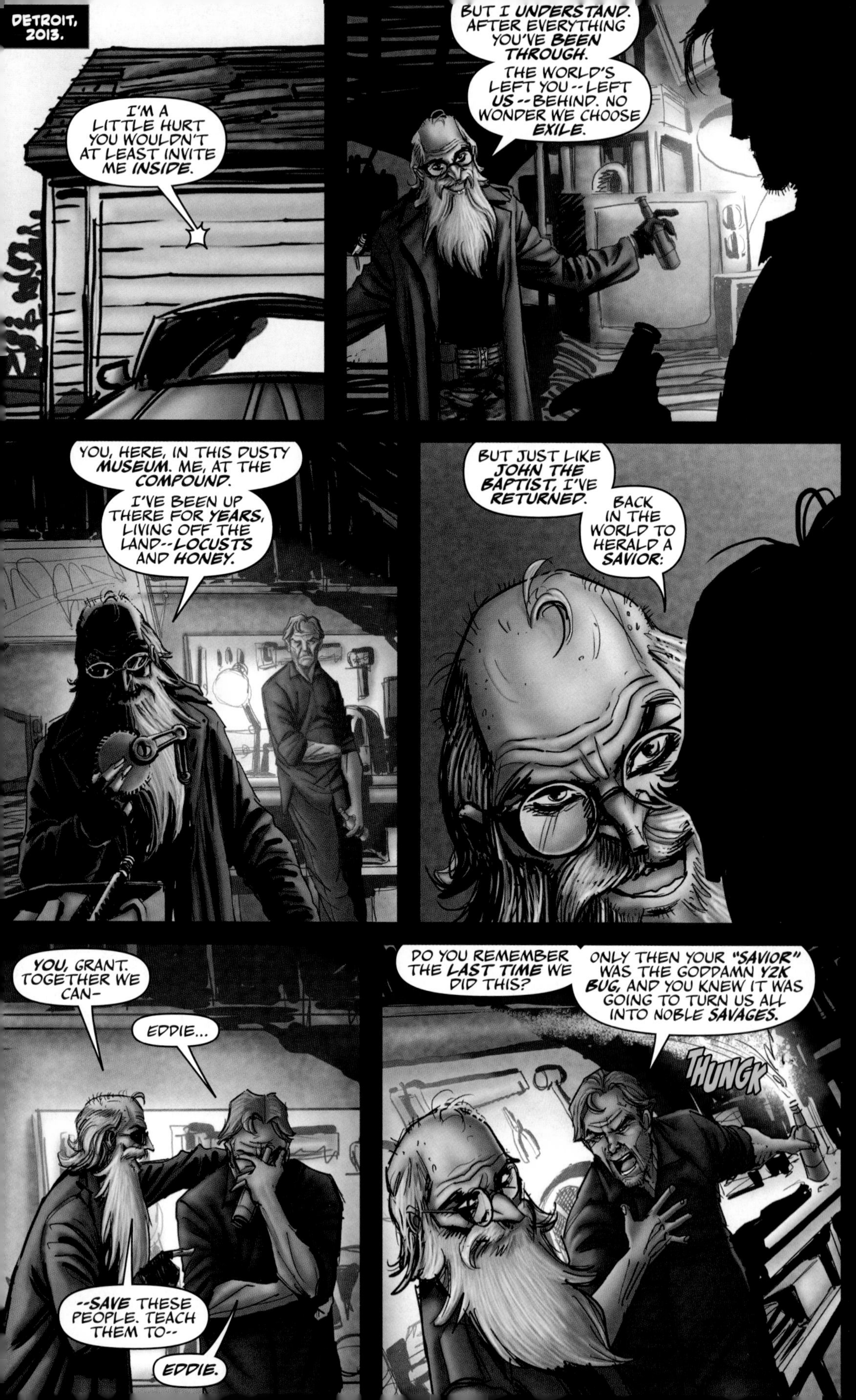
DETROIT, 2013.
I'M A LITTLE HURT YOU WOULDN'T AT LEAST INVITE ME INSIDE.
BUT I UNDERSTAND. AFTER EVERYTHING YOU'VE BEEN THROUGH.
THE WORLD'S LEFT YOU -- LEFT US -- BEHIND. NO WONDER WE CHOOSE EXILE.
YOU, HERE, IN THIS DUSTY MUSEUM. ME, AT THE COMPOUND.
I'VE BEEN UP THERE FOR YEARS, LIVING OFF THE LAND--LOCUSTS AND HONEY.
BUT JUST LIKE JOHN THE BAPTIST, I'VE RETURNED.
BACK IN THE WORLD TO HERALD A SAVIOR:
YOU, GRANT. TOGETHER WE CAN-
EDDIE...
--SAVE THESE PEOPLE. TEACH THEM TO--
EDDIE.
DO YOU REMEMBER THE LAST TIME WE DID THIS?
ONLY THEN YOUR "SAVIOR" WAS THE GODDAMN Y2K BUG, AND YOU KNEW IT WAS GOING TO TURN US ALL INTO NOBLE SAVAGES.
THUNGK

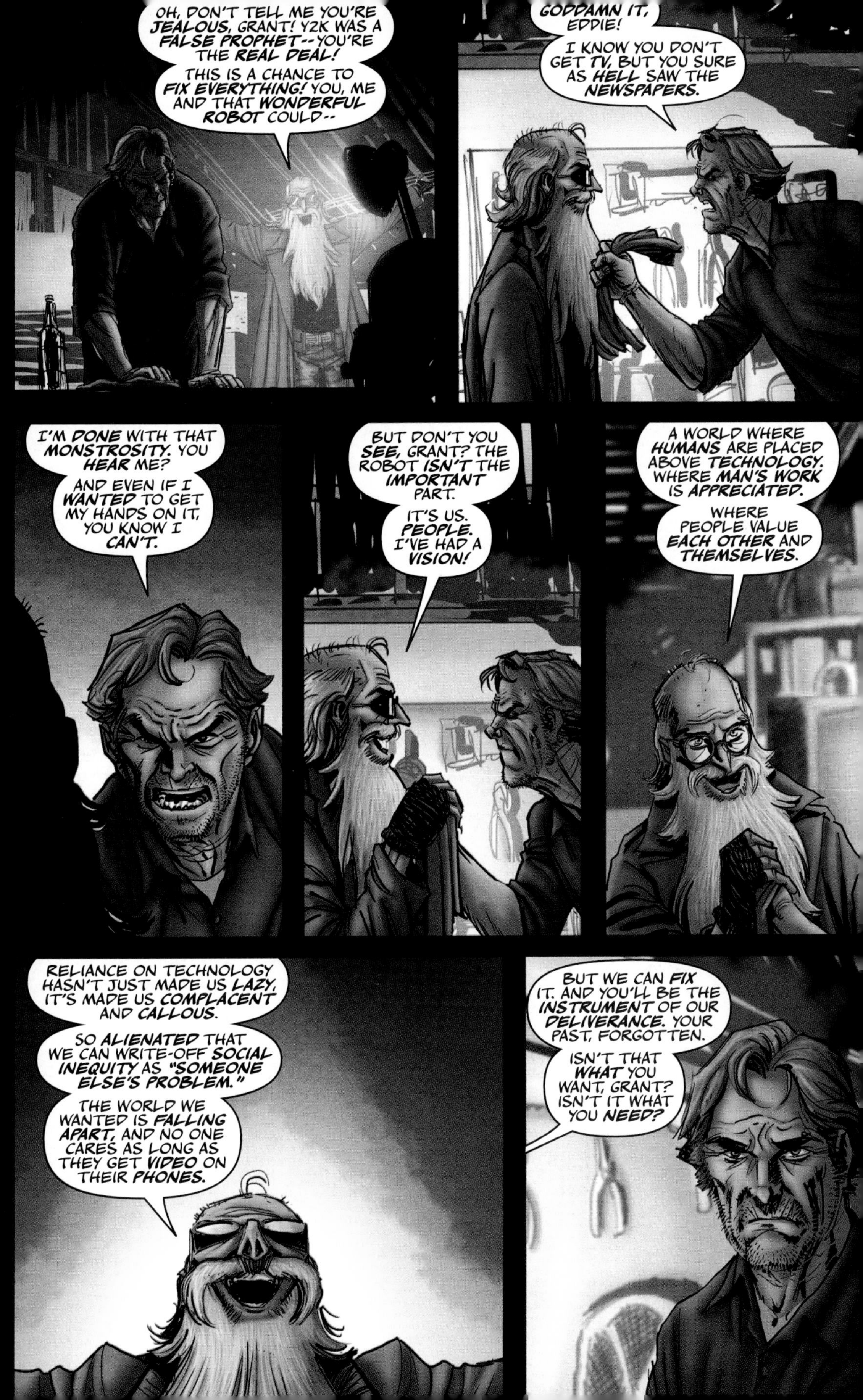
OH, DON'T TELL ME YOU'RE JEALOUS, GRANT! Y2K WAS A FALSE PROPHET--YOU'RE THE REAL DEAL!
THIS IS A CHANCE TO FIX EVERYTHING! YOU, ME AND THAT WONDERFUL ROBOT COULD--
GODDAMN IT, EDDIE!
I KNOW YOU DON'T GET TV, BUT YOU SURE AS HELL SAW THE NEWSPAPERS.
I'M DONE WITH THAT MONSTROSITY. YOU HEAR ME?
AND EVEN IF I WANTED TO GET MY HANDS ON IT, YOU KNOW I CAN'T.
BUT DON'T YOU SEE, GRANT? THE ROBOT ISN'T THE IMPORTANT PART.
IT'S US. PEOPLE. I'VE HAD A VISION!
A WORLD WHERE HUMANS ARE PLACED ABOVE TECHNOLOGY. WHERE MAN'S WORK IS APPRECIATED.
WHERE PEOPLE VALUE EACH OTHER AND THEMSELVES.
RELIANCE ON TECHNOLOGY HASN'T JUST MADE US LAZY, IT'S MADE US COMPLACENT AND CALLOUS.
SO ALIENATED THAT WE CAN WRITE-OFF SOCIAL INEQUITY AS "SOMEONE ELSE'S PROBLEM."
THE WORLD WE WANTED IS FALLING APART, AND NO ONE CARES AS LONG AS THEY GET VIDEO ON THEIR PHONES.
BUT WE CAN FIX IT. AND YOU'LL BE THE INSTRUMENT OF OUR DELIVERANCE. YOUR PAST, FORGOTTEN.
ISN'T THAT WHAT YOU WANT, GRANT? ISN'T IT WHAT YOU NEED?

I...IT'S...

MAYBE... MAYBE... I DON'T KNOW.

I KNOW. THIS IS OUR REDEMPTION. MY PLAN WILL--

WAIT...WHAT DO YOU HAVE PLANNED?

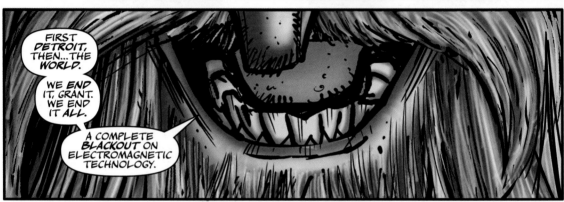

FIRST DETROIT, THEN...THE WORLD.

WE END IT, GRANT. WE END IT ALL.

A COMPLETE BLACKOUT ON ELECTROMAGNETIC TECHNOLOGY.

A BLACKOUT...?

EDDIE, HAVE YOU LOST YOUR GODDAMN MIND?!

WE'LL BE FREE! PEOPLE WILL START MATTERING AGAIN!

PEOPLE WILL DIE BY THE THOUSANDS! WHAT ABOUT HOSPITALS? EMERGENCY RESPONDERS? FOOD REFRIGERATION?

IT'S ALL JUST COLLATERAL DAMAGE!

YOU'RE NOT SEEING THE BIG PICTURE!

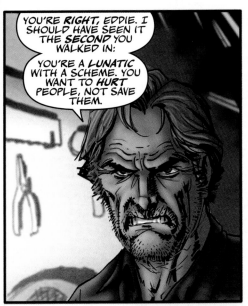

YOU'RE *RIGHT*, EDDIE. I SHOULD HAVE SEEN IT THE *SECOND* YOU WALKED IN:

YOU'RE A *LUNATIC* WITH A SCHEME. YOU WANT TO *HURT* PEOPLE, NOT SAVE THEM.

WE'RE *NOT* GOING THROUGH WITH *YOUR* PLAN. THIS CONVERSATION IS *OVER*.

YOU *MISUNDERSTAND* ME, GRANT. I WASN'T ASKING FOR *PERMISSION*.

YOU'RE THE PERFECT *SYMBOL:* THE MAN WHO CONTROLS MACHINES, *NOT* THE OTHER WAY AROUND.

BUT REST ASSURED, WHETHER YOU'RE INVOLVED OR NOT, YOU CAN'T STOP *THE FUTURE*.

AND *AFTERWARD?* I'LL BE AWAITING YOUR *GRATITUDE*.

JUST DO ME *ONE* FAVOR...

ONCE YOU'RE THE *MASTER OF MACHINES* IN A FALLEN WORLD. ONCE YOU'RE THE *ANOINTED ONE*...

...JUST DON'T FORGET YOUR *PROPHET*.

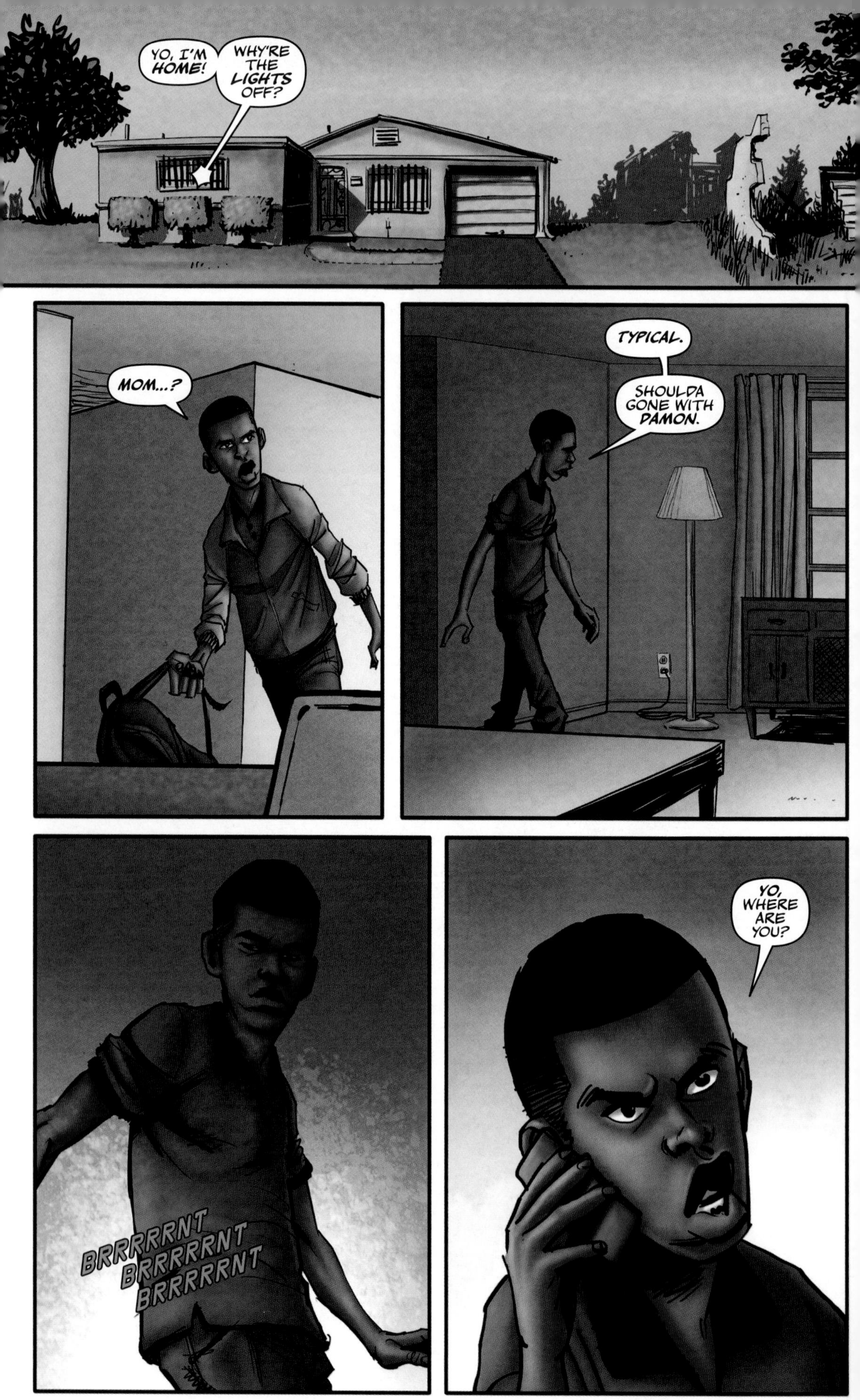
YO, I'M HOME!
WHY'RE THE LIGHTS OFF?
MOM...?
TYPICAL.
SHOULDA GONE WITH DAMON.
BRRRRRNT
BRRRRRNT
BRRRRRNT
YO, WHERE ARE YOU?

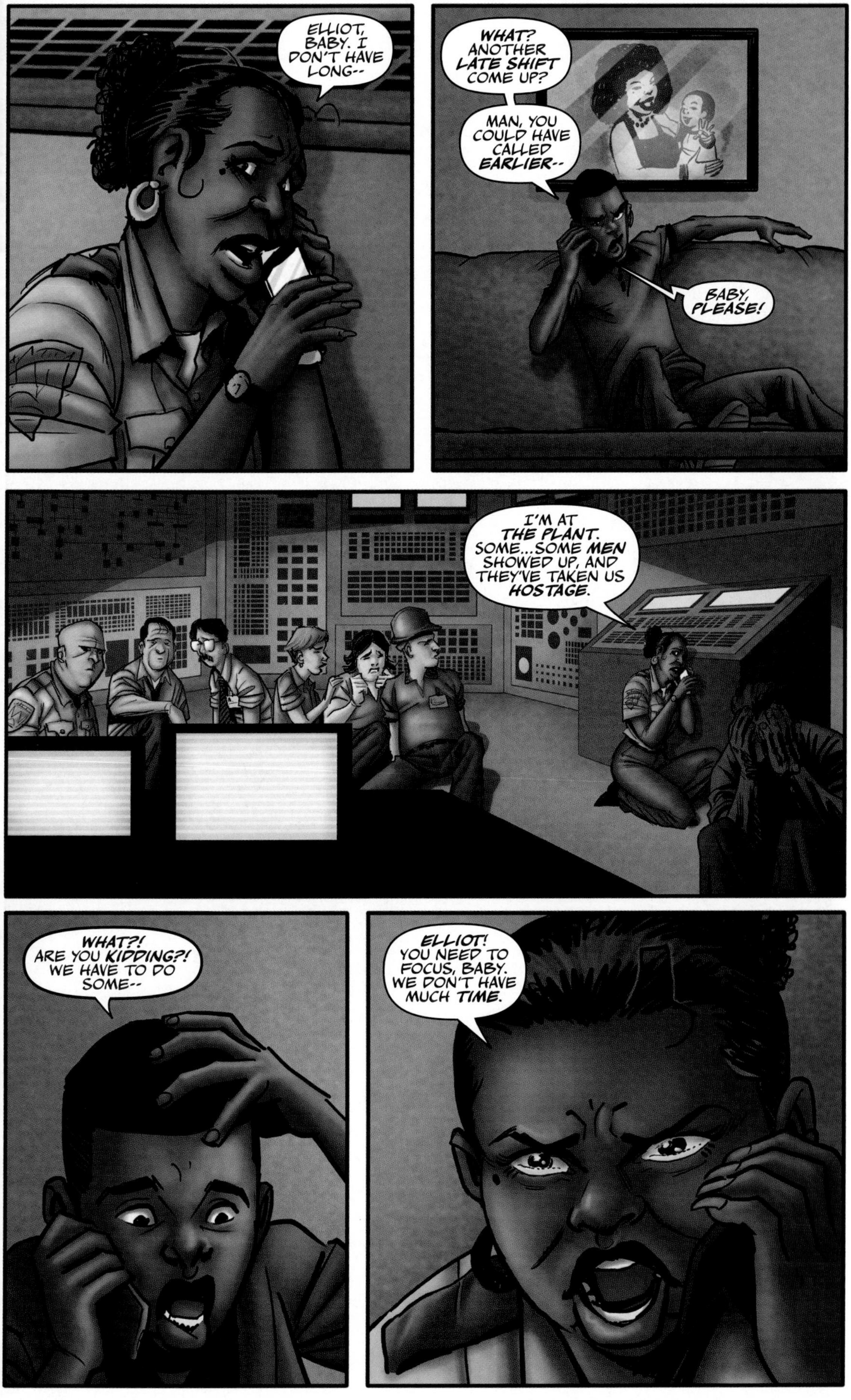
ELLIOT, BABY. I DON'T HAVE LONG--
WHAT? ANOTHER LATE SHIFT COME UP?
MAN, YOU COULD HAVE CALLED EARLIER--
BABY, PLEASE!
I'M AT THE PLANT. SOME...SOME MEN SHOWED UP, AND THEY'VE TAKEN US HOSTAGE.
WHAT?! ARE YOU KIDDING?! WE HAVE TO DO SOME--
ELLIOT! YOU NEED TO FOCUS, BABY. WE DON'T HAVE MUCH TIME.

"THESE MEN ARE *VIOLENT* AND WE DON'T KNOW WHAT THEY WANT."

"WORST OF ALL IS THEIR *BOSS.* HE'S OUT OF HIS MIND."

MOM, WE GOTTA *DO* SOMETHING! WE HAVE TO *CALL* SOMEONE!

NO, BABY, YOU *CAN'T!*

THEY SAID IF THE POLICE *MOVE IN,* THEY'LL START KILLING *HOSTAGES.*

LISTEN, BABY, I NEED YOU TO KNOW, I'M SORRY I WASN'T *AROUND* MORE, BUT...

...I LOVE YOU *SO* VERY MUCH.

ALMOST GOT IT...

...THERE!

NOW WORK, DAMN YOU.

HAH! KNEW I COULD GET YOU GOING AGAIN!

KNOCK KNOCK KNOCK KNOCK

GODDAMMIT.

EDDIE, I TOLD YOU THAT IF I HAD--

KNOCK KNOCK KNOCK KNOCK

THE HELL DO YOU WANT? GOT ANOTHER SCHOOL PROJECT DUE?

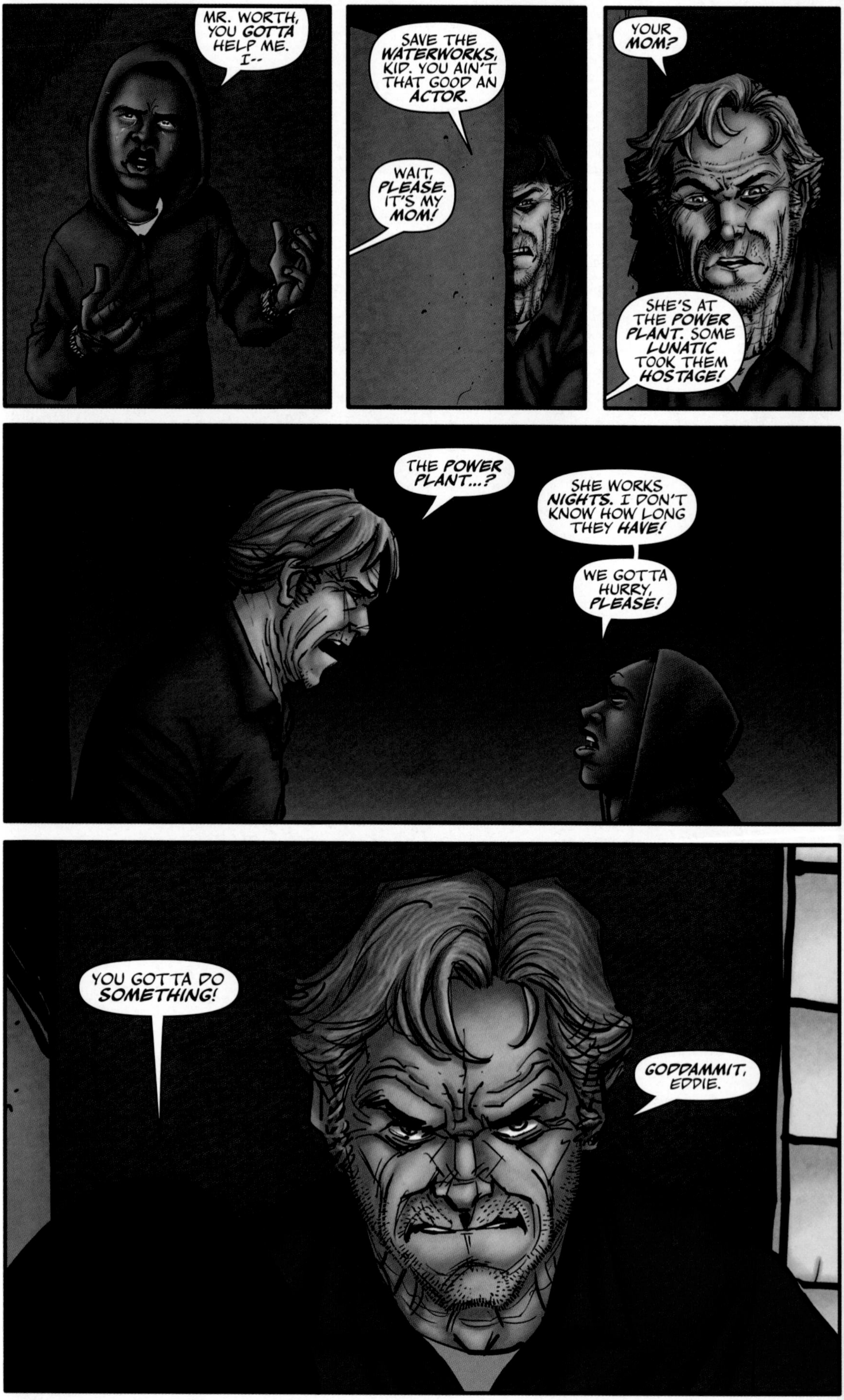
MR. WORTH, YOU GOTTA HELP ME. I--
SAVE THE WATERWORKS, KID. YOU AIN'T THAT GOOD AN ACTOR.
WAIT, PLEASE. IT'S MY MOM!
YOUR MOM?
SHE'S AT THE POWER PLANT. SOME LUNATIC TOOK THEM HOSTAGE!
THE POWER PLANT...?
SHE WORKS NIGHTS. I DON'T KNOW HOW LONG THEY HAVE!
WE GOTTA HURRY, PLEASE!
YOU GOTTA DO SOMETHING!
GODDAMMIT, EDDIE.

CHAPTER 5

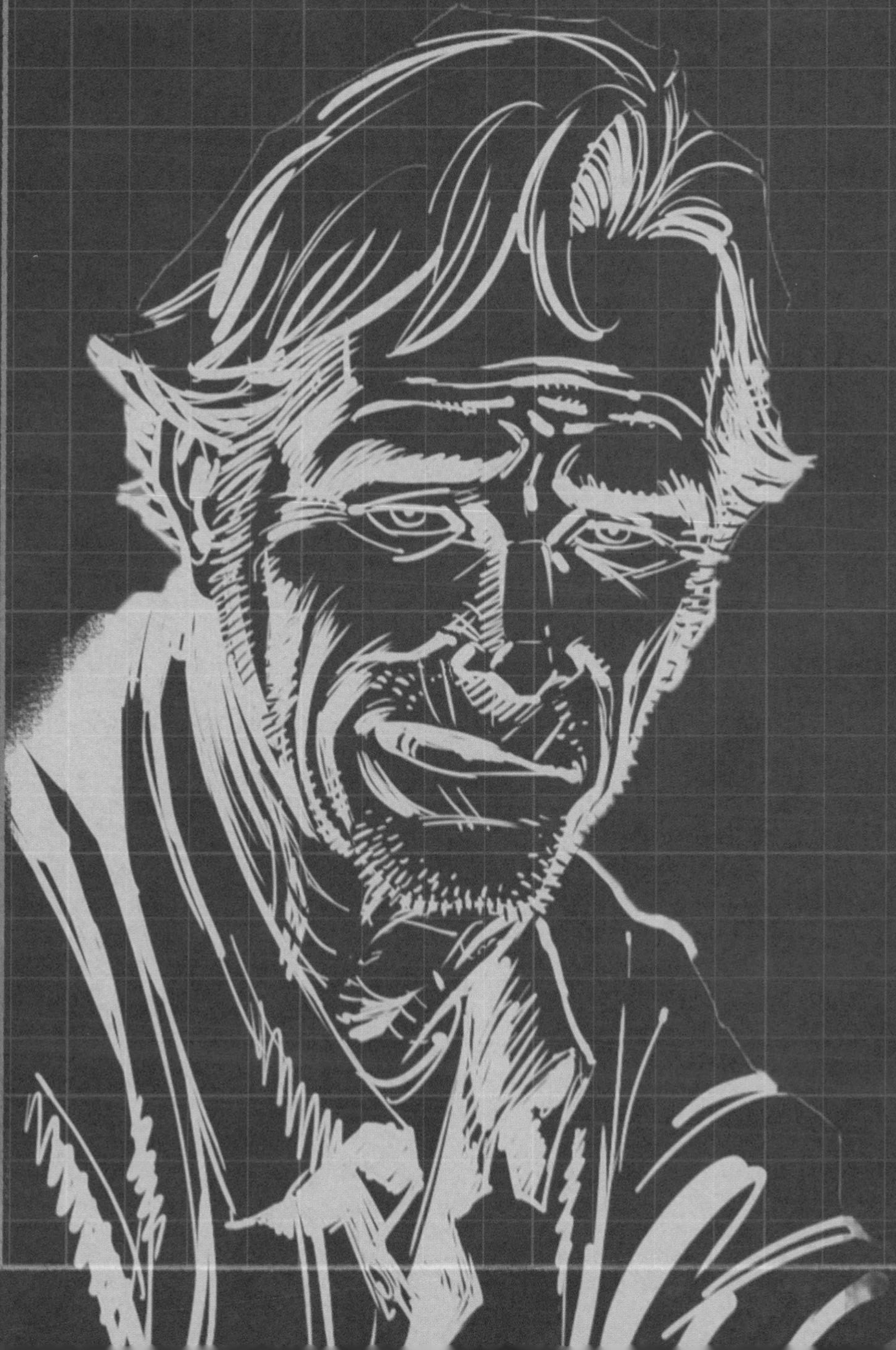

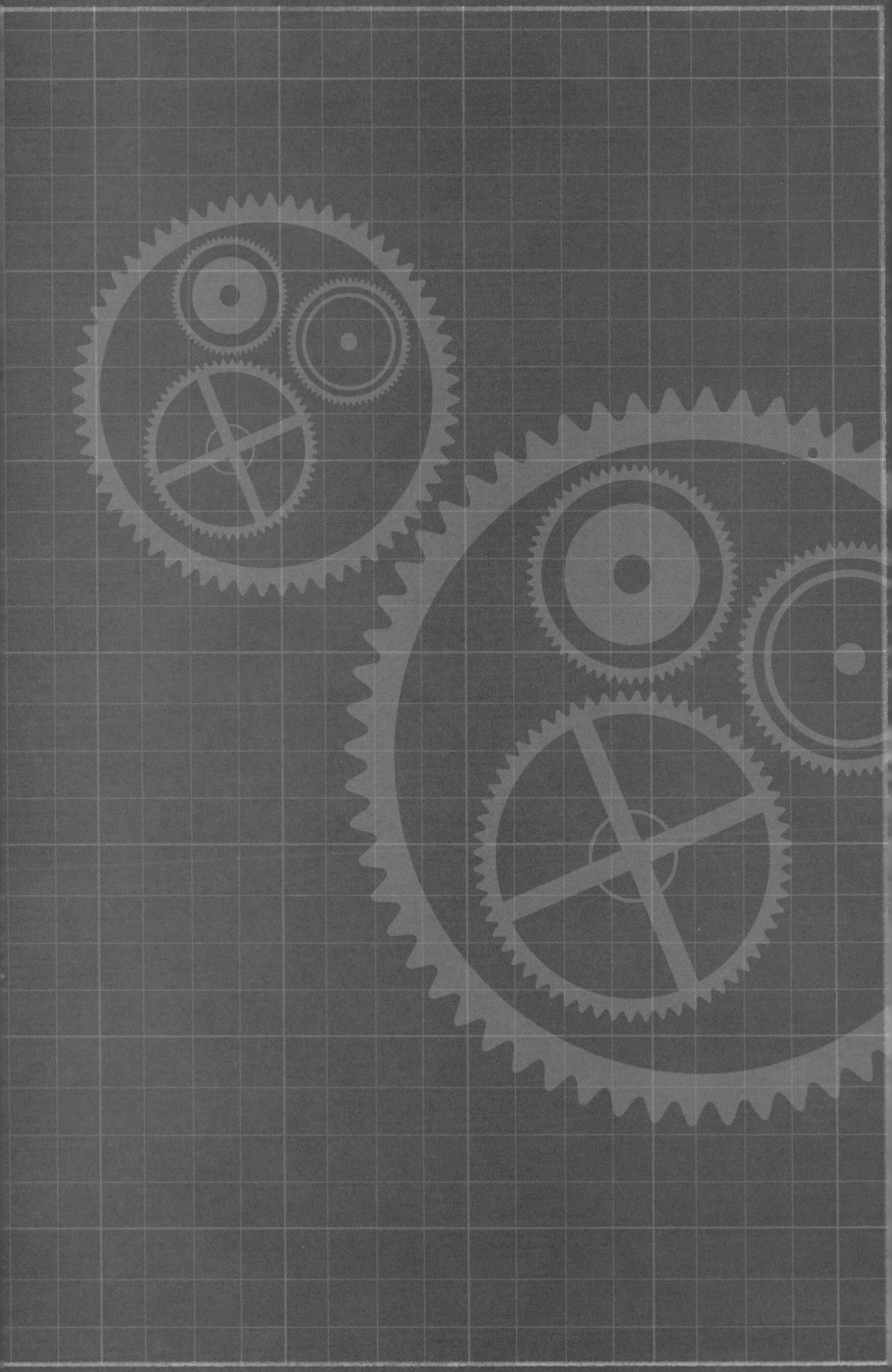

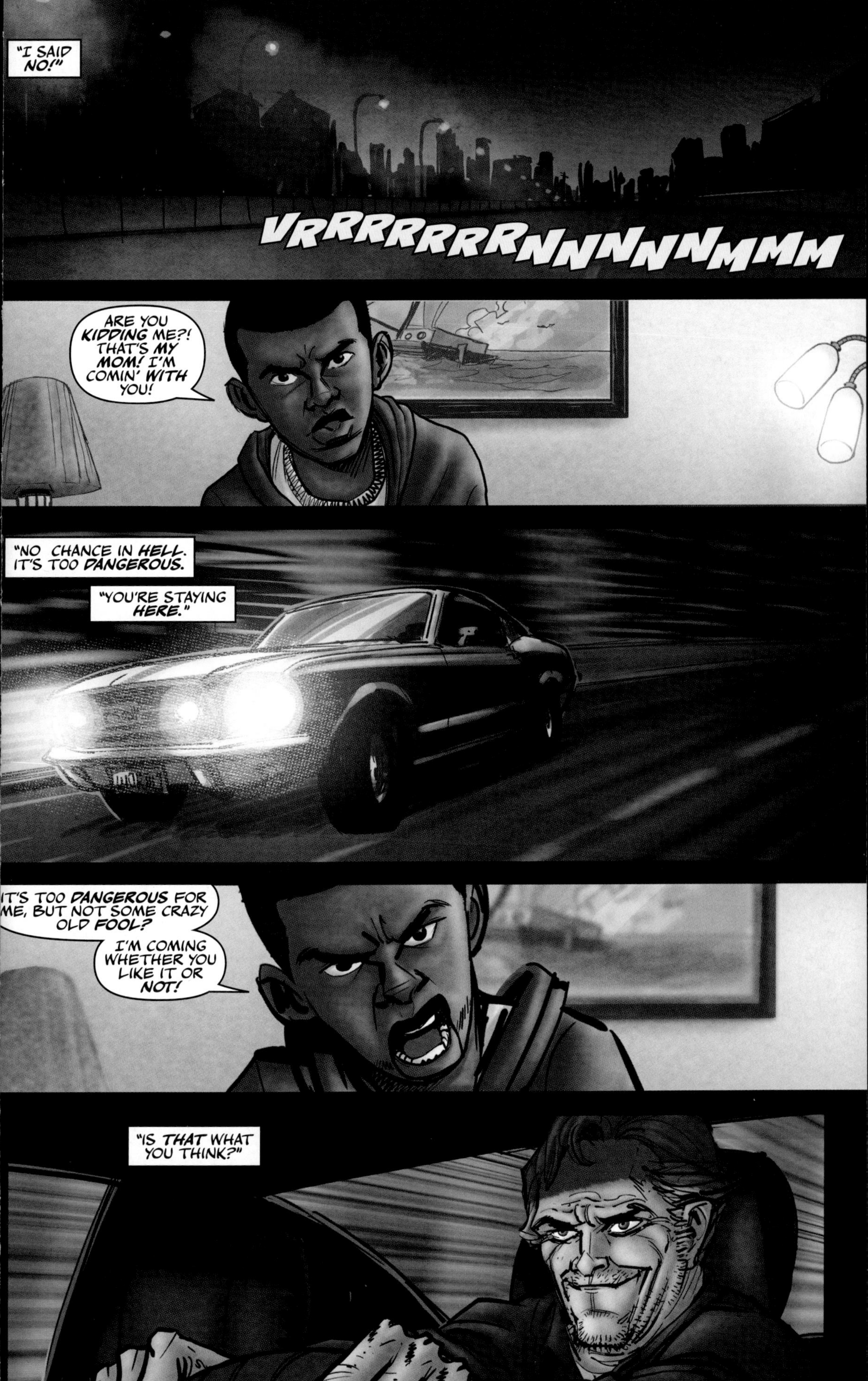
"I SAID NO!"
VRRRRRRRRNNNNNNMMM
ARE YOU KIDDING ME?! THAT'S MY MOM! I'M COMIN' WITH YOU!
"NO CHANCE IN HELL. IT'S TOO DANGEROUS.
"YOU'RE STAYING HERE."
IT'S TOO DANGEROUS FOR ME, BUT NOT SOME CRAZY OLD FOOL?
I'M COMING WHETHER YOU LIKE IT OR NOT!
"IS THAT WHAT YOU THINK?"

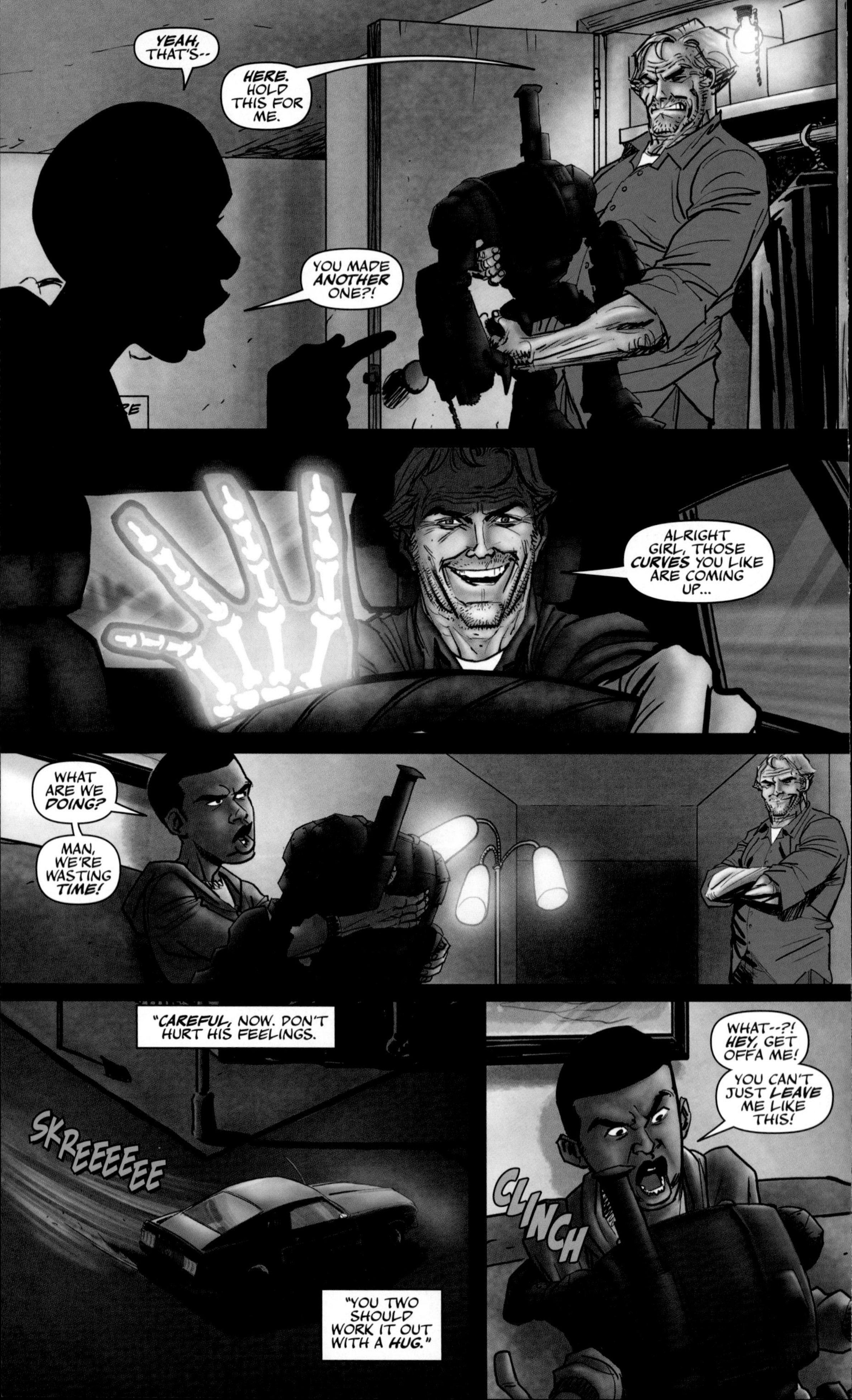
YEAH, THAT'S--
HERE. HOLD THIS FOR ME.
YOU MADE ANOTHER ONE?!
ALRIGHT GIRL, THOSE CURVES YOU LIKE ARE COMING UP...
WHAT ARE WE DOING?
MAN, WE'RE WASTING TIME!
"CAREFUL, NOW. DON'T HURT HIS FEELINGS.
SKREEEEEEE
"YOU TWO SHOULD WORK IT OUT WITH A HUG."
WHAT--?! HEY, GET OFFA ME!
YOU CAN'T JUST LEAVE ME LIKE THIS!
CLINCH

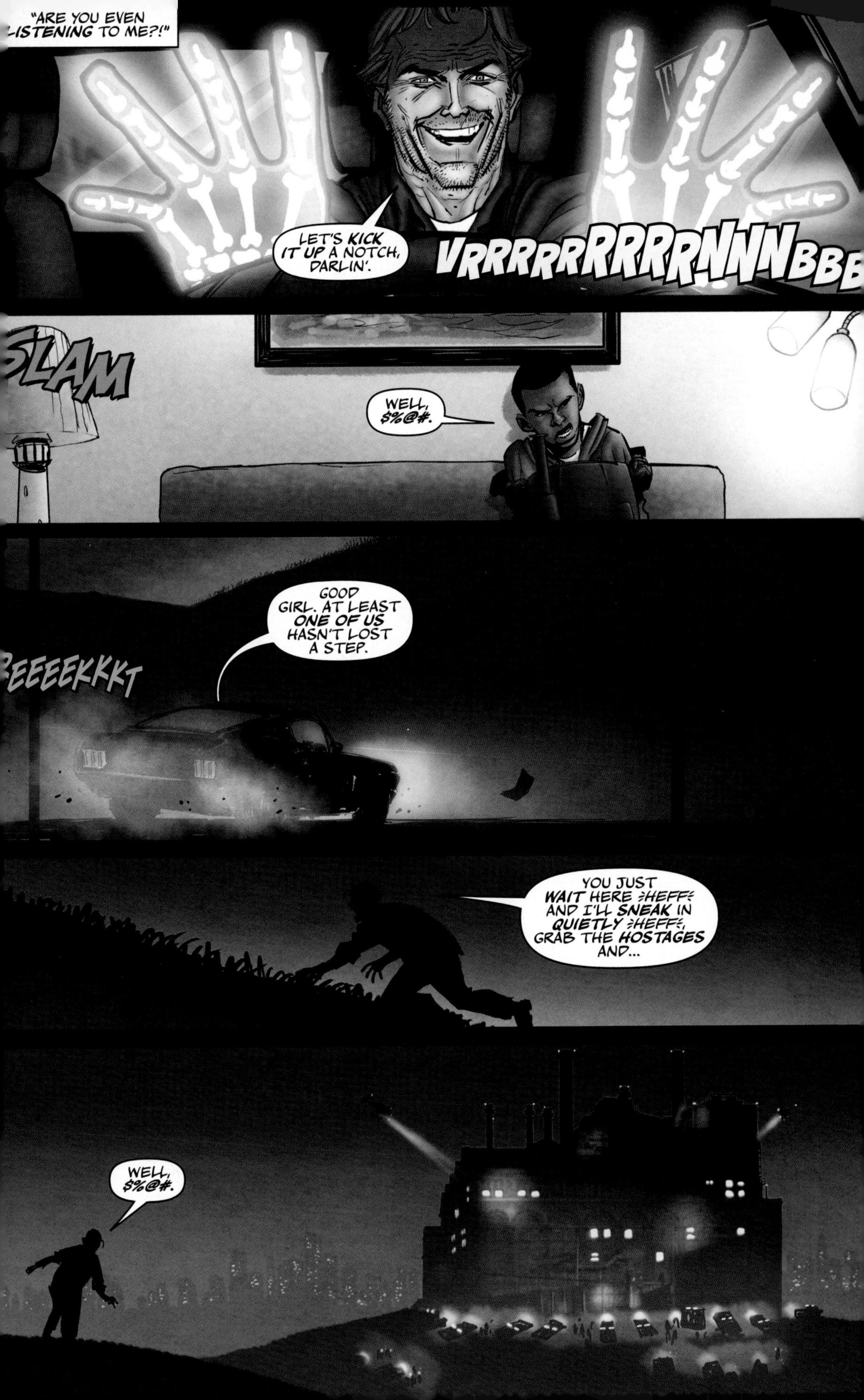
"ARE YOU EVEN LISTENING TO ME?!"
LET'S KICK IT UP A NOTCH, DARLIN'.
VRRRRRRRRRRNNNBBB
SLAM
WELL, $%@#.
GOOD GIRL. AT LEAST ONE OF US HASN'T LOST A STEP.
EEEEEKKKT
YOU JUST WAIT HERE ≈HEFF≈ AND I'LL SNEAK IN QUIETLY ≈HEFF≈, GRAB THE HOSTAGES AND...
WELL, $%@#.

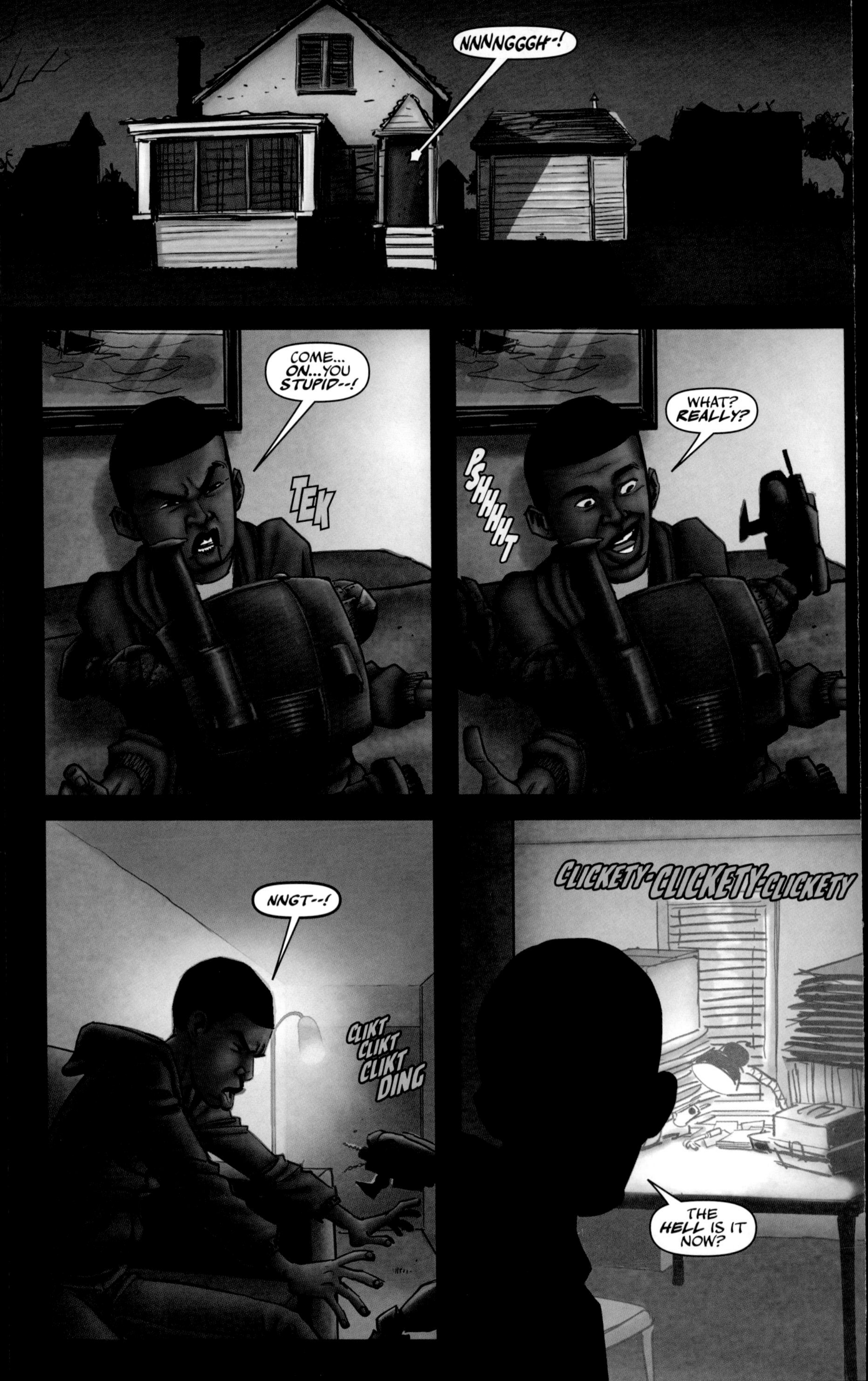
NNNNGGGH-!
COME... ON...YOU STUPID--!
TEK
WHAT? REALLY?
PSHHHHT
NNGT--!
CLIKT CLIKT CLIKT DING
CLICKETY-CLICKETY-CLICKETY
THE HELL IS IT NOW?

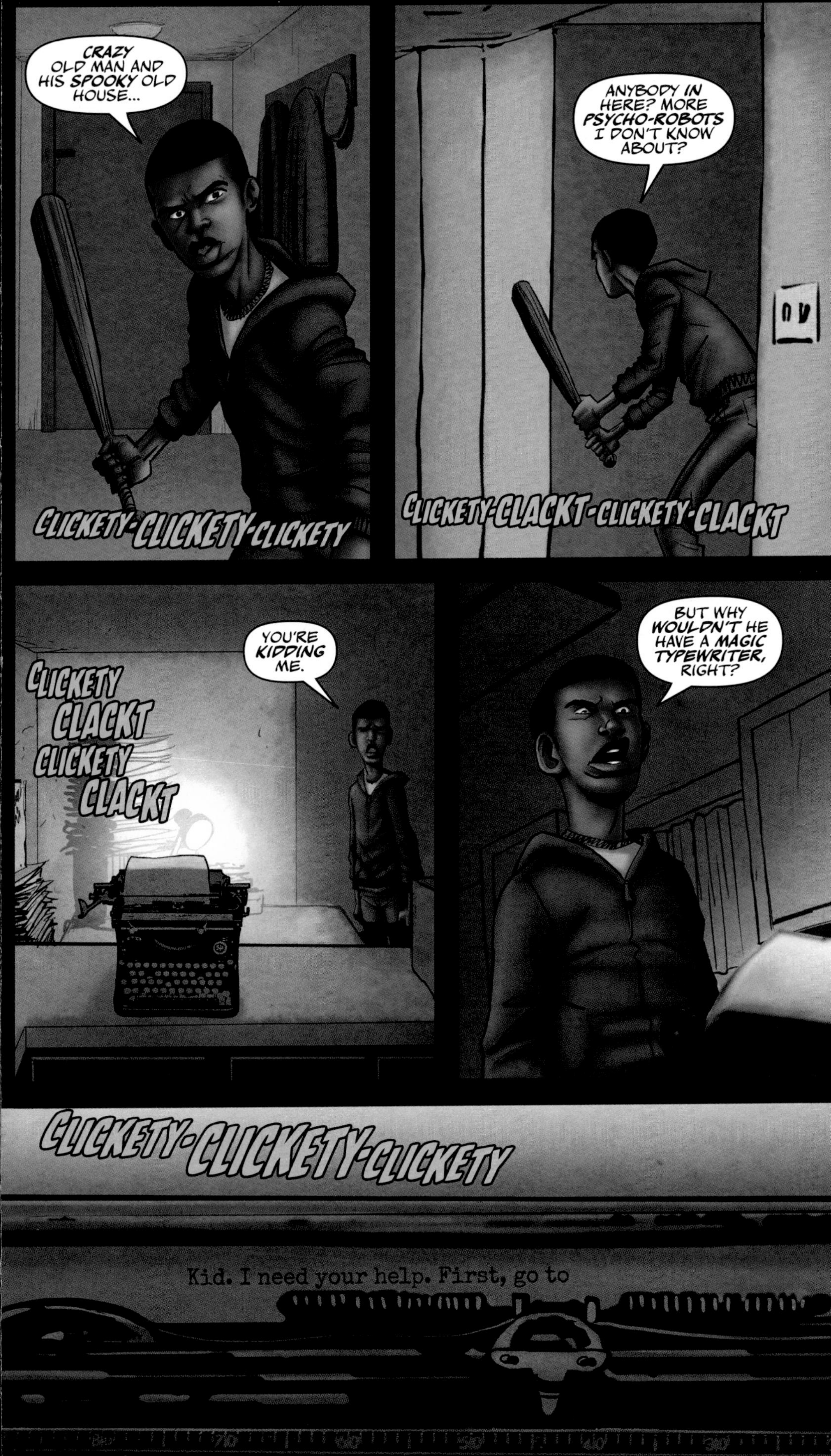
CRAZY OLD MAN AND HIS SPOOKY OLD HOUSE...
CLICKETY-CLICKETY-CLICKETY
ANYBODY IN HERE? MORE PSYCHO-ROBOTS I DON'T KNOW ABOUT?
CLICKETY-CLACKT-CLICKETY-CLACKT
CLICKETY CLACKT CLICKETY CLACKT
YOU'RE KIDDING ME.
BUT WHY WOULDN'T HE HAVE A MAGIC TYPEWRITER, RIGHT?
CLICKETY-CLICKETY-CLICKETY
Kid. I need your help. First, go to

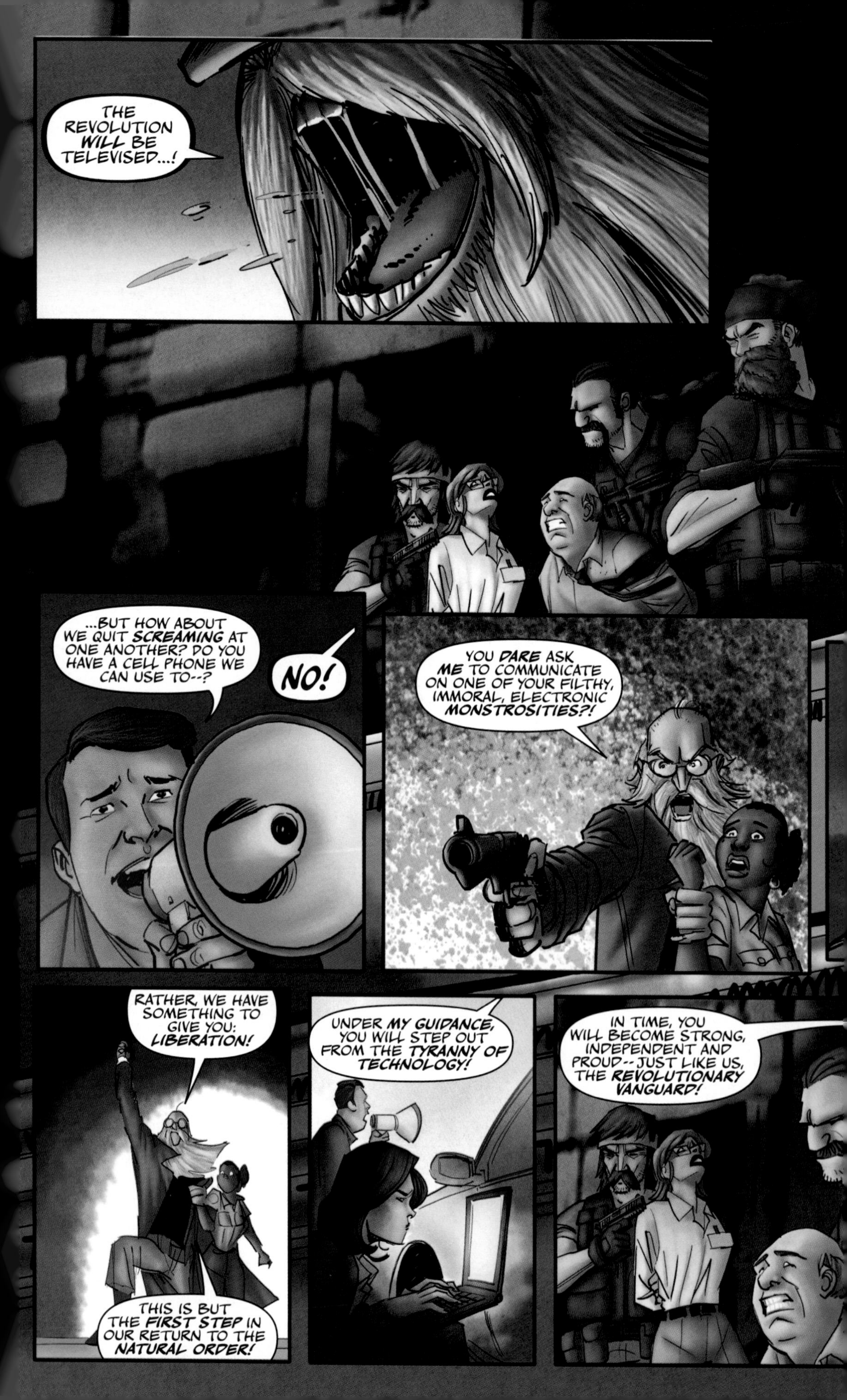
THE REVOLUTION WILL BE TELEVISED...!
...BUT HOW ABOUT WE QUIT SCREAMING AT ONE ANOTHER? DO YOU HAVE A CELL PHONE WE CAN USE TO--?
NO!
YOU DARE ASK ME TO COMMUNICATE ON ONE OF YOUR FILTHY, IMMORAL, ELECTRONIC MONSTROSITIES?!
RATHER, WE HAVE SOMETHING TO GIVE YOU: LIBERATION!
THIS IS BUT THE FIRST STEP IN OUR RETURN TO THE NATURAL ORDER!
UNDER MY GUIDANCE, YOU WILL STEP OUT FROM THE TYRANNY OF TECHNOLOGY!
IN TIME, YOU WILL BECOME STRONG, INDEPENDENT AND PROUD-- JUST LIKE US, THE REVOLUTIONARY VANGUARD!

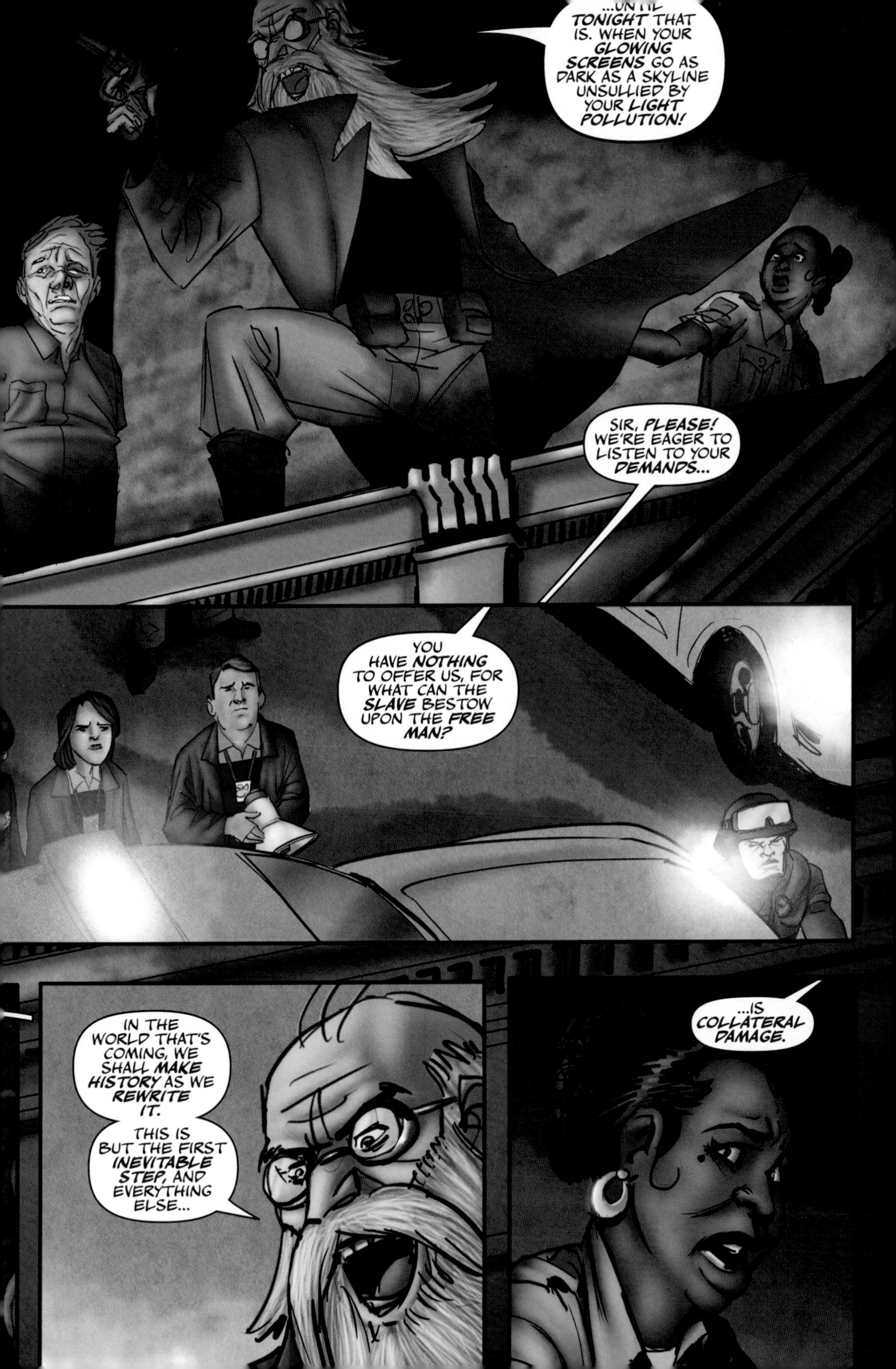
...UNTIL TONIGHT THAT IS. WHEN YOUR GLOWING SCREENS GO AS DARK AS A SKYLINE UNSULLIED BY YOUR LIGHT POLLUTION!
SIR, PLEASE! WE'RE EAGER TO LISTEN TO YOUR DEMANDS...
YOU HAVE NOTHING TO OFFER US, FOR WHAT CAN THE SLAVE BESTOW UPON THE FREE MAN?
IN THE WORLD THAT'S COMING, WE SHALL MAKE HISTORY AS WE REWRITE IT.
THIS IS BUT THE FIRST INEVITABLE STEP, AND EVERYTHING ELSE...
...IS COLLATERAL DAMAGE.

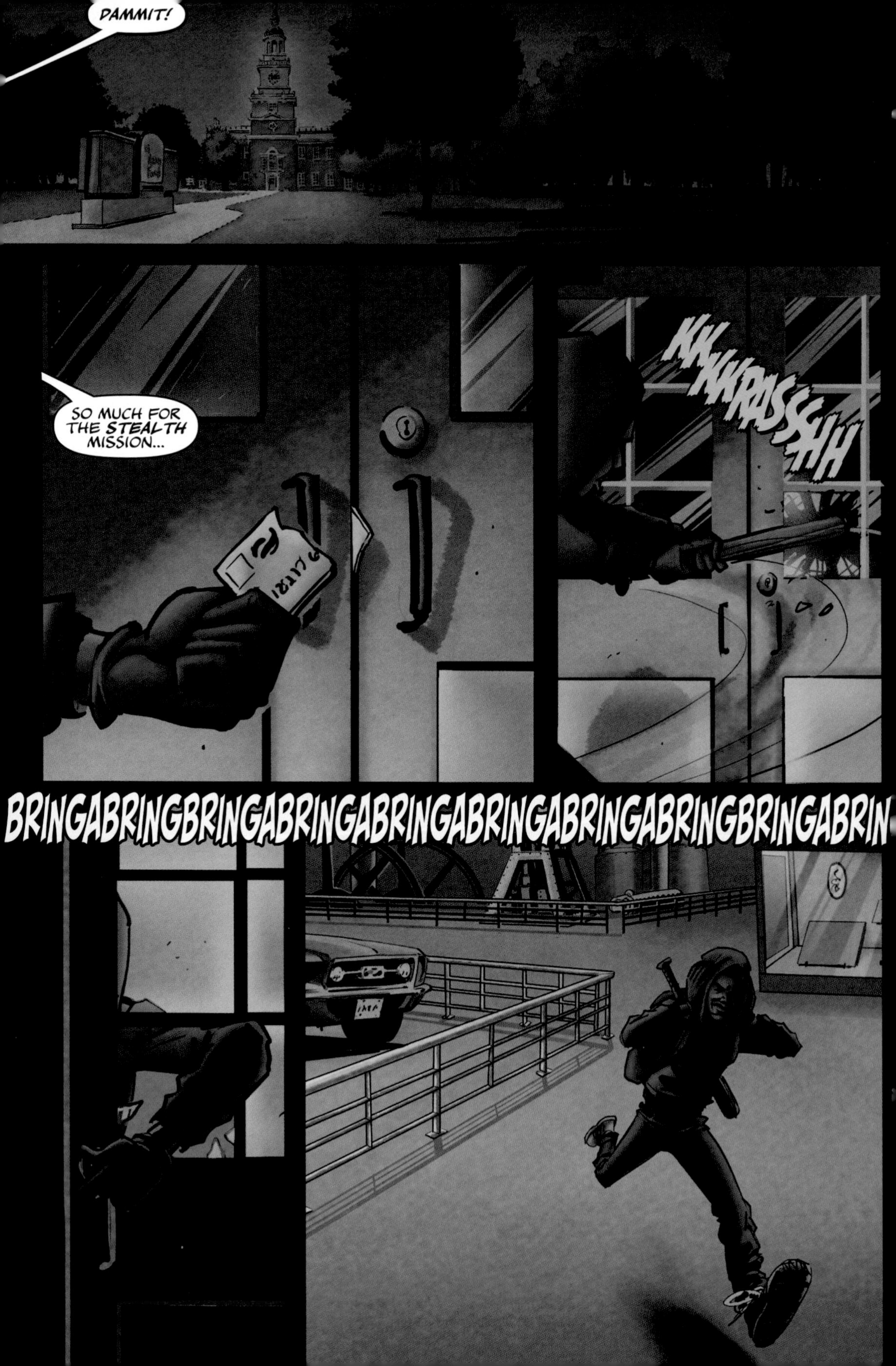
DAMMIT!
SO MUCH FOR THE STEALTH MISSION...
KKKKRASSSHH
BRINGABRINGBRINGABRINGABRINGABRINGABRINGBRINGABRIN

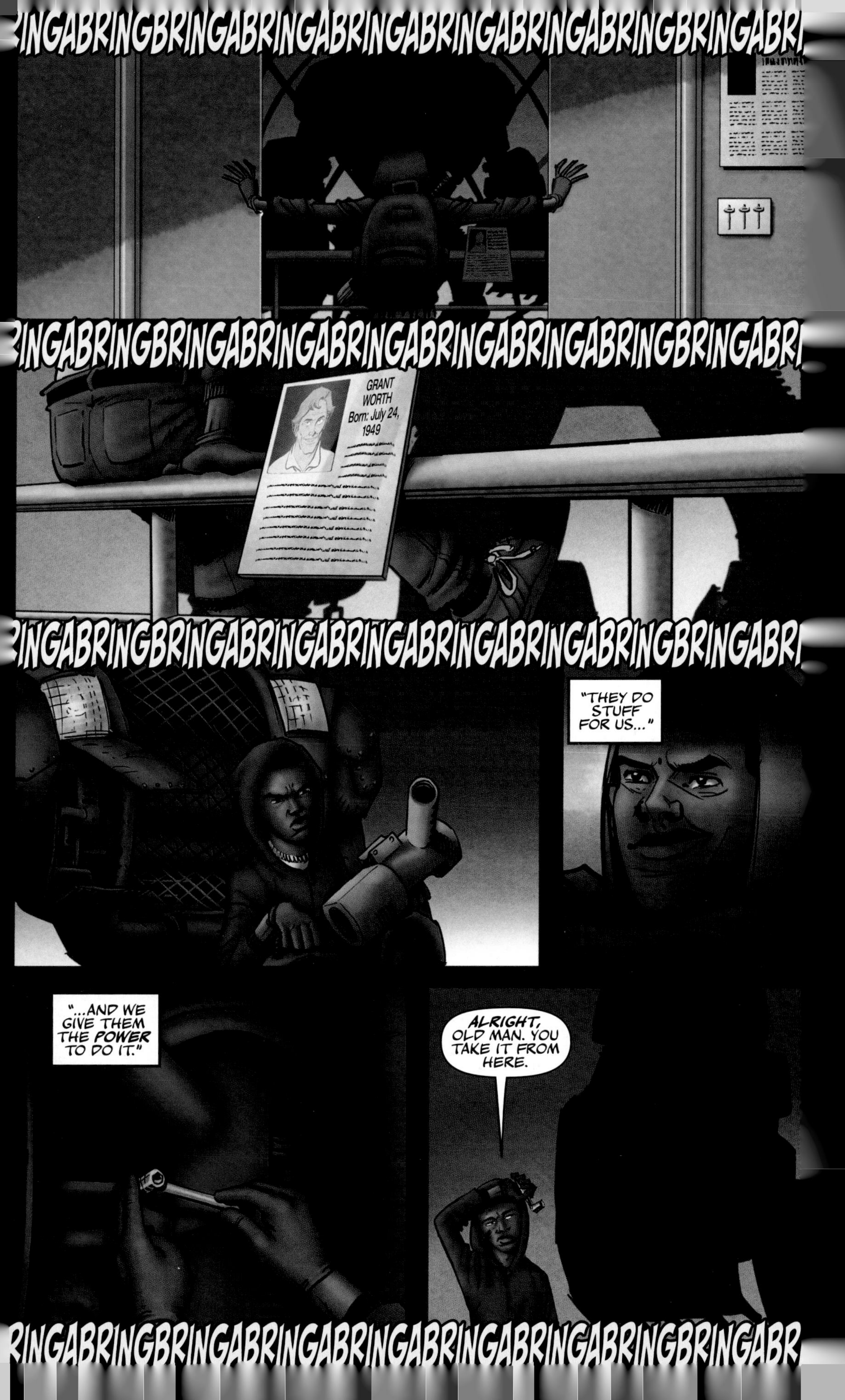
INGABRINGBRINGABRINGABRINGABRINGABRINGABRINGBRINGABR
RINGABRINGBRINGABRINGABRINGABRINGABRINGBRINGABR
GRANT WORTH Born: July 24, 1949
INGABRINGBRINGABRINGABRINGABRINGABRINGBRINGABR
"THEY DO STUFF FOR US..."
"...AND WE GIVE THEM THE POWER TO DO IT."
ALRIGHT, OLD MAN. YOU TAKE IT FROM HERE.
RINGABRINGBRINGABRINGABRINGABRINGABRINGBRINGABR

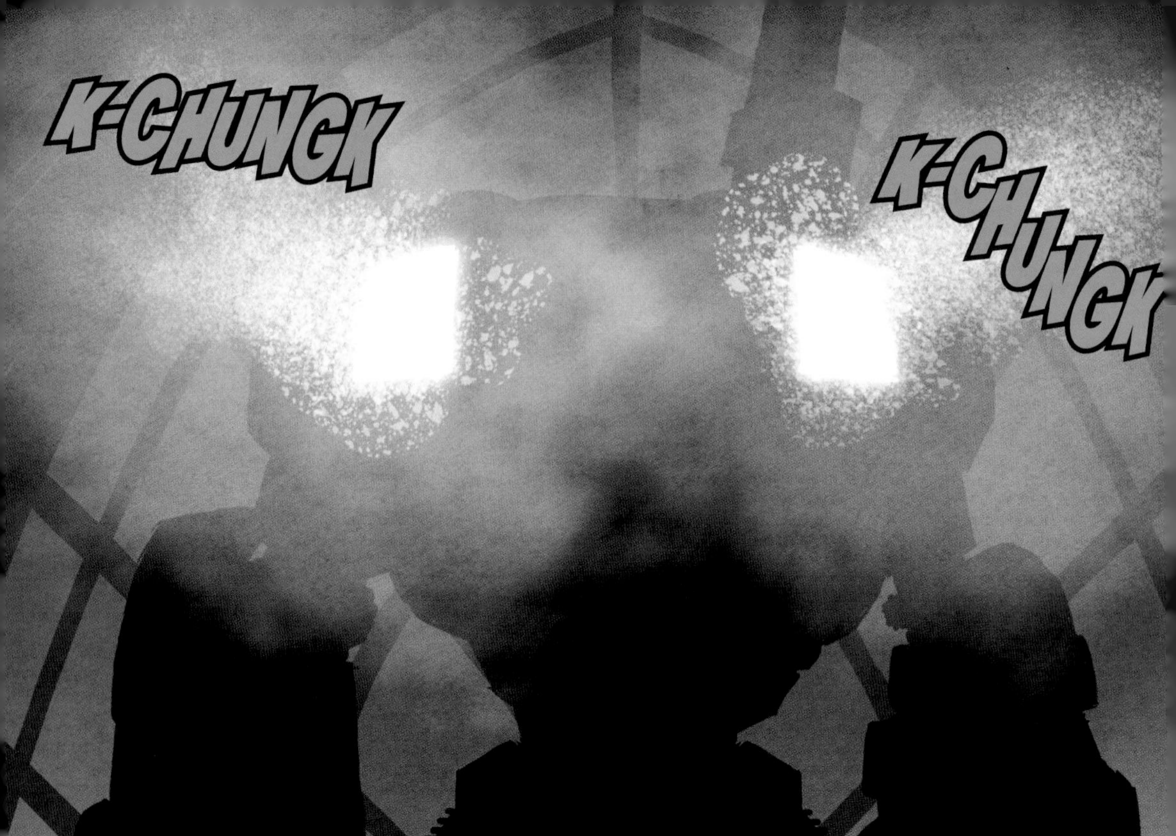
K-CHUNGK
K-CHUNGK

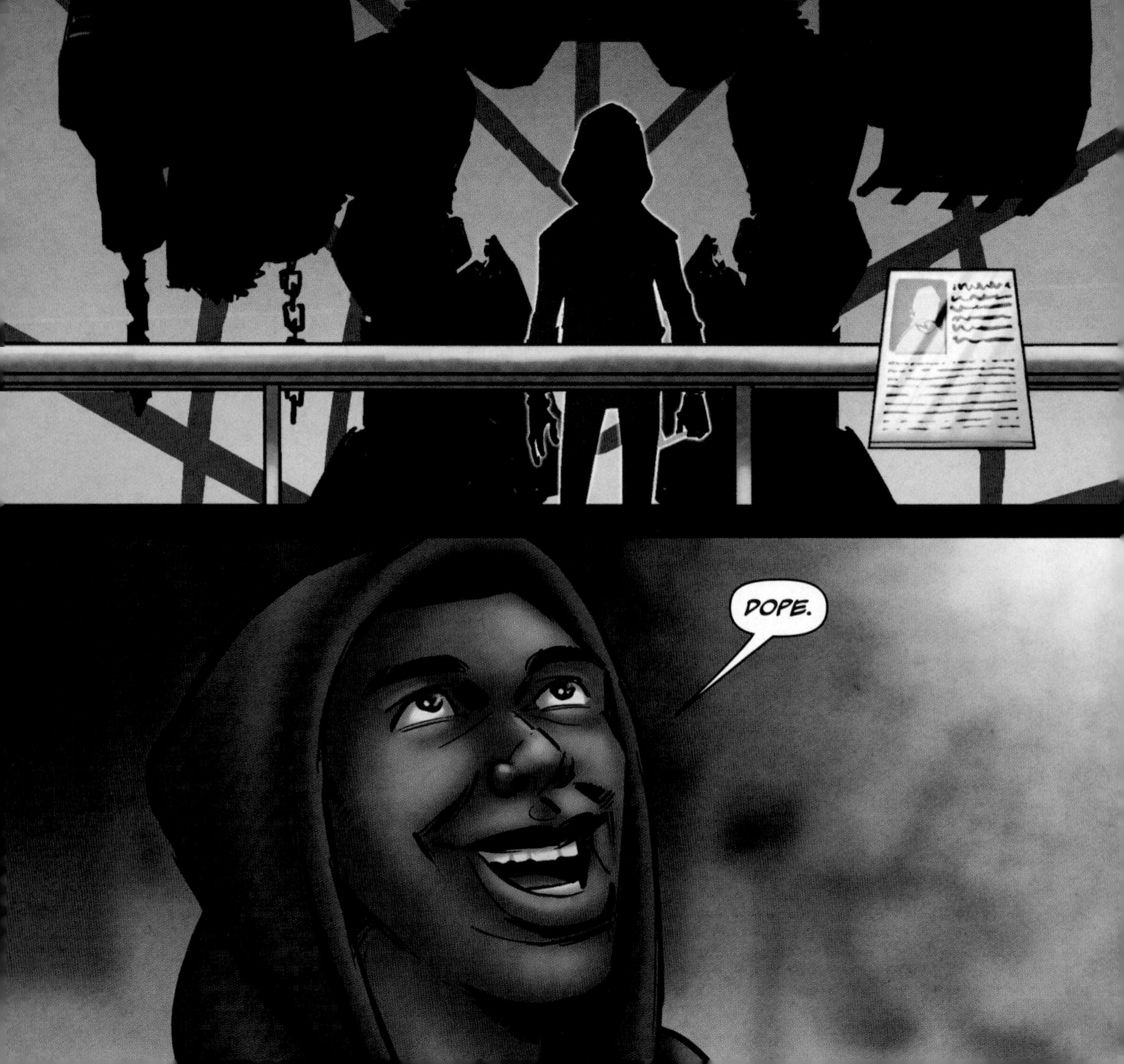
DOPE.

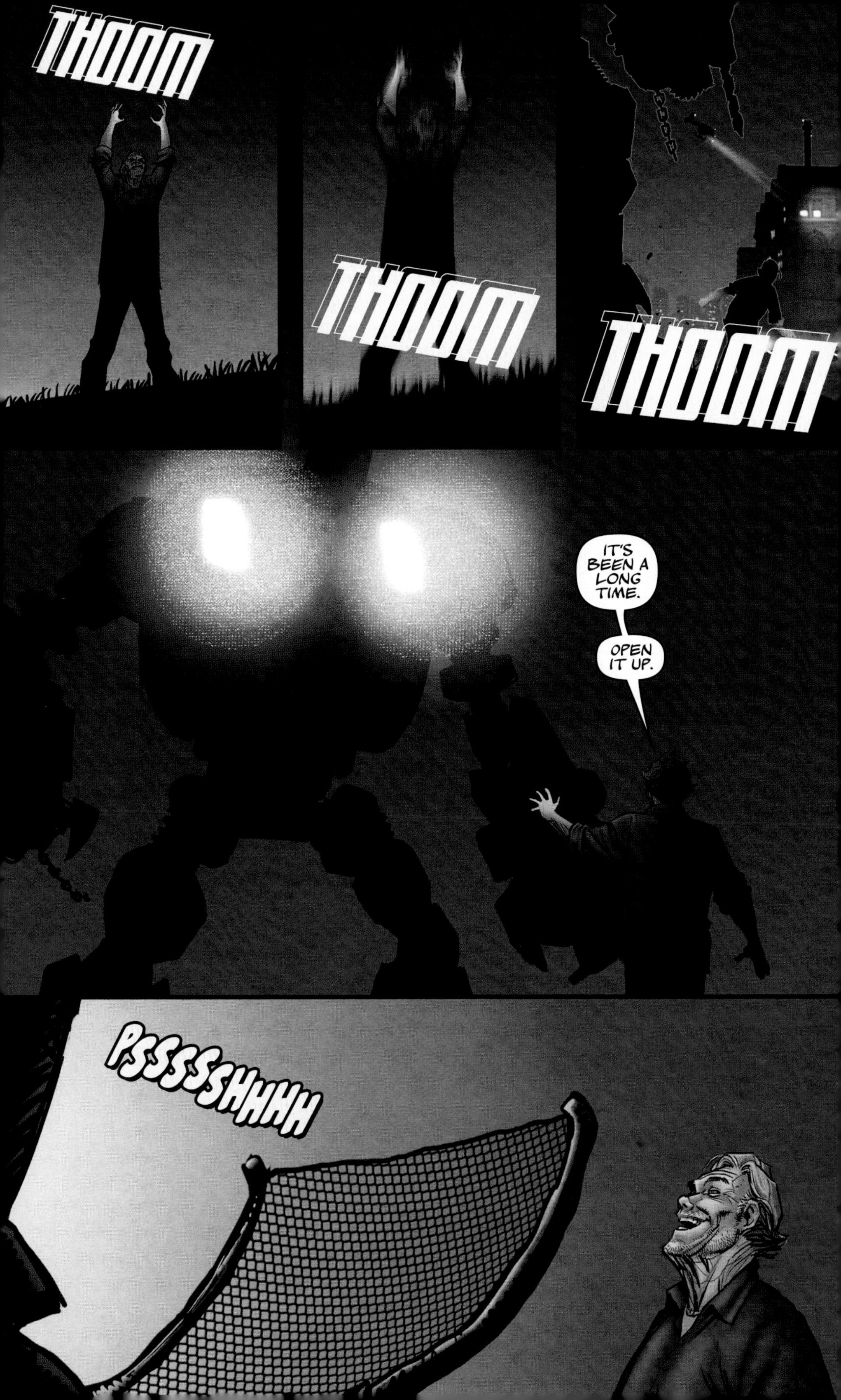
THOOM
THOOM
THOOM
IT'S BEEN A LONG TIME.
OPEN IT UP.
PSSSSSHHHH

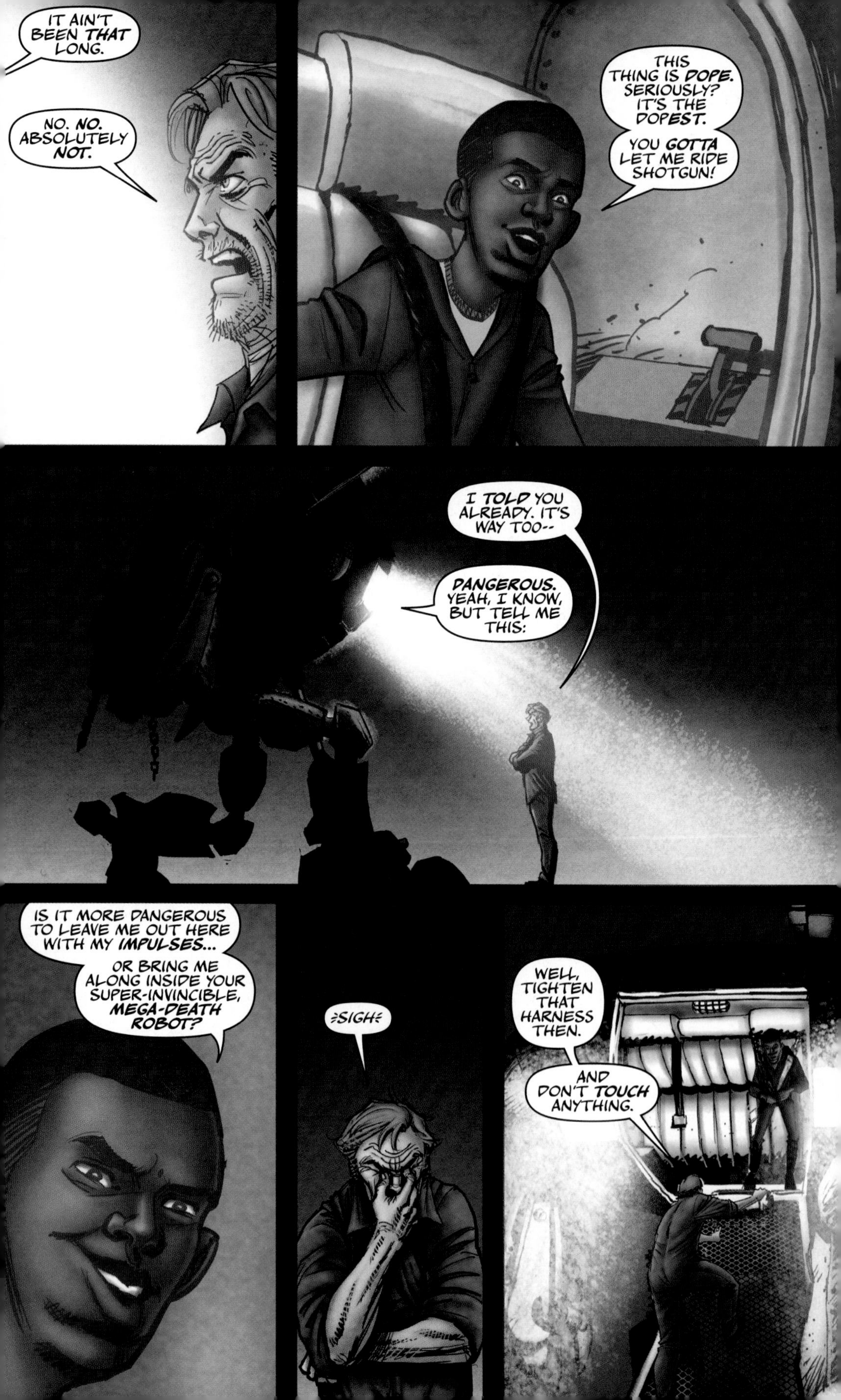
IT AIN'T BEEN THAT LONG.
NO. NO. ABSOLUTELY NOT.
THIS THING IS DOPE. SERIOUSLY? IT'S THE DOPEST.
YOU GOTTA LET ME RIDE SHOTGUN!
I TOLD YOU ALREADY. IT'S WAY TOO--
DANGEROUS. YEAH, I KNOW, BUT TELL ME THIS:
IS IT MORE DANGEROUS TO LEAVE ME OUT HERE WITH MY IMPULSES...
OR BRING ME ALONG INSIDE YOUR SUPER-INVINCIBLE, MEGA-DEATH ROBOT?
SIGH
WELL, TIGHTEN THAT HARNESS THEN.
AND DON'T TOUCH ANYTHING.

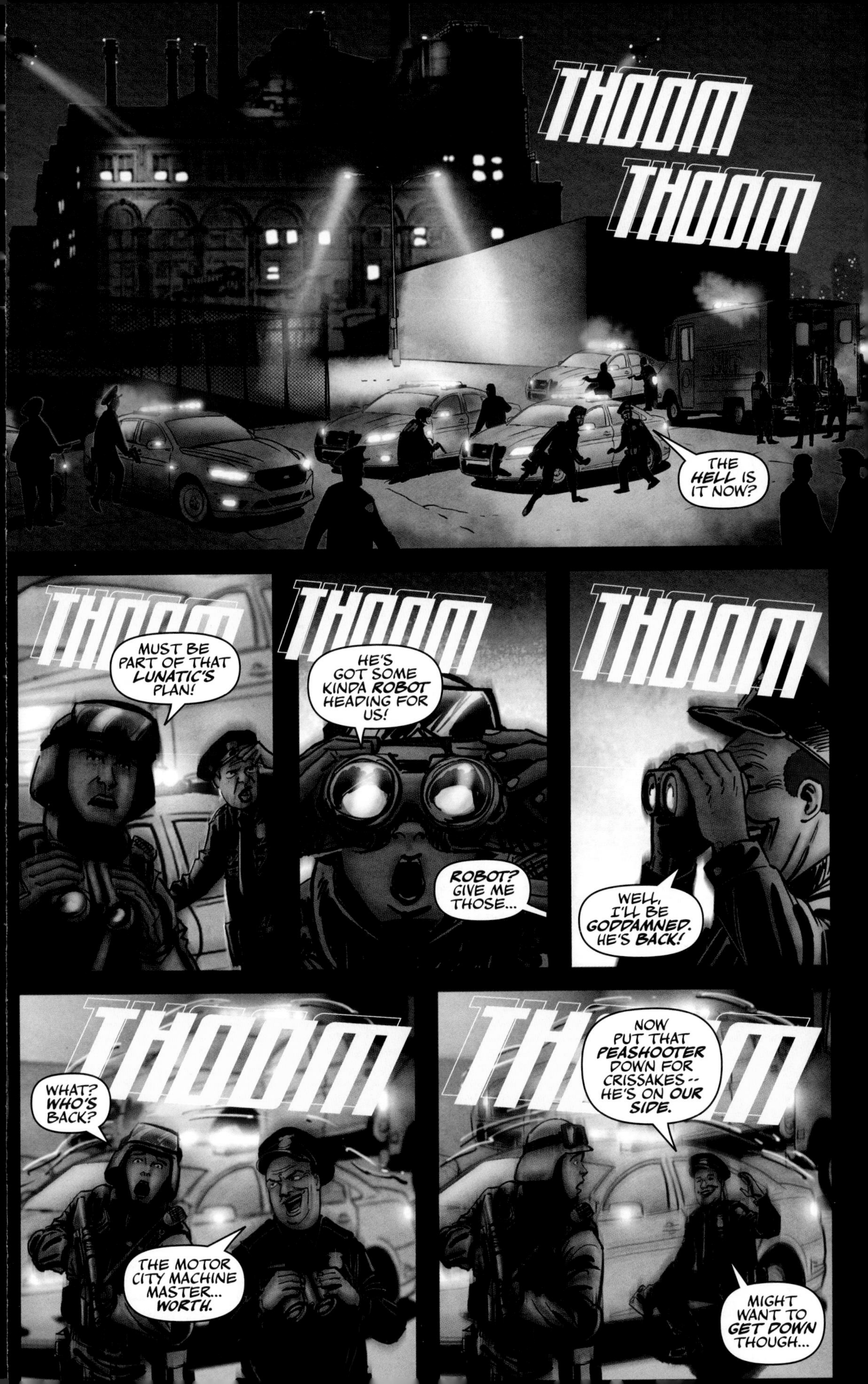
THOOM
THOOM
THE HELL IS IT NOW?
THOOM
MUST BE PART OF THAT LUNATIC'S PLAN!
THOOM
HE'S GOT SOME KINDA ROBOT HEADING FOR US!
ROBOT? GIVE ME THOSE...
THOOM
WELL, I'LL BE GODDAMNED. HE'S BACK!
THOOM
WHAT? WHO'S BACK?
THE MOTOR CITY MACHINE MASTER... WORTH.
THOOM
NOW PUT THAT PEASHOOTER DOWN FOR CRISSAKES -- HE'S ON OUR SIDE.
MIGHT WANT TO GET DOWN THOUGH...

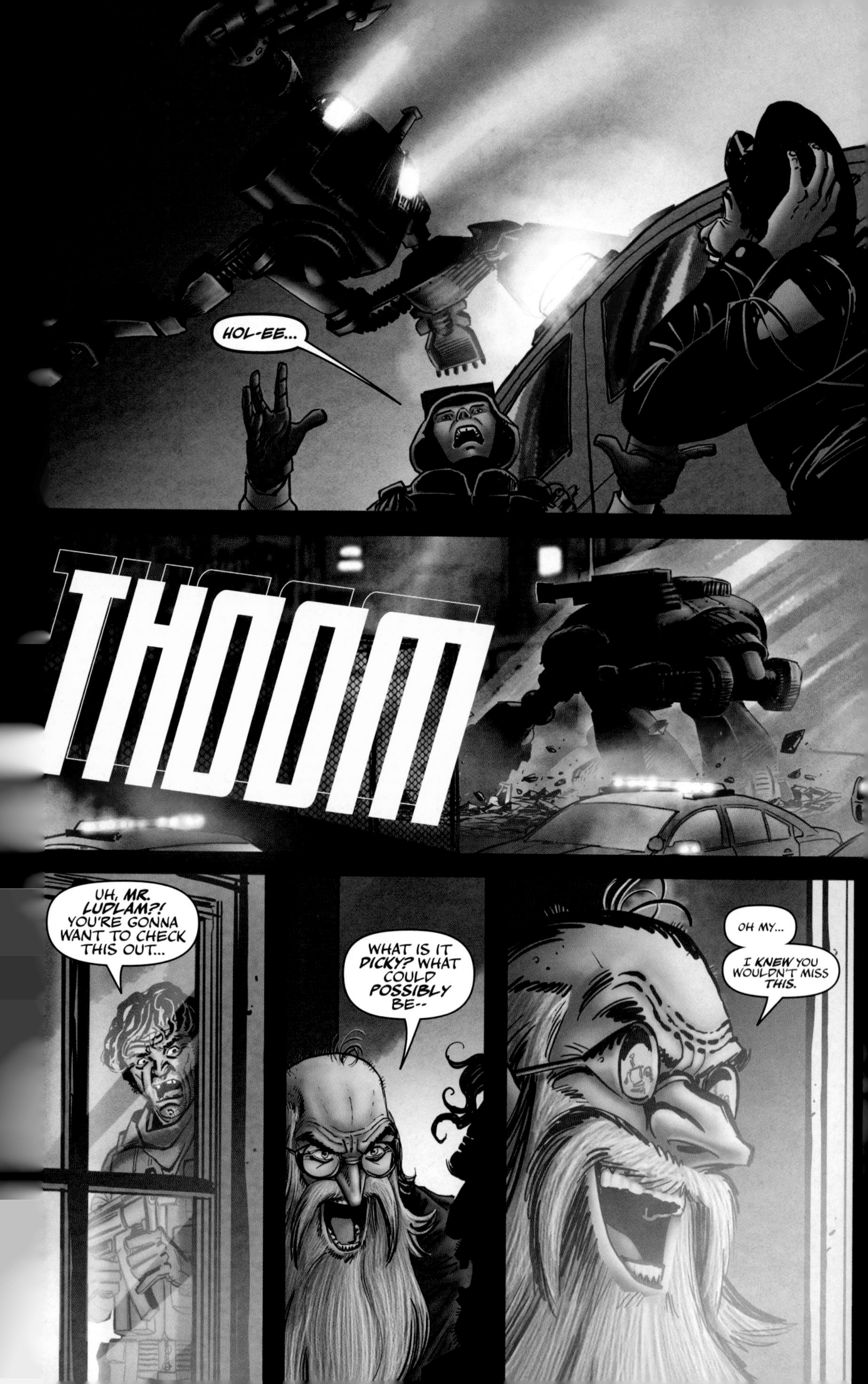
HOL-EE...
THOOM
UH, MR. LUDLAM?! YOU'RE GONNA WANT TO CHECK THIS OUT...
WHAT IS IT DICKY? WHAT COULD POSSIBLY BE--
OH MY...
I KNEW YOU WOULDN'T MISS THIS.

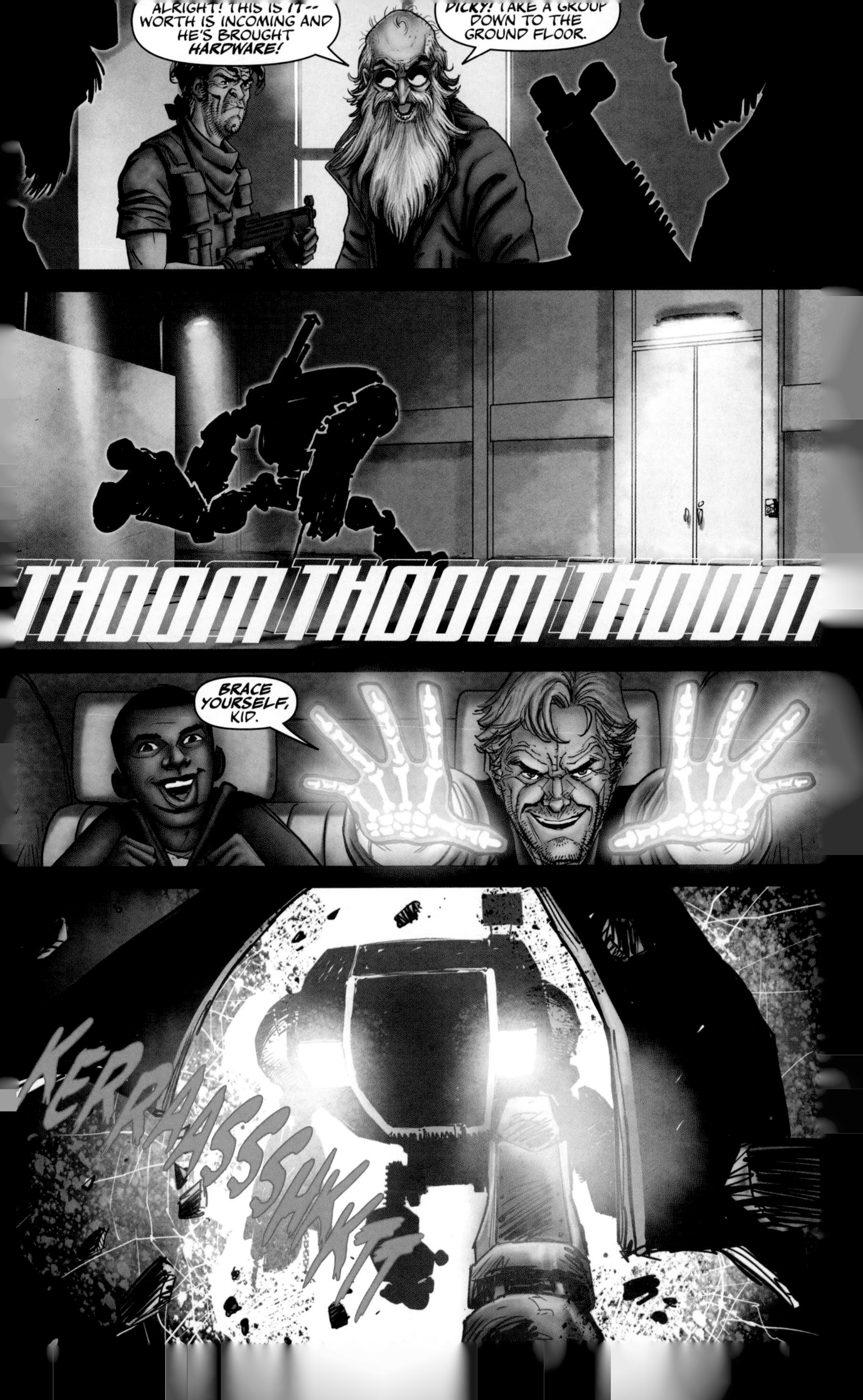
ALRIGHT! THIS IS IT-- WORTH IS INCOMING AND HE'S BROUGHT HARDWARE!
DICKY! TAKE A GROUP DOWN TO THE GROUND FLOOR.
THOOM THOOM THOOM
BRACE YOURSELF, KID.
KERRASSSHKT

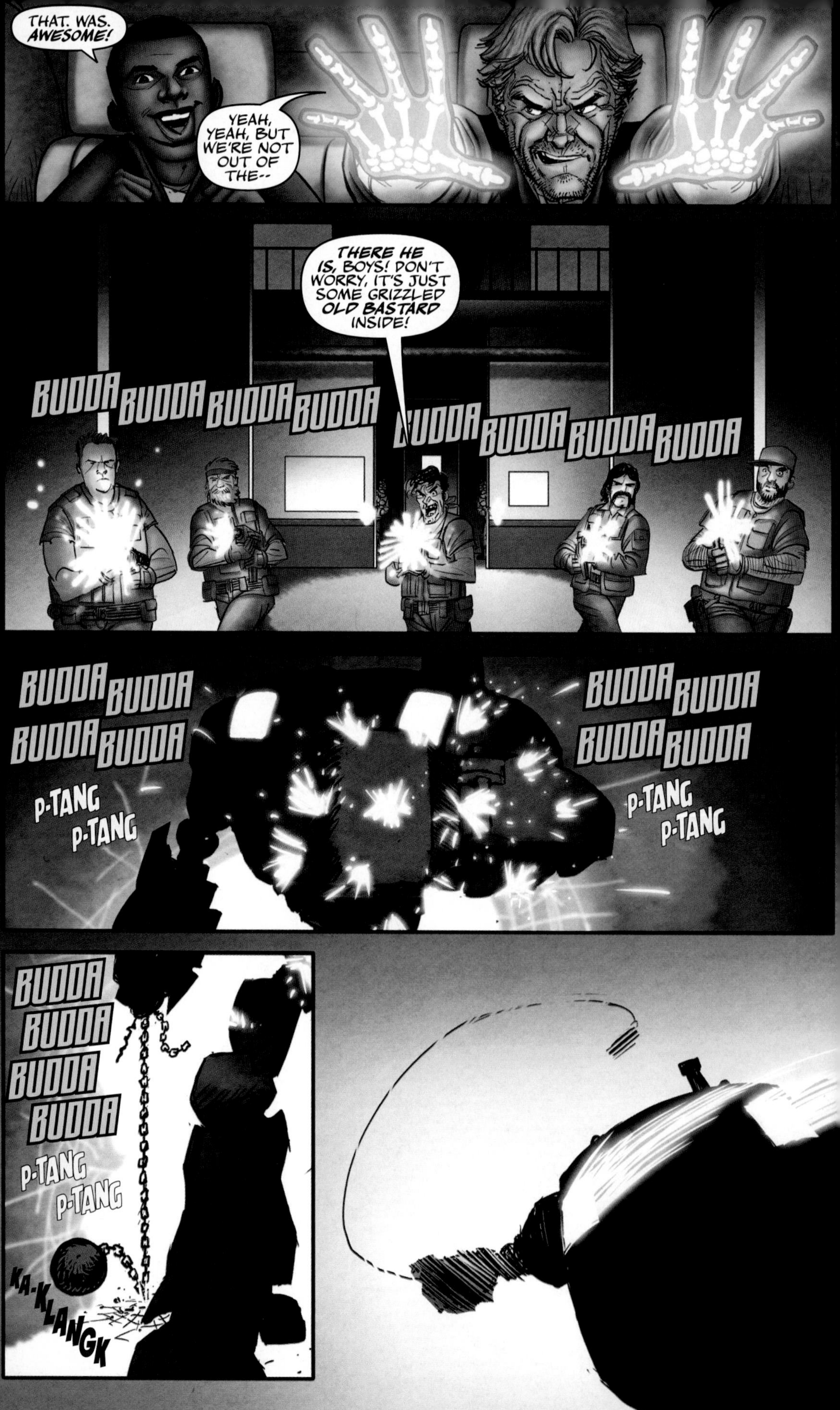
THAT. WAS. AWESOME!
YEAH, YEAH, BUT WE'RE NOT OUT OF THE--
THERE HE IS, BOYS! DON'T WORRY, IT'S JUST SOME GRIZZLED OLD BASTARD INSIDE!
BUDDA BUDDA BUDDA BUDDA
BUDDA BUDDA BUDDA BUDDA
BUDDA BUDDA BUDDA BUDDA
P-TANG P-TANG
BUDDA BUDDA BUDDA BUDDA
P-TANG P-TANG
BUDDA BUDDA BUDDA BUDDA
P-TANG P-TANG
KA-KLANGK

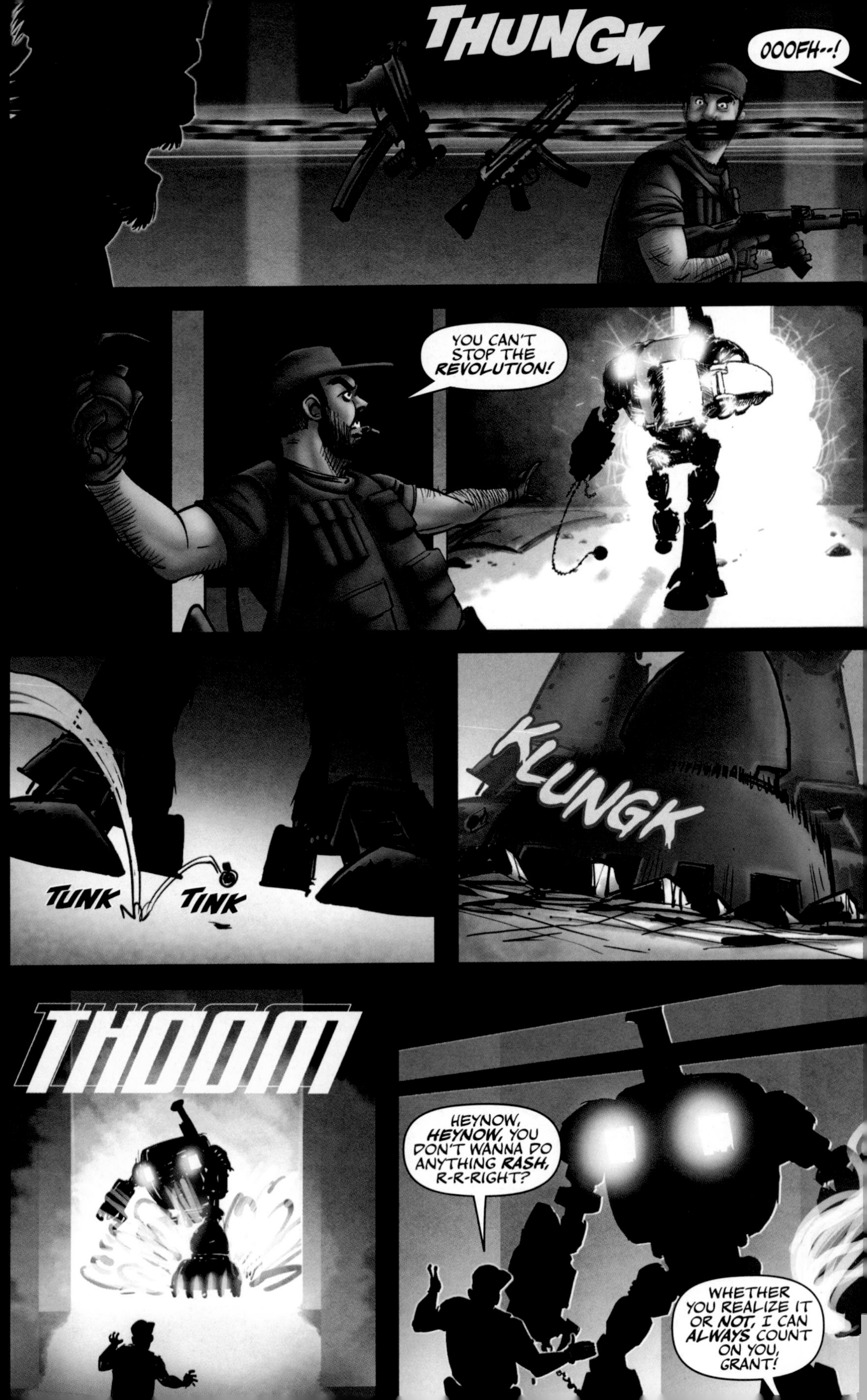
THUNGK
OOOFH--!
YOU CAN'T STOP THE REVOLUTION!
TUNK
TINK
KLUNGK
THOOM
HEYNOW, HEYNOW, YOU DON'T WANNA DO ANYTHING RASH, R-R-RIGHT?
WHETHER YOU REALIZE IT OR NOT, I CAN ALWAYS COUNT ON YOU, GRANT!

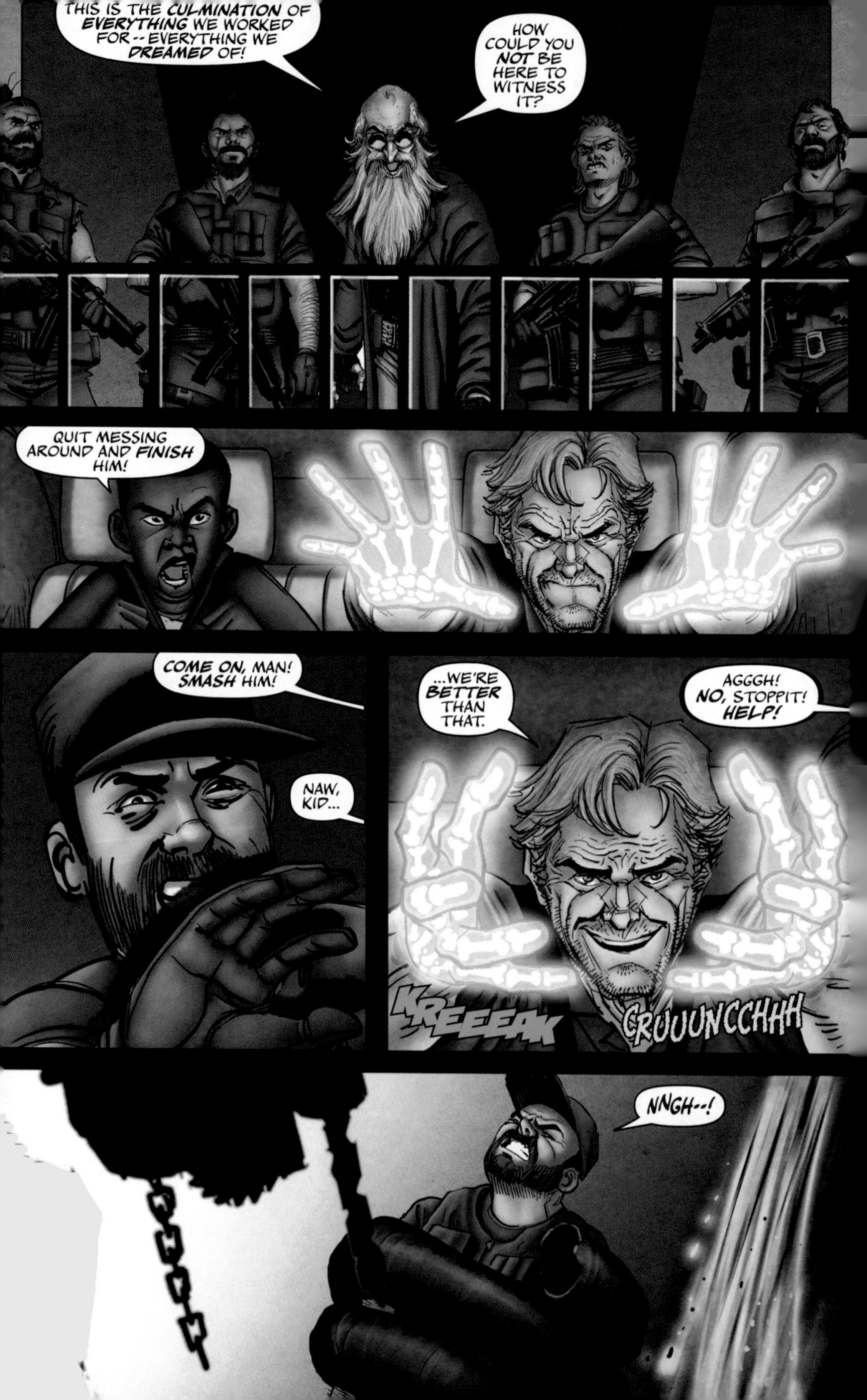
THIS IS THE CULMINATION OF EVERYTHING WE WORKED FOR -- EVERYTHING WE DREAMED OF!
HOW COULD YOU NOT BE HERE TO WITNESS IT?
QUIT MESSING AROUND AND FINISH HIM!
COME ON, MAN! SMASH HIM!
NAW, KID...
...WE'RE BETTER THAN THAT.
AGGGH! NO, STOPPIT! HELP!
KREEEAK
CRUUUNCCHHH
NNGH--!

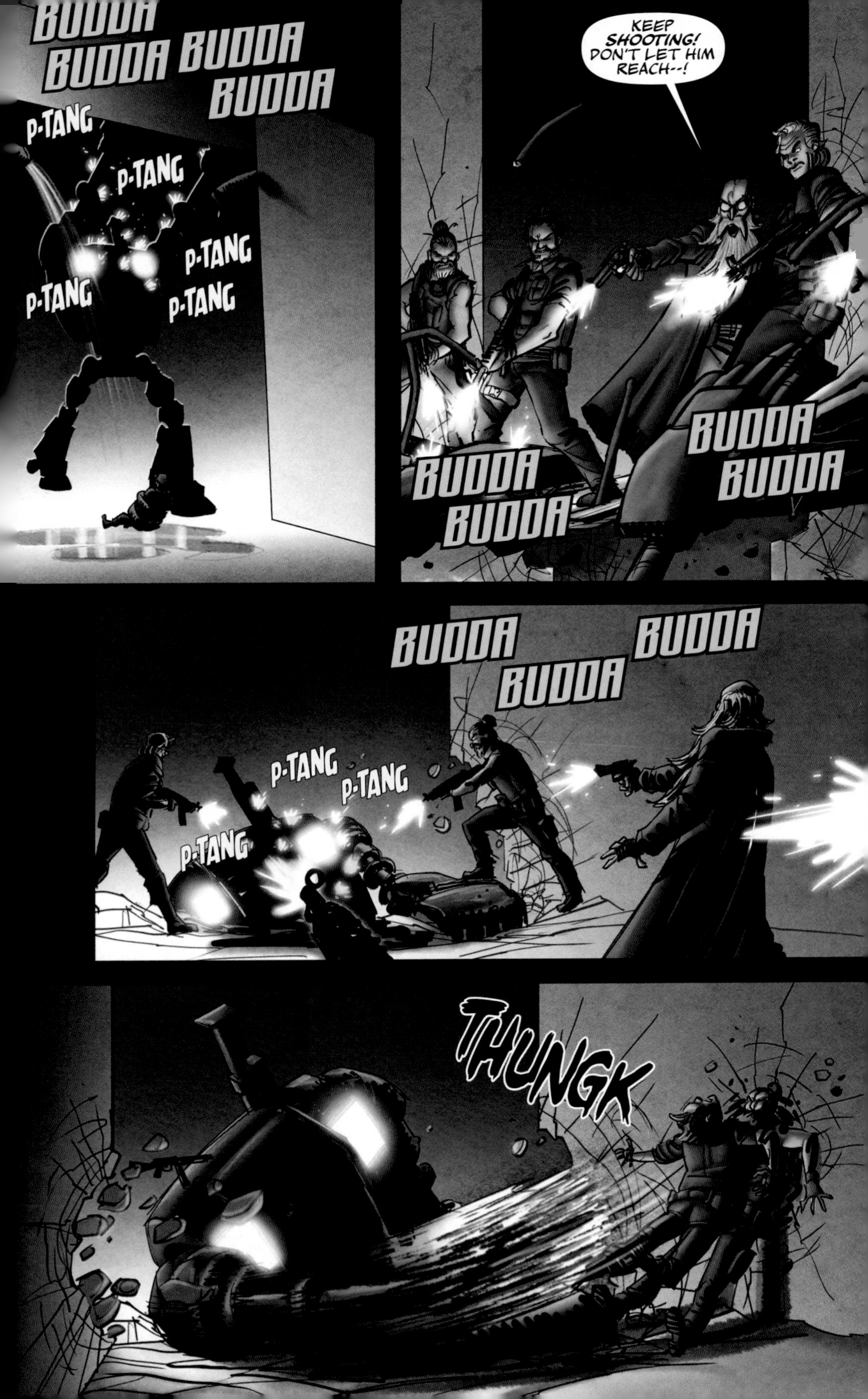
BUDDA
BUDDA BUDDA
BUDDA
P-TANG
P-TANG
P-TANG
P-TANG
P-TANG
KEEP SHOOTING! DON'T LET HIM REACH--!
BUDDA
BUDDA
BUDDA
BUDDA
BUDDA
BUDDA
BUDDA
P-TANG
P-TANG
P-TANG
THUNGK

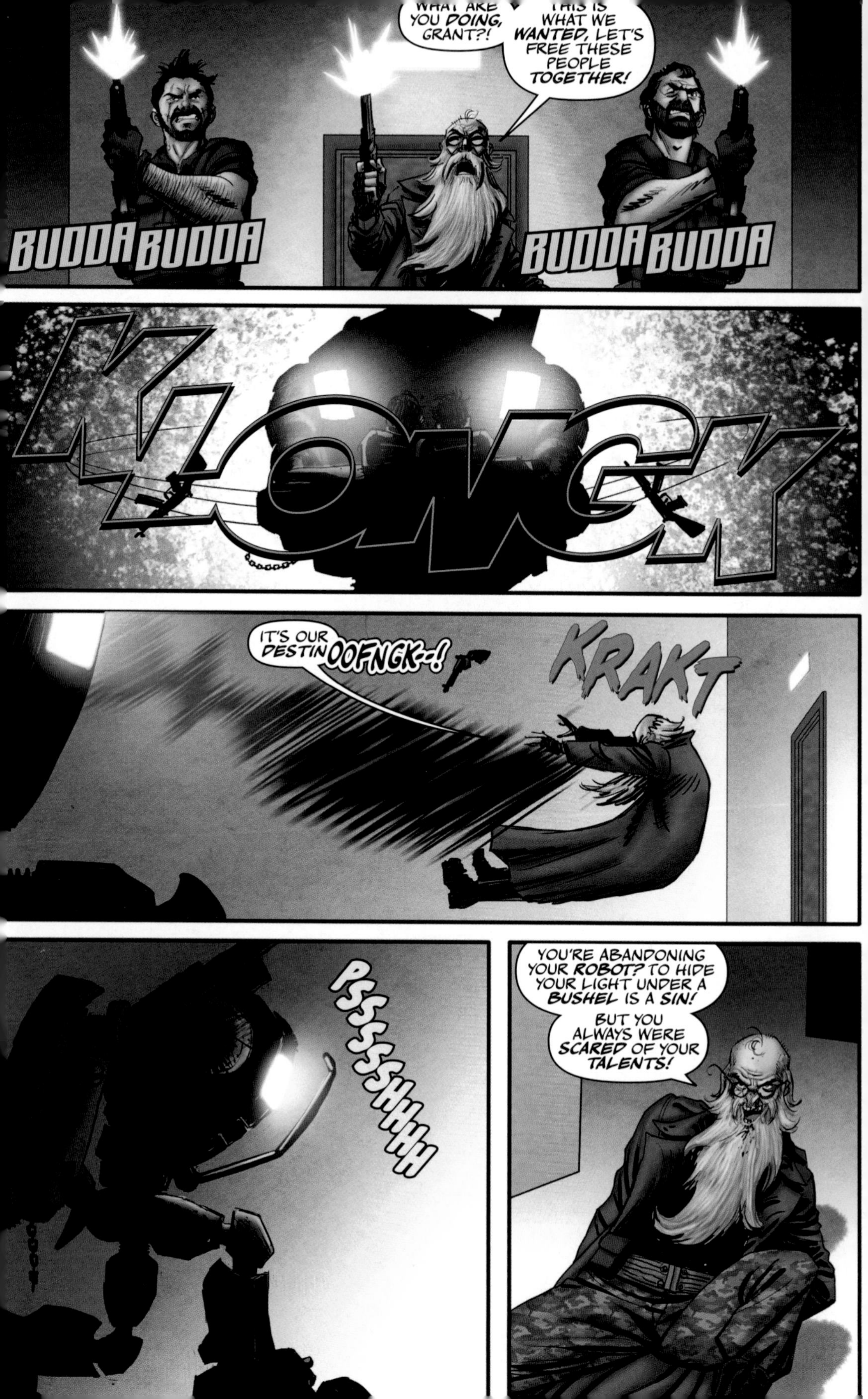
WHAT ARE YOU DOING, GRANT?!
THIS IS WHAT WE WANTED, LET'S FREE THESE PEOPLE TOGETHER!
BUDDA BUDDA
BUDDA BUDDA
KLONGK
IT'S OUR DESTIN OOFNGK--!
KRAKT
PSSSSHHHH
YOU'RE ABANDONING YOUR ROBOT? TO HIDE YOUR LIGHT UNDER A BUSHEL IS A SIN!
BUT YOU ALWAYS WERE SCARED OF YOUR TALENTS!

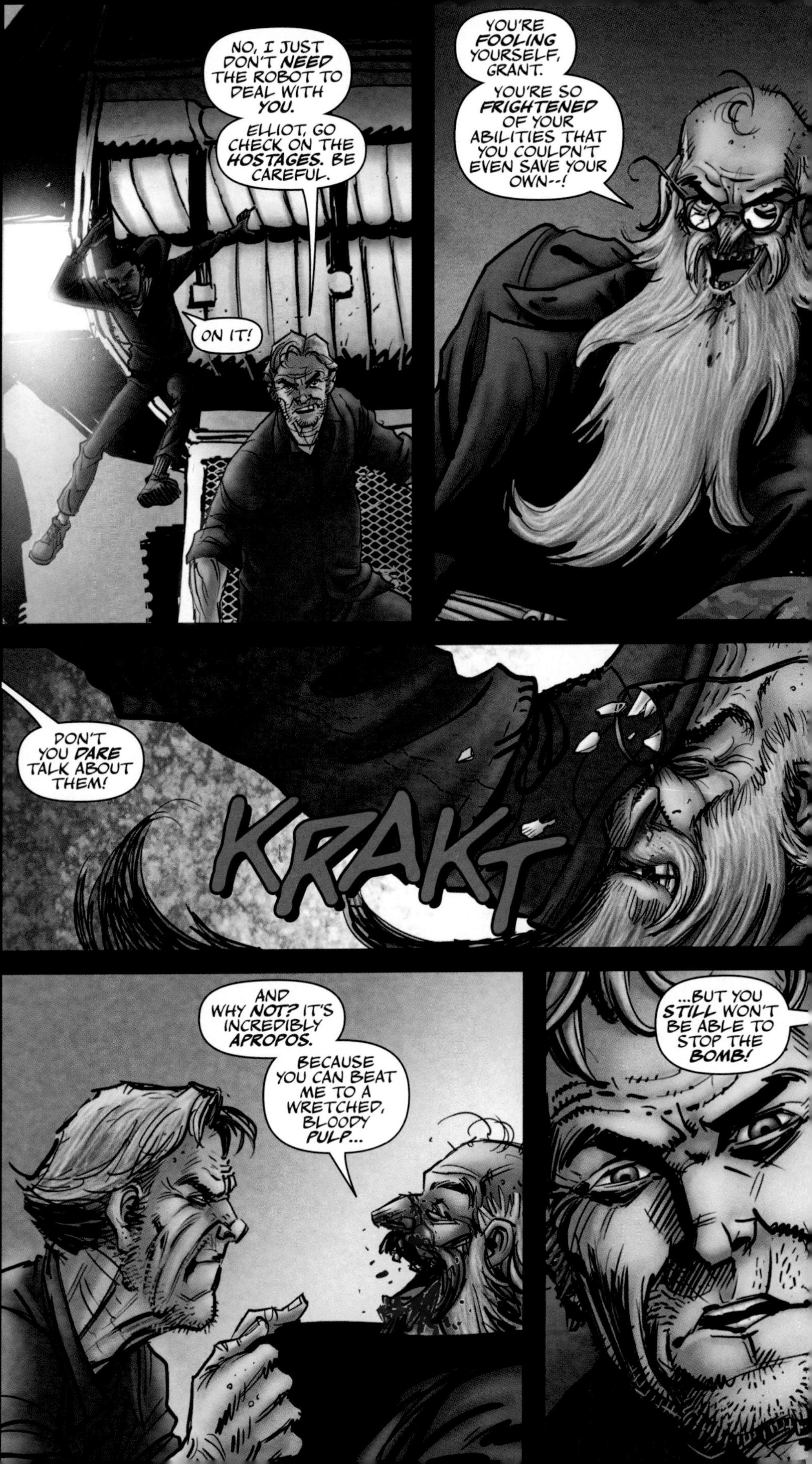
NO, I JUST DON'T NEED THE ROBOT TO DEAL WITH YOU.
ELLIOT, GO CHECK ON THE HOSTAGES. BE CAREFUL.
ON IT!
YOU'RE FOOLING YOURSELF, GRANT.
YOU'RE SO FRIGHTENED OF YOUR ABILITIES THAT YOU COULDN'T EVEN SAVE YOUR OWN--!
DON'T YOU DARE TALK ABOUT THEM!
KRAKT
AND WHY NOT? IT'S INCREDIBLY APROPOS.
BECAUSE YOU CAN BEAT ME TO A WRETCHED, BLOODY PULP...
...BUT YOU STILL WON'T BE ABLE TO STOP THE BOMB!

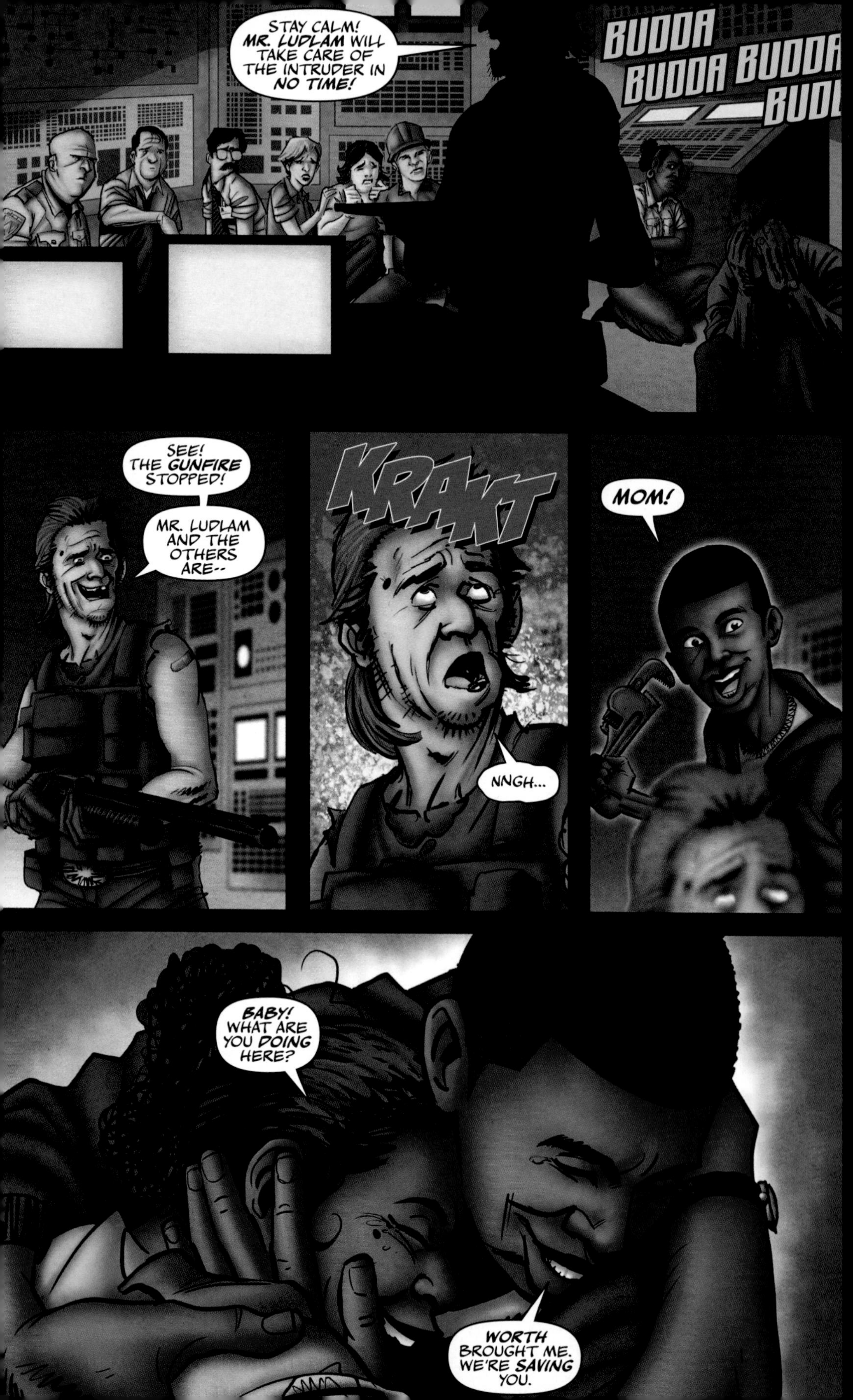
STAY CALM! MR. LUDLAM WILL TAKE CARE OF THE INTRUDER IN NO TIME!
BUDDA BUDDA BUDDA
SEE! THE GUNFIRE STOPPED!
MR. LUDLAM AND THE OTHERS ARE--
KRAKT
NNGH...
MOM!
BABY! WHAT ARE YOU DOING HERE?
WORTH BROUGHT ME. WE'RE SAVING YOU.

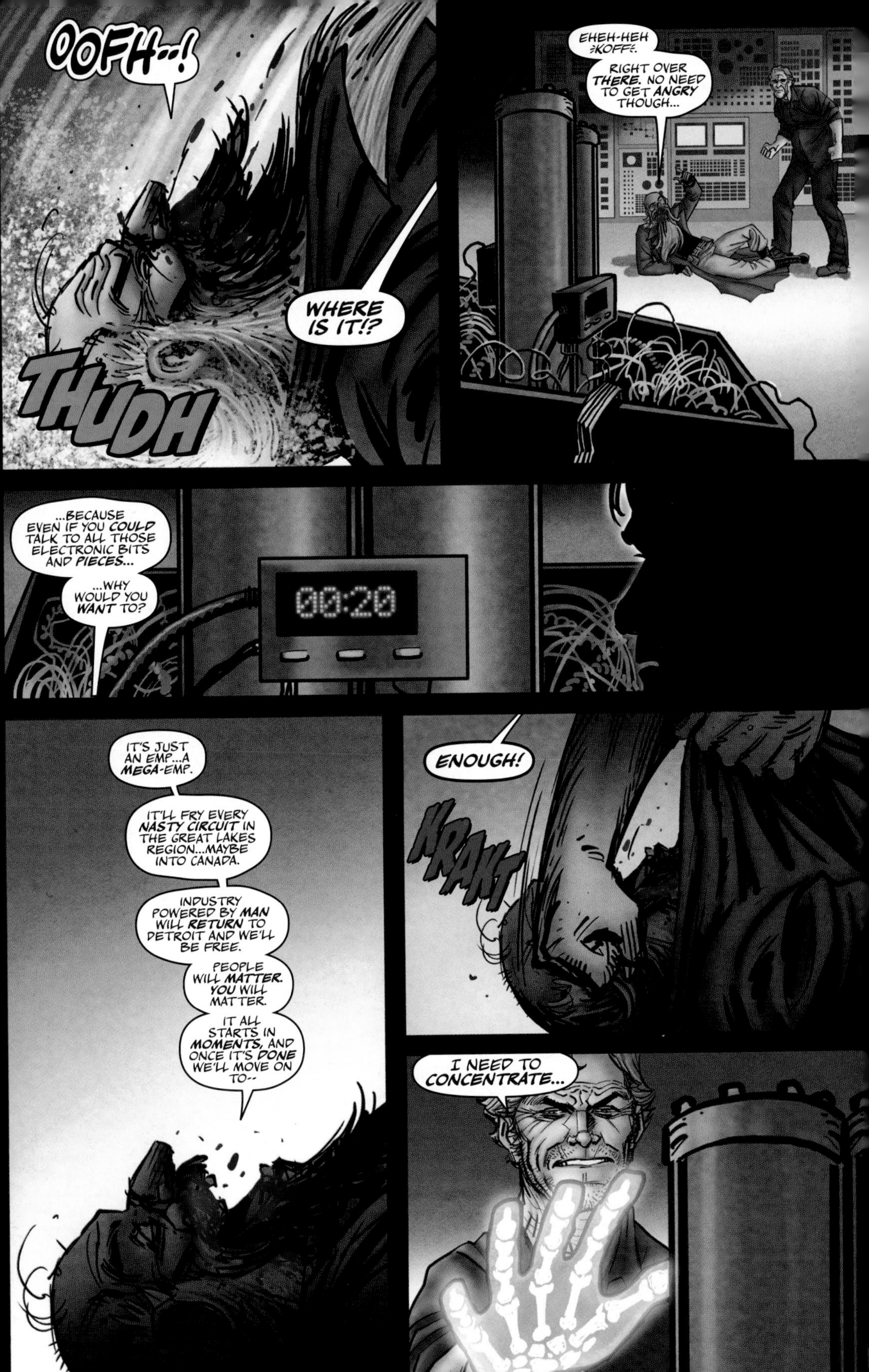
OOFH--!
THUDH
WHERE IS IT!?
EHEH-HEH *KOFF*.
RIGHT OVER THERE. NO NEED TO GET ANGRY THOUGH...
...BECAUSE EVEN IF YOU COULD TALK TO ALL THOSE ELECTRONIC BITS AND PIECES...
...WHY WOULD YOU WANT TO?
00:20
IT'S JUST AN EMP...A MEGA-EMP.
IT'LL FRY EVERY NASTY CIRCUIT IN THE GREAT LAKES REGION...MAYBE INTO CANADA.
INDUSTRY POWERED BY MAN WILL RETURN TO DETROIT AND WE'LL BE FREE.
PEOPLE WILL MATTER. YOU WILL MATTER.
IT ALL STARTS IN MOMENTS, AND ONCE IT'S DONE WE'LL MOVE ON TO--
ENOUGH!
KRAKT
I NEED TO CONCENTRATE...

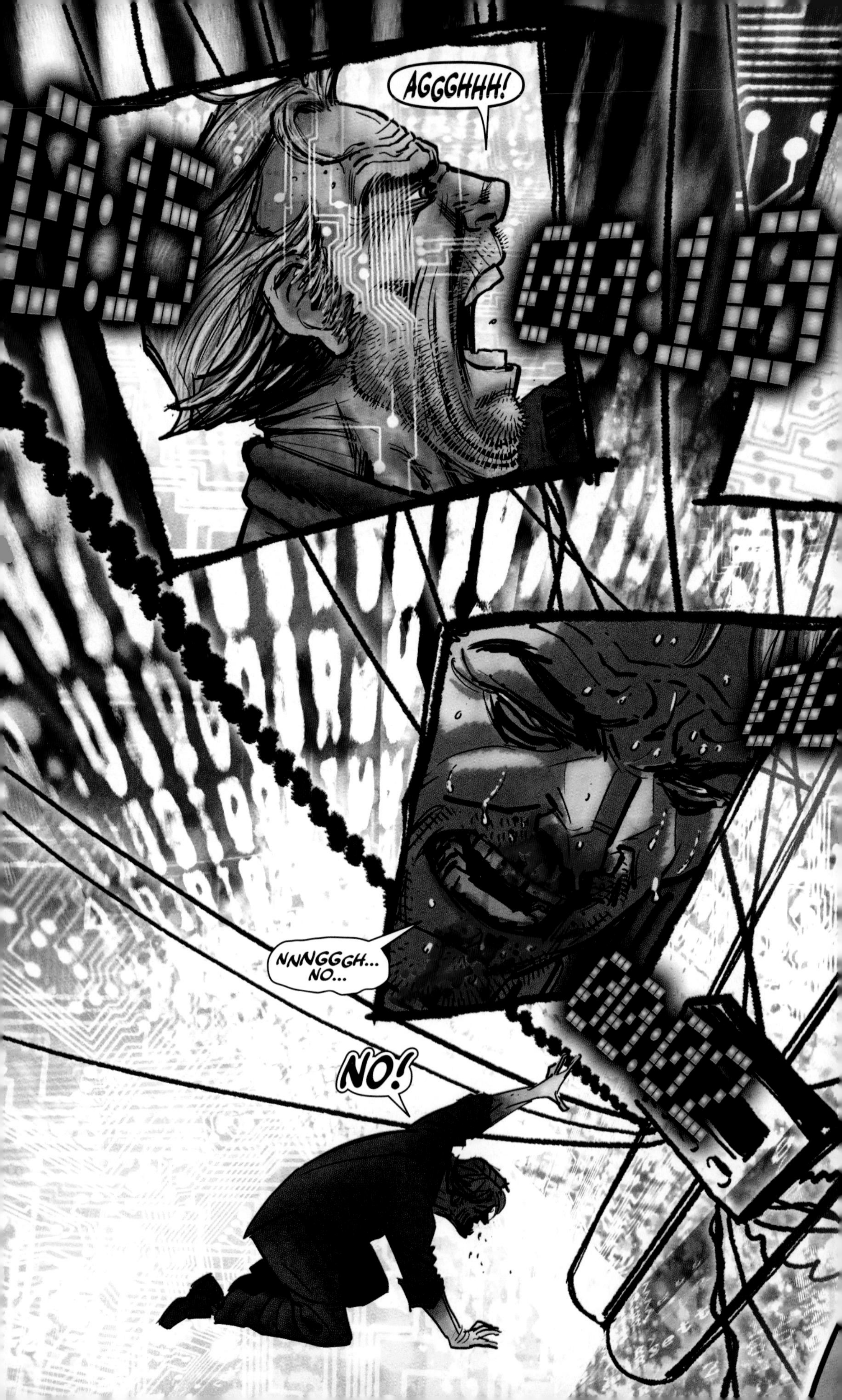
AGGGHHH!
NNNGGGH... NO...
NO!

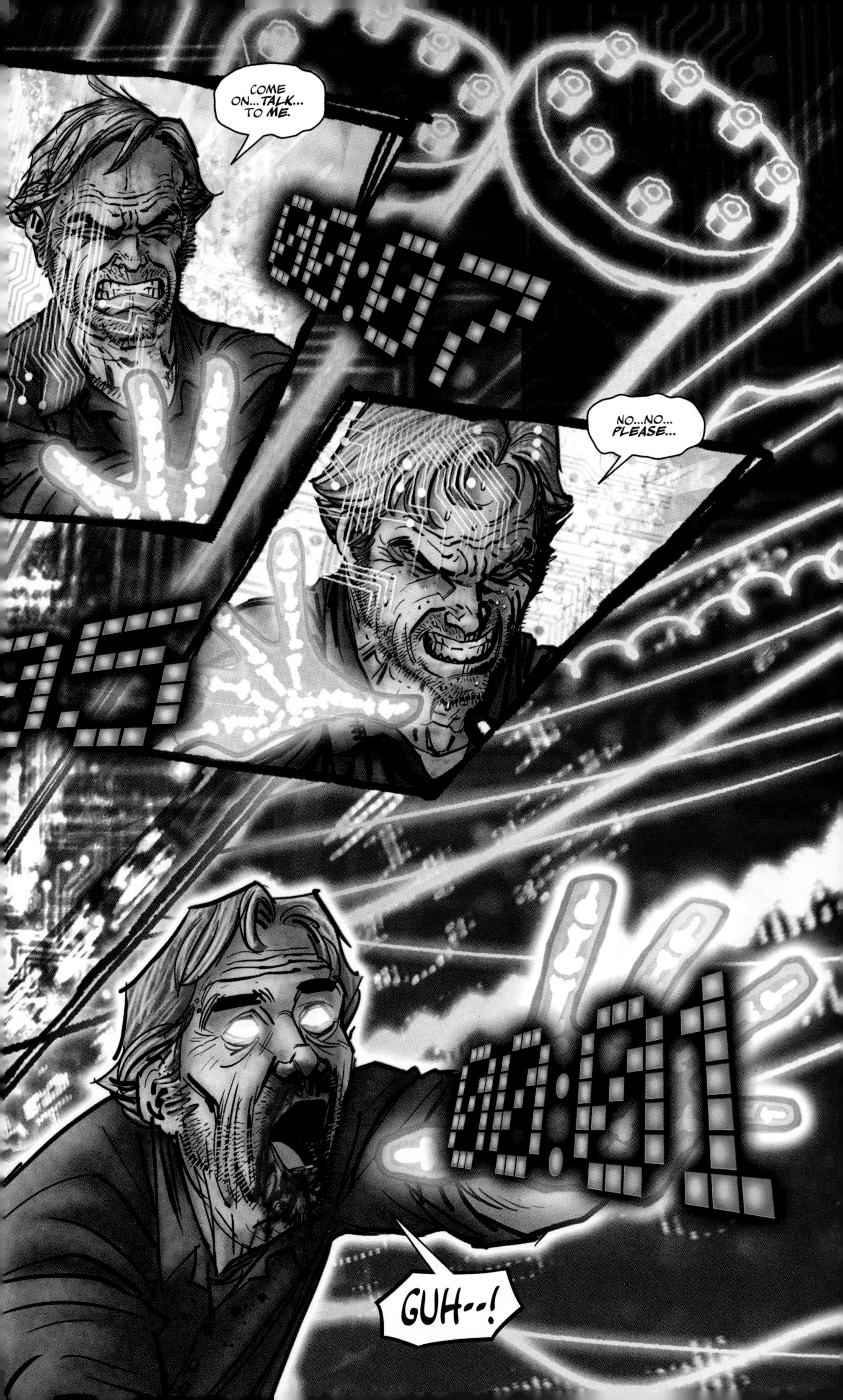
COME ON...TALK... TO ME.
00:07
NO...NO... PLEASE...
00:01
GUH--!

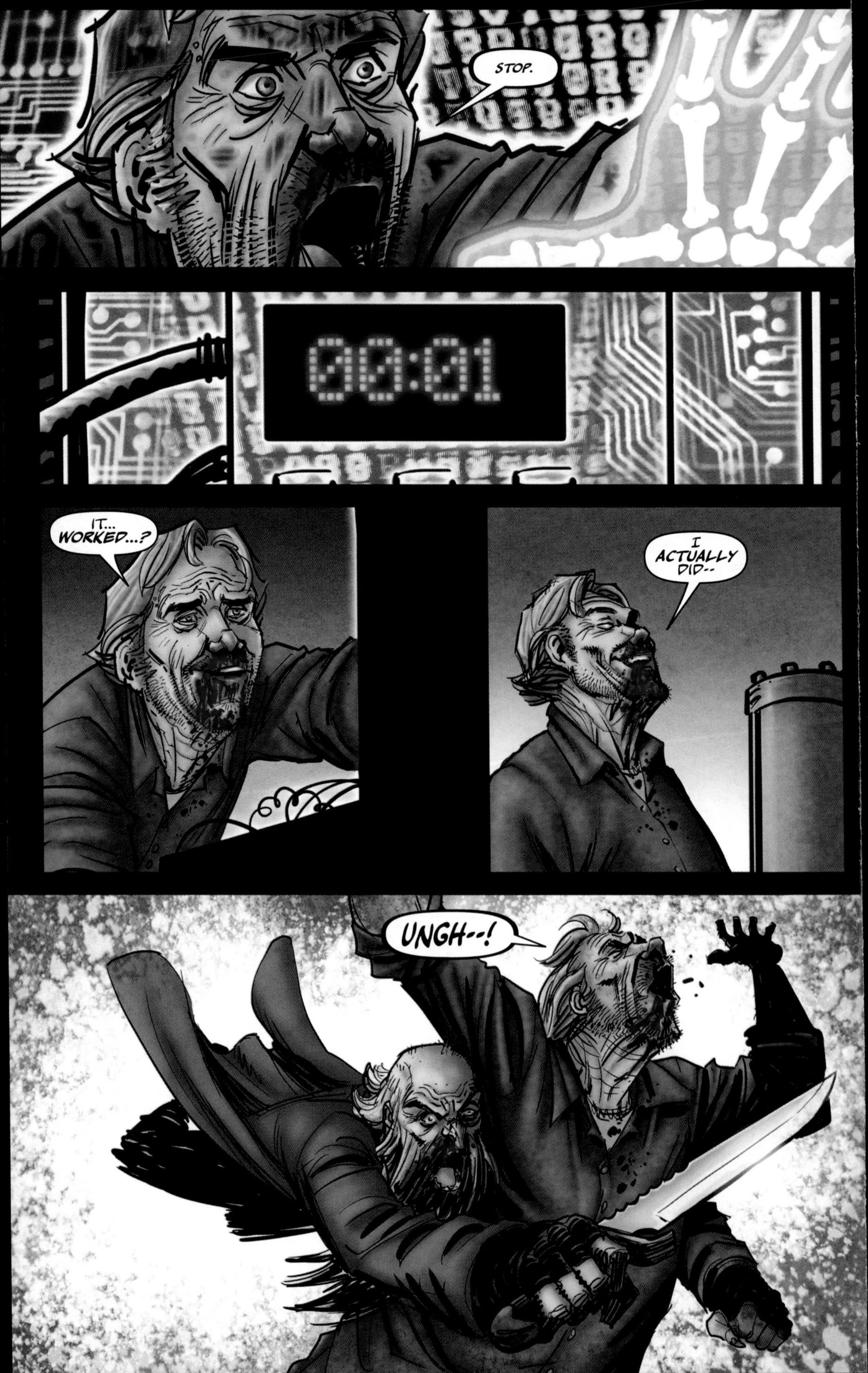
STOP.
00:01
IT... WORKED...?
I ACTUALLY DID--
UNGH--!

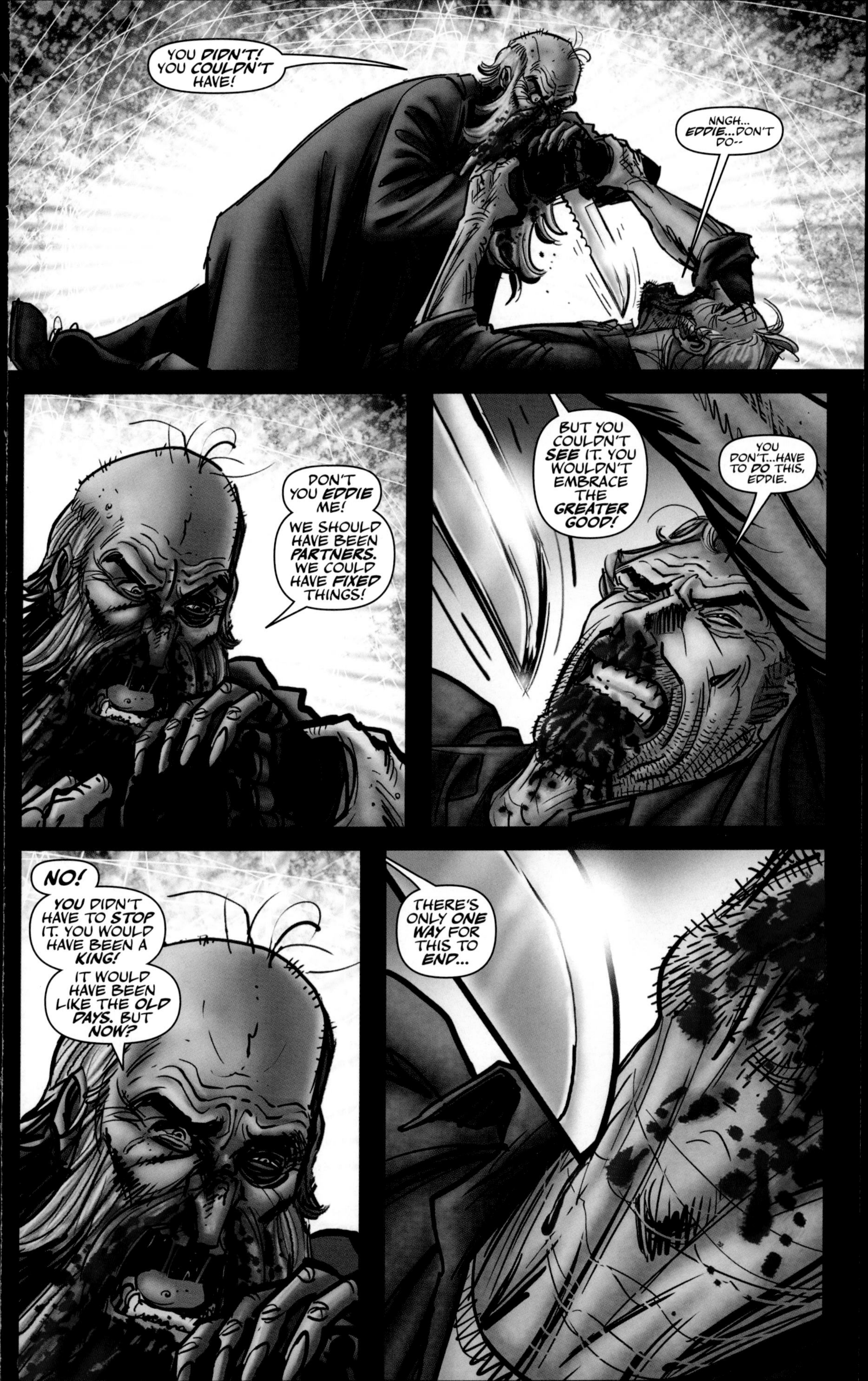
YOU DIDN'T! YOU COULDN'T HAVE!
NNGH... EDDIE...DON'T DO--
DON'T YOU EDDIE ME!
WE SHOULD HAVE BEEN PARTNERS. WE COULD HAVE FIXED THINGS!
BUT YOU COULDN'T SEE IT. YOU WOULDN'T EMBRACE THE GREATER GOOD!
YOU DON'T...HAVE TO DO THIS, EDDIE.
NO!
YOU DIDN'T HAVE TO STOP IT. YOU WOULD HAVE BEEN A KING!
IT WOULD HAVE BEEN LIKE THE OLD DAYS. BUT NOW?
THERE'S ONLY ONE WAY FOR THIS TO END...

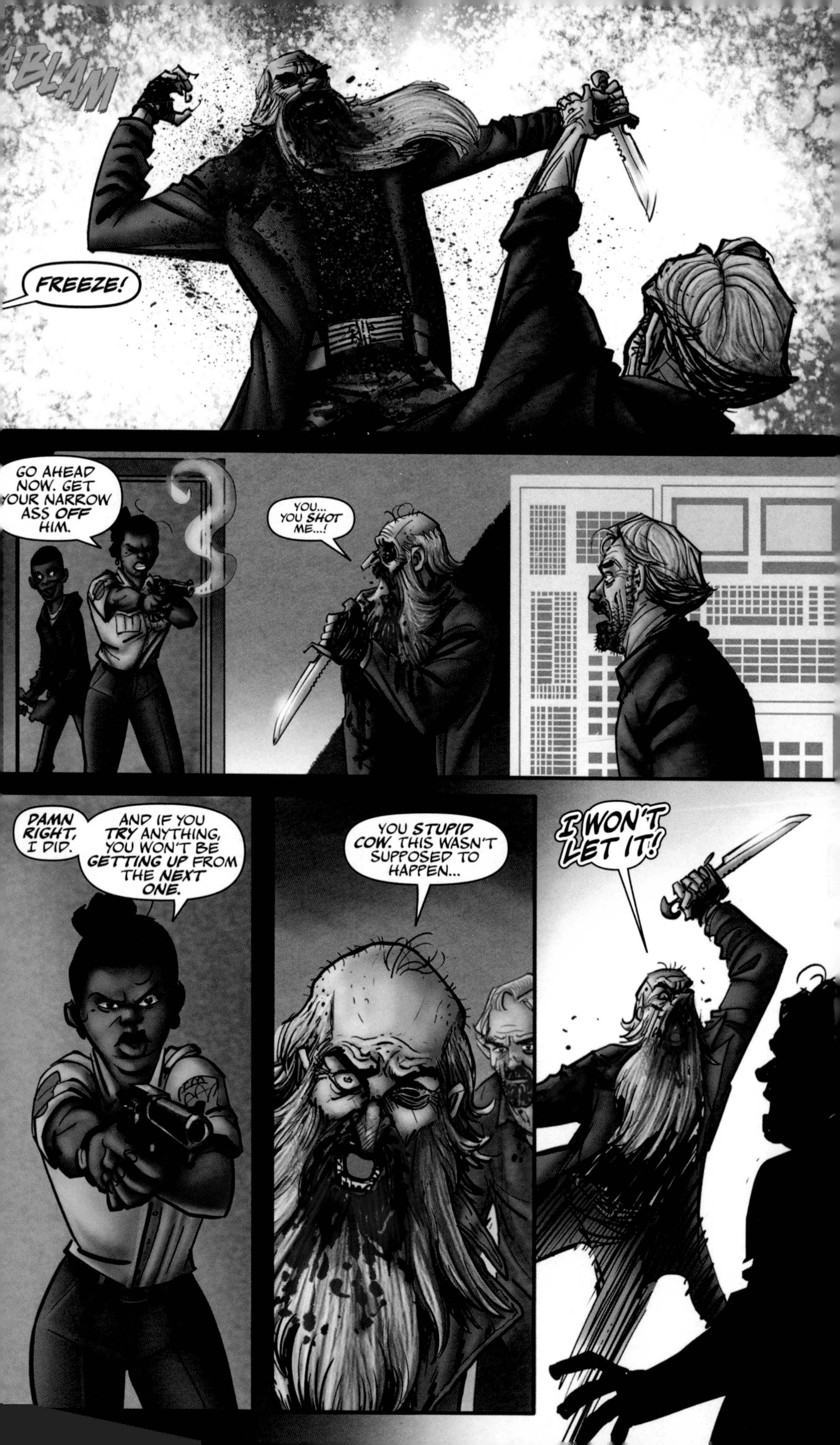
BLAM
FREEZE!
GO AHEAD NOW. GET YOUR NARROW ASS OFF HIM.
YOU... YOU SHOT ME...!
DAMN RIGHT, I DID.
AND IF YOU TRY ANYTHING, YOU WON'T BE GETTING UP FROM THE NEXT ONE.
YOU STUPID COW. THIS WASN'T SUPPOSED TO HAPPEN...
I WON'T LET IT!

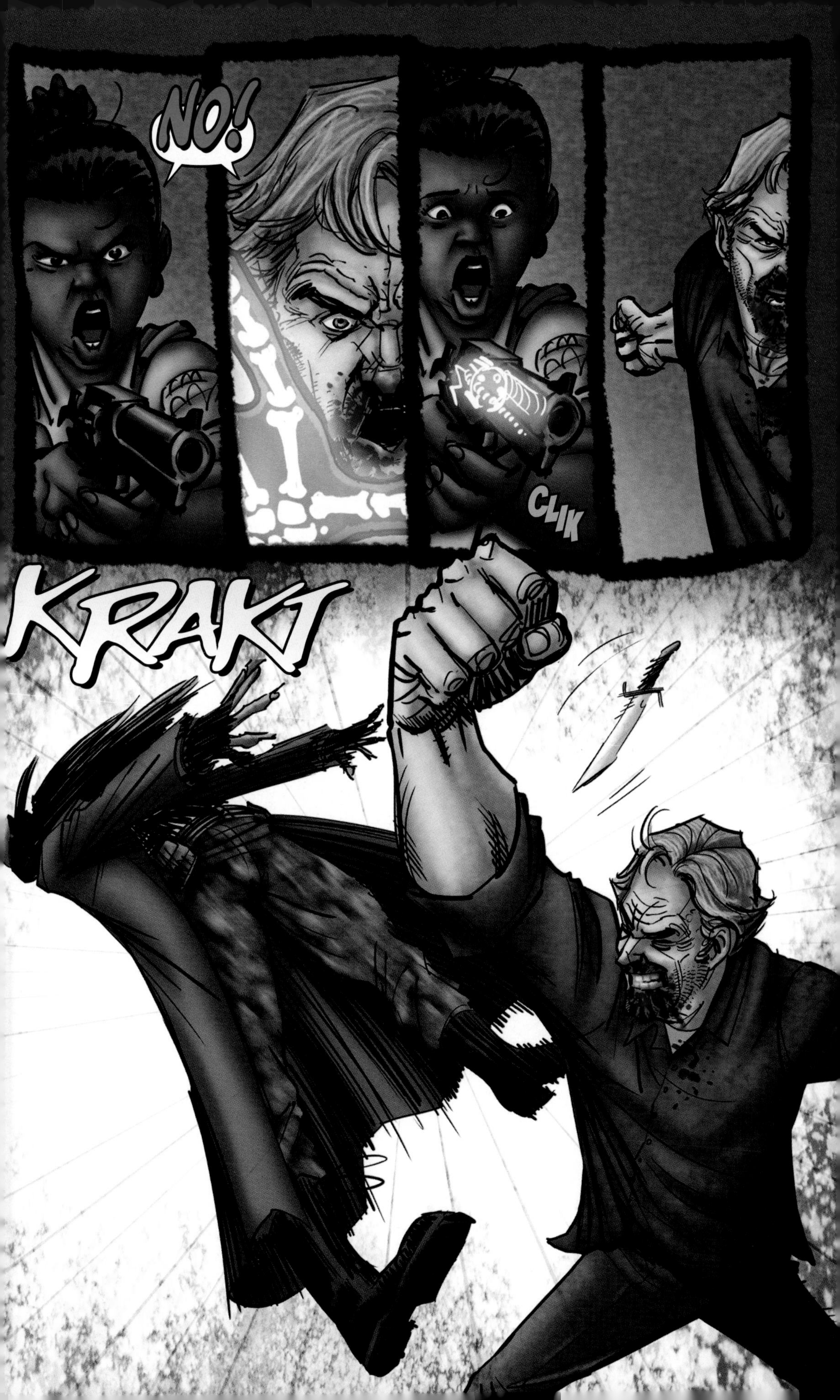
NO!
CLIK
KRAK!

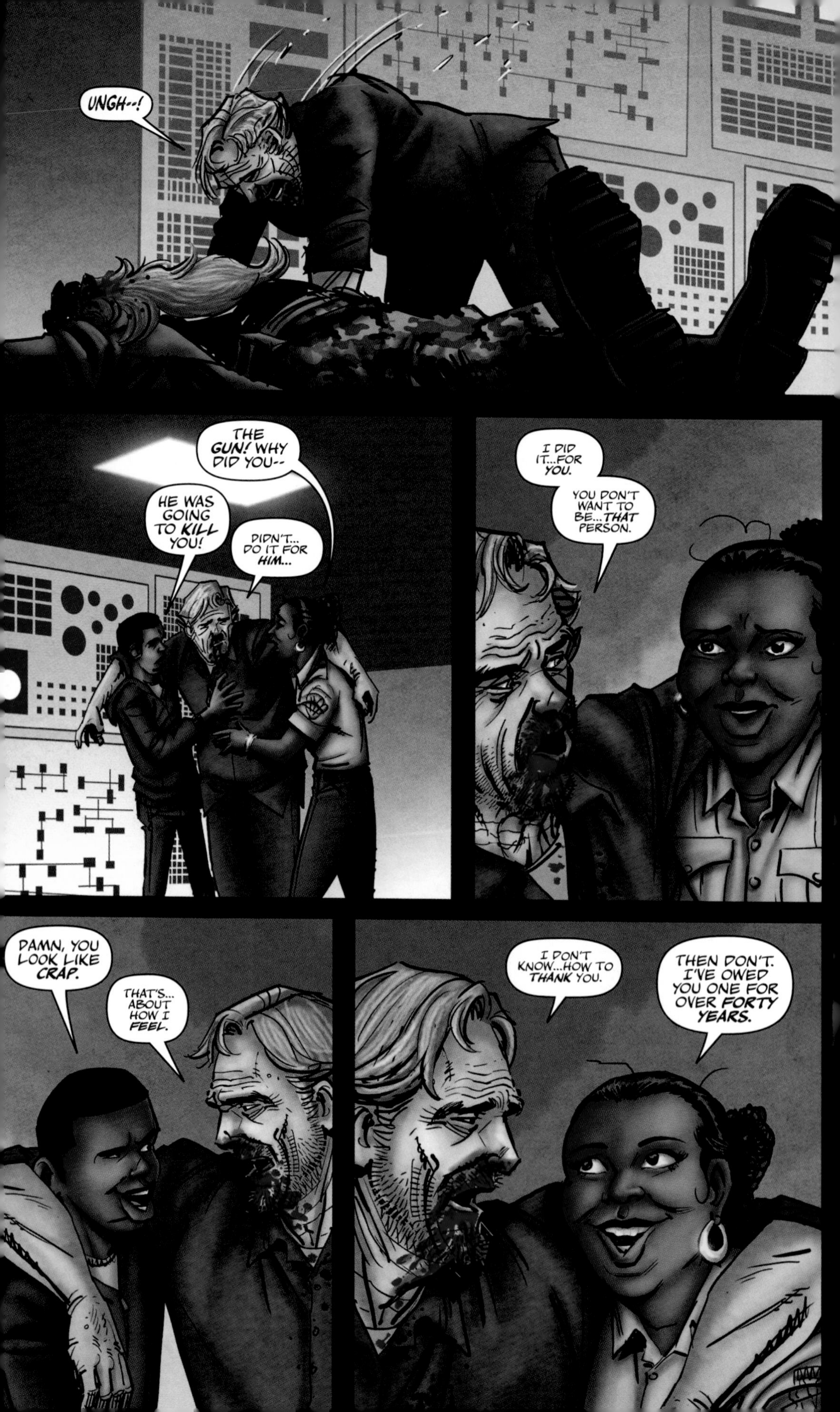
UNGH--!
THE GUN! WHY DID YOU--
HE WAS GOING TO KILL YOU!
DIDN'T... DO IT FOR HIM...
I DID IT...FOR YOU.
YOU DON'T WANT TO BE...THAT PERSON.
DAMN, YOU LOOK LIKE CRAP.
THAT'S... ABOUT HOW I FEEL.
I DON'T KNOW...HOW TO THANK YOU.
THEN DON'T. I'VE OWED YOU ONE FOR OVER FORTY YEARS.

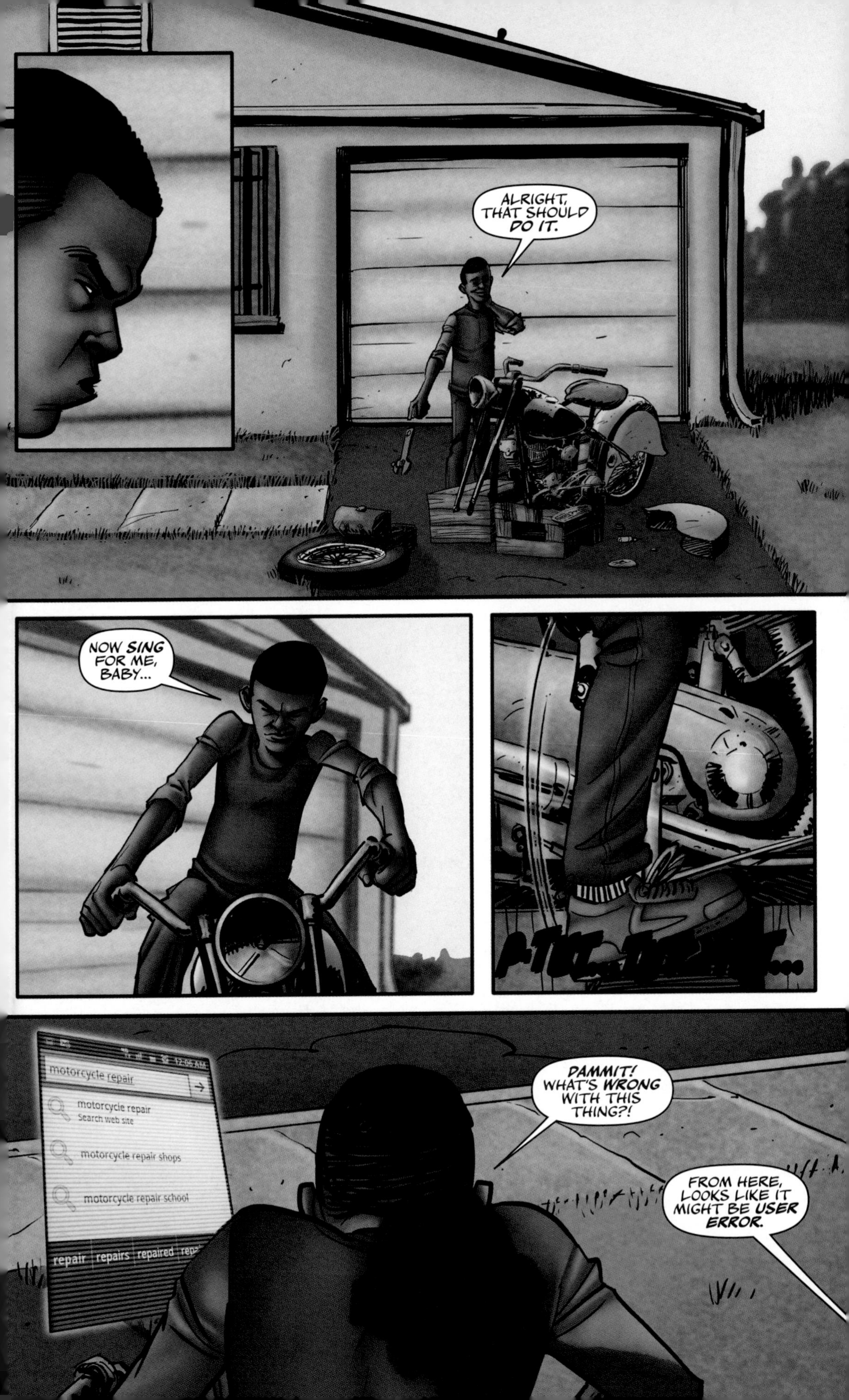
ALRIGHT, THAT SHOULD DO IT.
NOW SING FOR ME, BABY...
motorcycle repair
motorcycle repair
Search web site
motorcycle repair shops
motorcycle repair school
repair | repairs | repaired
DAMMIT! WHAT'S WRONG WITH THIS THING?!
FROM HERE, LOOKS LIKE IT MIGHT BE USER ERROR.

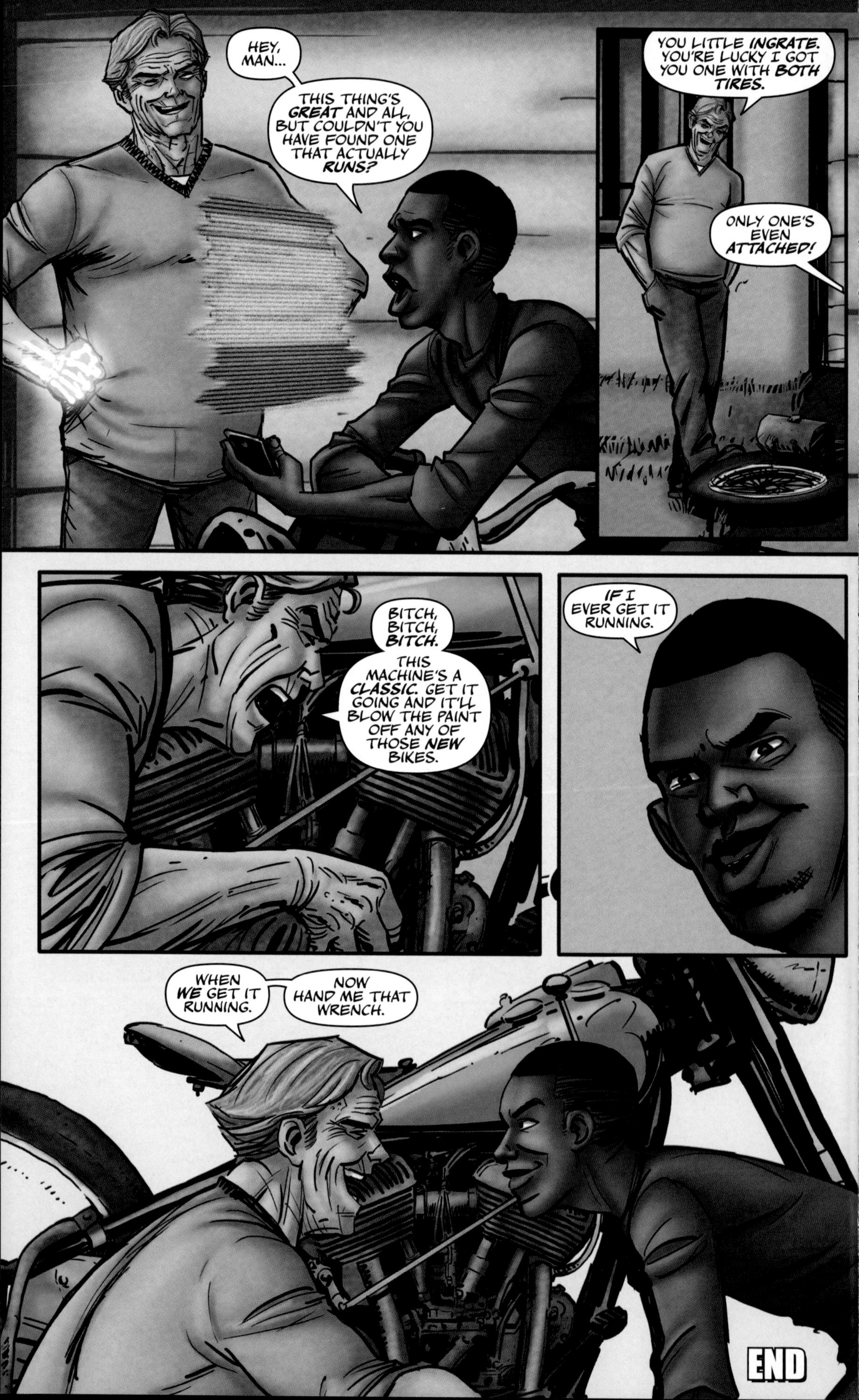
HEY, MAN...
THIS THING'S GREAT AND ALL, BUT COULDN'T YOU HAVE FOUND ONE THAT ACTUALLY RUNS?
YOU LITTLE INGRATE. YOU'RE LUCKY I GOT YOU ONE WITH BOTH TIRES.
ONLY ONE'S EVEN ATTACHED!
BITCH, BITCH, BITCH.
THIS MACHINE'S A CLASSIC. GET IT GOING AND IT'LL BLOW THE PAINT OFF ANY OF THOSE NEW BIKES.
IF I EVER GET IT RUNNING.
WHEN WE GET IT RUNNING.
NOW HAND ME THAT WRENCH.
END

GRANT WORTH

STAT SHEET

AGE: 65
HEIGHT: 5' 11"
WEIGHT: 231 lbs
HAIR COLOR: Gray
EYE COLOR: Blue
OCCUPATION:
Mechanic/Restoration Specialist

ABILITY:

mech•an•o•path•y *[me-kan-ō-paTH-ē]*
–**noun**

The ability to communicate with[1] and/or control machines[2]. Simple levers and basic machines can be easily manipulated. As machines gain intricacies they become more difficult to access, requiring the mechanopath to communicate through the "brain" of the device – a central access point that mechanical complexity requires. The brain is often associated with the machine's motor or mechanisms related to physical human control of the machine like a steering wheel.*

[1]Mechanopathy is a singularly directional ability. That is to say that communications from machine to mechanopath are impossible. As much as a mechanopath might speak to a machine, that machine cannot answer or actively engage in any form of communication.

[2]**ma•chine** *[muh-sheen]* –**noun**
An apparatus consisting of interrelated parts with separate functions, used in the performance of some kind of work.

*Mechanopathy is not to be confused with an ability that includes the power of telekinesis. A mechanopath can communicate and control an electric drill. He can turn it on, request that it moves its gears and get the bit spinning at full speed. A mechanopath cannot move the drill, stand it up and or it to float into position for the actual drilling of a screw into the wall. The mechanopath is constrained by whatever limitations the machine itself engenders.

LIMITATIONS:

Since the brain of any complex machine is its portal for mechanopathic instruction, communication with such a machine is predicated on the machine being turned on and the brain being operational. If a machine's function is dependent on a power source such as batteries or being plugged into the wall, then mechanopathic control of such a machine is dependent on it being connected to that source. Only once a machine is awakened and its brain operational (should it have one) then the machine can appropriately receive the Worth's desires/directions.

Computers, microchips, Intel processors and nano-bytes are Worth's kryptonite. When technology of that form and magnitude is connected to or integrated into a machine, it creates a block for Worth's mechanopathic connection – a buffer based in ones and zeros. In this case the complexity of the machine's brain seemingly surpasses Worth's ability to speak to it.

Examples provided for clarification:

Handheld Can Opener

Worth can ask it to clamp down, turn its gears and unlatch. He can communicate completely with such a device and it will respond affirmatively to each of his requests.

Toaster

Worth can ask its levers to move, and its knobs to twist, resulting in the heating of bread or even the cooking of a steak. However, communication with a machine of this type is dependent on the machine's ability to operate, and its brain's capacity to receive Worth's request, which means it has to be plugged in.

Lawn Mower

A "walk behind" lawn mower is another example of a machine with which Worth is able to converse. That said, a lawn mower also requires a power source to run, and thus to hear Worth. In this case the power source is not electricity (usually), it's fuel. The fuel would have to be activated by the pull crank mechanism, in order to turn on the mower's engine and allow it to dialogue with Worth.

iMac Computer

Stick a fork in him. When it comes to computers, Worth is done. Having a conversation with a machine with this magnitude of technology is like a first year Spanish student from New York trying to converse with a native Brazilian about the economics of Latin American agriculture.

PHILOSOPHICAL OUTLOOK:

Mechanopath or not, the relationship between man and machine is symbiotic in nature. The machine is built and maintained by man, and man created that machine to serve a purpose or function in his life.

Worth doesn't see what he can do as controlling machines. In his mind, he has a relationship with them. He understands, that while they are far from sentient, machines have a soul and deserve a great deal of respect.

"To appreciate machines you need look no further than the human body. What are humans but organic machines. We are intricate elements that work together to achieve movement and thought. We have need for food instead of batteries but the interworkings are very similar. The body and the way it works is no different than a machine and I doubt that anyone would tell you it's not worth your appreciation." – Grant Worth

WORTH

SKETCHBOOK

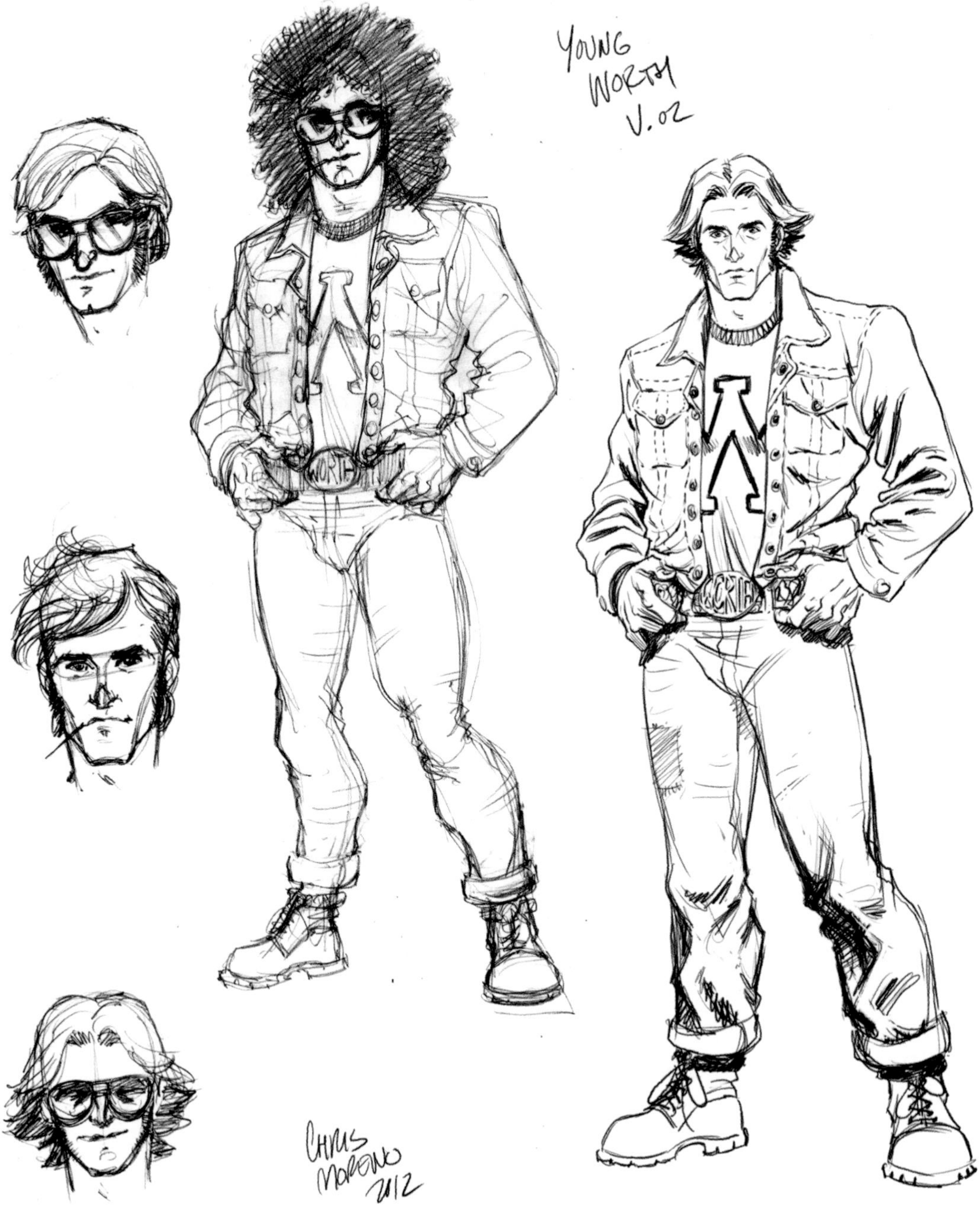

YOUNG WORTH V.02
CHRIS MORENO 2012

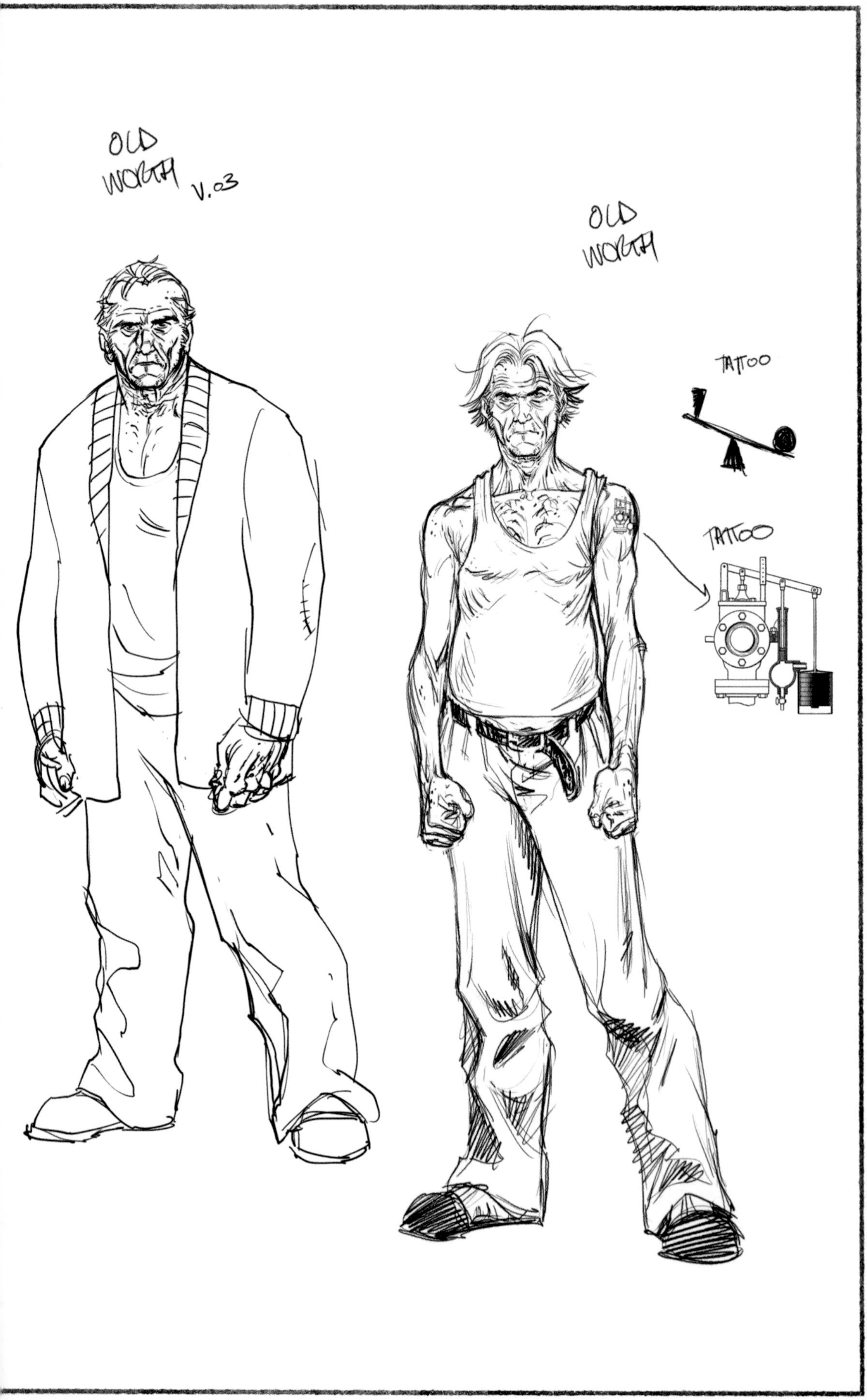
OLD WORTH V.03
OLD WORTH
TATTOO
TATTOO

MECHS

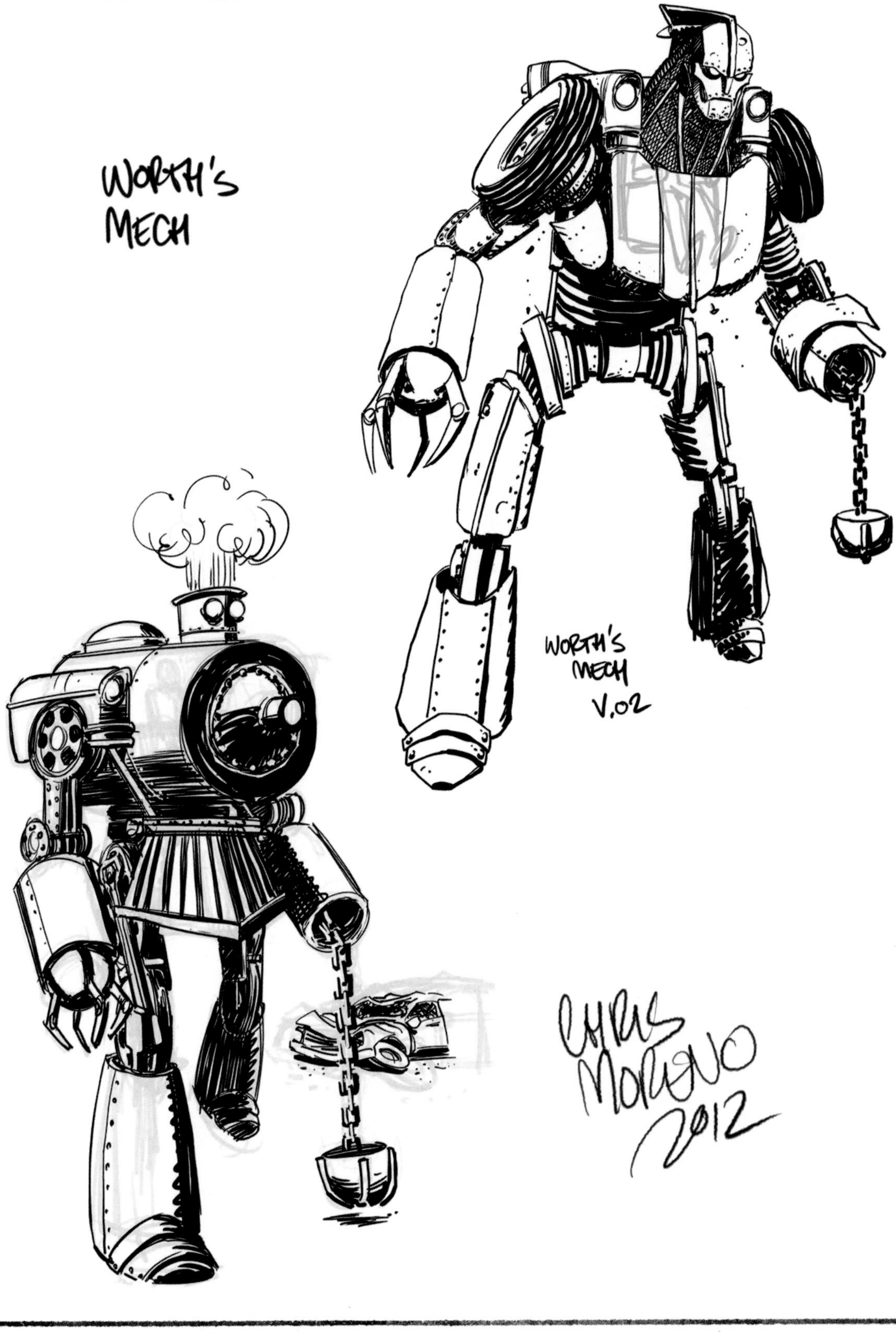

WORTH'S
MECH
WORTH'S
MECH
V.02
CHRIS
MORENO
2012

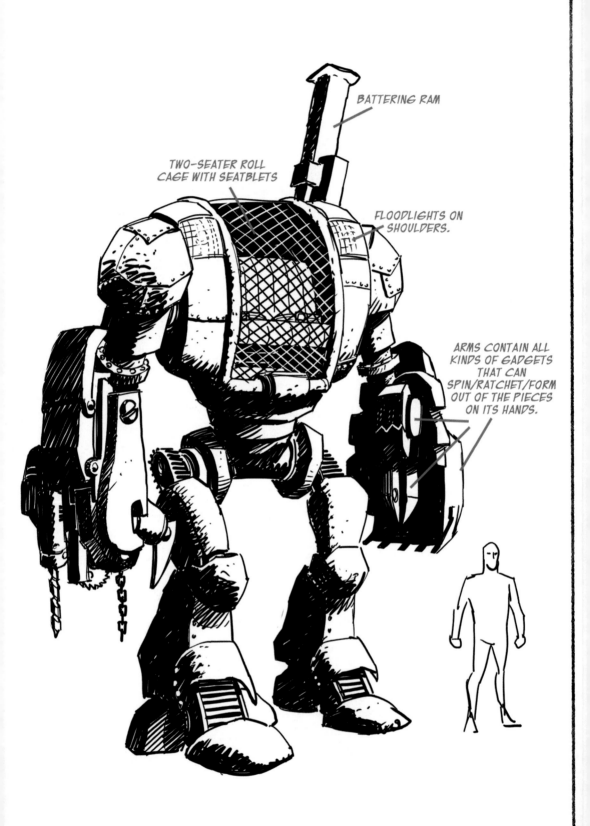

BATTERING RAM

TWO-SEATER ROLL CAGE WITH SEATBLETS

FLOODLIGHTS ON SHOULDERS.

ARMS CONTAIN ALL KINDS OF GADGETS THAT CAN SPIN/RATCHET/FORM OUT OF THE PIECES ON ITS HANDS.

WORTH AFTERWORDS

by Trevor Roth

One of the things we take great pride in when it comes to upholding the traditions of Gene Roddenberry is finding a novel approach for our subject matter. With Worth we wanted to avoid the <u>origin</u> story. Sure you might be wondering, Where did Worth come from? How did he get his powers? And the answers to those questions could prove to be a very compelling story. But for this book, we wanted to forgo the normality of starting at the beginning. We wanted to take this one all the way around the corner to see what happens to a hero after it's all over. Exploring Worth on a grounded, human level, we wanted to ask, What happens when someone so extraordinary is normalized and even becomes obsolete?

If you've read the book and are still willing to read this afterward, we're hopeful we can take that as a sign that we did our job. That said, I do feel a bit badly about cheating readers out of some kind of origin story. And while I don't think we are prepared to share the origin of Grant Worth the man, I thought I might share the origin of Worth the concept.

The day was ominous. The mist had rolled in from the ocean shore and a full moon was on the rise…. OK so it was a regular day at the office.

STEPS 1 – 4 FROM THE ELEVATOR:
I was headed to my car after a long day's work and, while fumbling my irregularly large set of keys, I realized how convenient it might be to have the power to shape shift my index finger into the shape of any key, something along the lines of Terminator 2. If that were the case, then I would never have to find the right key on my keychain. Heck, I wouldn't even need a keychain.

STEPS 5 & 6 TOWARDS MY CAR:
This might have been the creation of the best power ever imagined. A person with this simple little power would undoubtedly be the most renowned thief in history.

STEPS 7 - 11 TOWARDS MY CAR:
Unfortunately, my grandiose ideas came crashing down only steps later when I saw a building neighbor get into her car using a keyless remote. I quickly looked around at other vehicles and noticed keypads on the outside of car doors and one car with no visible entry system at all. I instantaneously searched my memory banks to remember my cousin's house in Michigan. The one with the front door that had a code to open it. It dawned on me, keys are going the way of the dinosaur. And my ground-breaking ability to change my finger into any key might soon be the most useless power I could have invented. Idiot!

STEP 12 AT MY CAR:
Still, now that I had spawned the power I couldn't just throw it away. I was stuck with it. So I can change my finger into a key. Well a decade or two ago, assuming I was willing be a crook, I would have been on the top of the world. And a decade from now I would be the most obsolete, non-super superhero the world has ever known.

TURNING THE IGNITION & DRIVING HOME:
Wow would that suck! What if, by no fault of your own, if through the passage of time and the evolution of technology, you became completely worthless. And how many people in the world have actually lived through a similar experience. The Industrial Revolution, Henry Ford's assembly lines, the automation of the workforce, and the advent the Internet – each one represents an amazing time of human accomplishment and the human causalities of those left behind. It's not a problem unlike many feel today – the need to keep up with technology or fall by the wayside – and it deserves a discussion.

PARKING MY CAR AT HOME:
Worth is born.

SPECIAL THANKS

A number of people deserve high praise and huge thanks for helping this book come to fruition. Sincere appreciation for each of the following: Aubrey Sitterson – who wove layer upon layer upon layer of interconnected social commentary, human drama and thrilling story. Chris Moreno – whose art choices for both present day and flashbacks have brought Worth to a truly experiential level. Paul Morrisey – whose editing talents were key in guiding this story and making the tough decisions along the way. Tory Mell – who, along with producing the book, was a constant source of creativity and problem-solving.